The School for Scandal

NEW MERMAIDS

General editor: Brian Gibbons
Professor of English Literature, University of Münster

Reconstruction of an eighteenth-century
stage by C. Walter Hodges

NEW MERMAIDS

NEW MERMAIDS

Richard Brinsley
Sheridan

The
School
for Scandal

edited by F. W. Bateson

Late Fellow and Tutor in English
Corpus Christi College, Oxford

with amendments and a new article
by David Crane

A & C Black • London
W W Norton • New York

Second edition 1995
Reprinted 1996, 1999
Published by A & C Black (Publishers) Limited
35 Bedford Row, London WC1R 4JH

ISBN 0–7136–4259–9

First published in this form 1979
by Ernest Benn Limited

Published in the United States of America by
W. W. Norton & Company Inc.
500 Fifth Avenue, New York, NY 10110
ISBN 0–393–90077–0 (USA)

A CIP catalogue record for this book
is available from the British Library.

Printed and bound in Great Britain by
Biddles Limited, Guildford and King's Lynn

CONTENTS

PREFACE TO FIRST EDITION

THE MILLS OF SCHOLARSHIP grind slowly. In the couple of centuries since its first public performance *The School for Scandal* has only been edited—*really* edited—once. Cecil Price's *Dramatic Works of Sheridan* (2 vols., 1973) is an edition I have come to admire increasingly over the years. The amount of relevant information unpretentiously packed in its 875 pages is staggering and makes my own bits and pieces of discovery and the contributions of my old but always genial contestants in the past—notably R. Crompton Rhodes and George H. Nettleton—look very small indeed. I have tried to pay the proper acknowledgement for each item I derive from Professor Price in this edition, but I hope he will excuse the occasional omission.

No doubt in the final analysis *The School for Scandal* is primarily light entertainment. It gets us giggling, but is it possible to take our giggles seriously? What emotion is being purged? This is not the place to re-examine Shaftesbury's doctrine that ridicule is the best test of truth, but one generalization may be permitted. It is that a healthy society is only possible where what is said is what is meant. The brilliance of a Sheridan is in his total commitment to 'good English' rather than good behaviour; but the precision of the language 'places' and reflects the degree of sincerity in the speaker. It is human to err; it is comic when error of intention is betrayed in the failure of one's words to conceal it.

I have tried to supplement Price rather than supersede him by raising such questions, in the textual notes, in particular instances. His text like mine is essentially eclectic, but he hardly ever tells us in his useful lists of variants why one reading appears in his text and the others lurk in a textual note. I have also paid more attention than he does to the theatrical setting. The modern reader will tend when reading the play to set it in a theatre of the mind in which characters do not enter from anywhere special but are found talking in a vaguely eighteenth-century room. That Sheridan encouraged such a habit in what I have called the 'presentation' MSS—culminating in the famous Crewe MS given to his *inamorata*—must be conceded. But he wrote the play to be acted rather than read privately, and the modern editor should in my opinion construct a text which as far as possible is capable of being acted publicly *and* read to oneself.

ix

I have been fortunate—through the kindness of Mr Hoffmann (of Hoffmann and Freeman) and the Bodleian Library—in being allowed the use at home of the Tickell MS, which embodies the play's text in its final—or conceivably penultimate—form. Mr Robert H. Taylor has lent me copies of the pre-performance MSS in his remarkable Sheridan collection (now on loan at Princeton University), and I have had similar courtesies from the Theatre Collection at Harvard, the Victoria and Albert Museum, Yale University, the Henry E. Huntington Library (California), and the Royal Irish Academy. The print of the Tickell title-page is by courtesy of the Bodleian Library; that of the collapse of the screen by courtesy of the Victoria and Albert Museum.

My manuscript was skilfully typed by Geraldine Aylott. Roma Gill, of Sheffield University, who is now one of the General Editors of this series, has the penitent gratitude of the retired dictator of a similar series.

F.W.B.

GENERAL EDITOR'S NOTE TO FIRST EDITION

IN 1799 SHERIDAN wrote to a publisher who had been pestering him for the manuscript of *The School for Scandal*.

> The fact is, Mr R., I have been nineteen years endeavouring to satisfy my own taste in this play, and have not yet succeeded.

The dramatist's enduring concern for the minutiae of his creation was shared by his latest editor, F. W. Bateson. Freddy's notes extend over many years and many miles, marking with loving care the variants, even in stage directions, between versions of the play in Oxford, London, the United States of America, and (by courtesy of The Bodleian Library) his home in Brill. The present edition is an inadequate representation of such care and effort; it could never have been otherwise, for the insights were far too numerous to be encapsulated in an economically viable form.

But the edition has also suffered because of Freddy's sudden death, shortly after he had delivered his manuscript to Ernest Benn. At the point where a General Editor, personally less involved with the play, and mindful of the needs of student readers, could have asked for the occasional clarification, it was too late. To call in a second specialist editor—and many, in affection and respect for Freddy, offered their services—would have risked altering the tones and emphasis that he wanted. Consequently, apart from the occasional checking of references and smoothing-out of some inconsistencies (with the gratefully acknowledged help of Professor Cecil Price), we have left this edition as Freddy left it—perhaps as he found *The School for Scandal*: incomplete, but the work of a master.

ROMA GILL 1979

xi

ABBREVIATIONS AND ORIGINS OF PRINCIPAL TEXTS, EDITIONS, ETC.

THE PRINCIPAL MSS, editions, and standard biographies, etc. are listed here in what appears to be their chronological order. In the Notes to the text and in the Introduction they are referred to in italics. Further information on the manuscripts is provided by Cecil Price, *Dramatic Works of Sheridan* (1973), I, 333–45; II, 837–9. Price's abbreviations are normally adopted here.

1. Manuscripts and Editions

Manuscripts

FRAMPTON COURT. Copied and revised by Sheridan himself, *c.* March 1777, from earlier drafts now almost all lost. (Robert H. Taylor Collection, Princeton.) Ed. W. Fraser Rae (in *Sheridan's Plays now printed as he wrote them* (1902)) = RAE.

SHARGL (misreading of 'Spangle' by Sotheby's cataloguer at Clare Sheridan sale). Theatre copy of preceding MS with many corrections by Sheridan, *c.* April 1777. Act I only. (British Library.) For a detailed description see Textual Appendix (below, pp. 140–4).

LORD CHAMBERLAIN. Theatre copy submitted for licence 7 May 1777 to William Chetwynd, the Lord Chamberlain's Examiner of Plays. (Yale.) Three loose sheets in Frampton Court MS may be last-minute additions used in first-night performance and not submitted for licence (see *Price*, pp. 337–8).

1778. Theatre copy of prompt-book ('1778' on cover) as used in 1778–79 season. (British Library.)

1779. Theatre copy. Each of Acts II, III, IV is subscribed 'Portsmouth, 1779'; earliest extant 'vamped' text. Act V is missing. For Act I see under 'POWELL' below. (Harvard Theatre Collection.)

BUCKINGHAMSHIRE. First of surviving presentation copies, *c.* 1779. Sheridan has identified author of Epilogue in his own hand. Text close to *1778*, but less careless. Fly-leaf signed 'Albinia Buckinghamshire'. (She became countess of Buckinghamshire in 1804, but is likely to have acquired MS much earlier.)

CREWE B (second Crewe MS). Bookplate with separate, superadded coronet, so later than 1806. MS may have been inherited by Frances Anne Crewe from mother, Frances Greville, to whom *The Critic* is dedicated. Title-page date '1777' refers to first production. Many

xiii

autograph insertions, especially of stage directions. (Still in private hands.) The first Crewe MS, apparently lost, was sent with 'A Portrait' (c. July 1777).

BANBURY. Said to have been presented to Frederick Augustus, duke of York (1763–1827). Inscribed (but not in Sheridan's hand) 'From the Author'. Owned in the early nineteenth century by Catharine Banbury. Copied by William Hopkins, Drury Lane prompter, from his prompt-book. Text is intermediate between the two extant Crewe MSS. (Robert H. Taylor Collection, Princeton.)

GEORGETOWN (third Crewe MS). Inscribed 'To Mrs. Crewe From the Author', and has Mrs Crewe's bookplate. Many autograph insertions. Wrongly described by Thomas Moore as 'the last, I believe, ever revised' by Sheridan (*Memoirs*, I, 260). (Georgetown University, Washington, D.C.) Ed. G. H. Nettleton in *British Dramatists from Dryden to Sheridan*, ed. Nettleton and A. E. Case (1939) = NETTLETON.

SPUNGE. Revision by Sheridan, perhaps c. 1787, of early theatre copy similar in text to LORD CHAMBERLAIN. Trip appears as Spunge in *Dramatis Personae* (as in Frampton Court), then deleted. A long passage early in IV. i, here deleted, only found elsewhere in Frampton Court.

POWELL. Copy of I. i and part of ii from Drury Lane prompt-book by William Powell, the prompter, in connection with J. G. Raymond's proposal, 1809, to publish Sheridan's writings; now prefixed to *1779* (see above). (Harvard Theatre Collection.)

TICKELL. Owned and perhaps copied by Sheridan's niece Elizabeth Ann Tickell. His last thorough revision of play, c. 1812. First extant MS to include 'A Portrait'. (Bodleian.)

FAWCETT. Copy of Drury Lane prompt-book made by James Fawcett, an actor there and at Covent Garden, c. 1813. (Harvard Theatre Collection; contemporary copy in Henry E. Huntington Library, California.)

HOLL. Apparently c. 1840. Dialogue notable for large number of short cuts. Of interest for stage directions—fuller than FAWCETT, but similar. (Harvard Theatre Collection.)

Editions

1780. First of 'Dublin' editions. Unauthorized and corrupt text. *The School for Scandal, a Comedy; as it is performed at the Theatres-Royal, in London and Dublin* ('Dublin', 1780). Some 30 reprints by 1830. A corruption of the London version and not of the authentic Dublin text printed in 1799. Scolar Press facsimile (1969) has 6 pp. photocopied from Georgetown MS.

1786. The School for Scandal . . . From a Manuscript Copy in the Possession of John Henry, Esquire, Joint Manager of the American Company, given him by the Author (New York, 1786). A somewhat less corrupt text than *1780*, also reprinted several times in the United States and England. Although Henry did act once or twice at Drury Lane, Sheridan is most unlikely to have given him a copy of the play. Though certainly corrupt, the text has some readings of interest.

1799. Text derived from MS given by Sheridan to his sister Alicia, who sold to Ryder, manager of Smock Alley Theatre, Dublin, 1772–82. Text similar to LORD CHAMBERLAIN, but less advanced.

MURRAY. Included in Murray, Wilkie, Ridgway edition of Sheridan's *Works* (1821); Murray, alone (1823). Apparently printed from a copy of TICKELL, with gaps filled from late 'Dublin' edition. Seen through press by Thomas Wilkie.

CUMBERLAND. John Cumberland's edition 'taken from the acting copy', i.e., the current Drury Lane prompt-book (1826). George Daniel provided an introduction.

2. Works of Reference

MOORE. Thomas Moore's *Memoirs of the Life of . . . Sheridan* (2nd edition, 2 vols., 1825). Based upon the family papers, which Moore does not seem to have always returned.

RAE. W. Fraser Rae, *Sheridan. A Biography* (2 vols., 1896). (Rae's *The School for Scandal* (in his *Sheridan's Plays now printed as he wrote them*, 1902) transcribed the Frampton Court MS; it has no notes.)

SICHEL. Walter Sichel's *Sheridan* (2 vols., 1909). The fullest of the biographies.

RHODES. *The Plays and Poems of . . . Sheridan*, ed. R. Crompton Rhodes (3 vols., 1928). Contains much relevant information in its introductions and appendices, but its collations are incomplete and it has no explanatory notes.

LONDON STAGE. *The London Stage, 1660–1800: Part 5, 1777–1800*, ed. C. B. Hogan (Carbondale, Illinois, 1960–68). Indispensable for details of performances, actors, and staging.

LETTERS. *Letters of Richard Brinsley Sheridan*, ed. Cecil Price (3 vols., 1966).

PRICE. *The Dramatic Works of . . . Sheridan*, ed. Cecil Price (2 vols., 1973). The definitive edition.

3. Other Abbreviations

MLN   *Modern Language Notes*
N&Q   *Notes and Queries*

OED	*Oxford English Dictionary*
RES	*Review of English Studies*
TLS	*Times Literary Supplement*
om.	omit(s)
s.d.	stage direction

INTRODUCTION

THE AUTHOR

THE EXACT DATE of Sheridan's birth is not known; he was christened, however, on 4 November 1751 at St Mary's Anglican Church, Dublin. By a mistake of identity appropriate in a future comic dramatist, who was often to depend upon the device, the event is recorded in the church's register as that of 'Thos. Brinsley Sheridan'. His father, an actor of talent, especially in tragic parts, and at the time the successful if dictatorial manager of Dublin's Smock Alley Theatre, *was* a Thomas—as *his* father, Swift's versifying crony, had also been. The Sheridans, as the name's Celtic origin implies, were native Irish, even if now Protestant, and only some three or four generations separated them from the O'Sheridans of the primeval bog.[1]

It was the opinion of the marquis of Dufferin and Ava, Sheridan's one Victorian descendant to be ennobled, that apart from his poverty the greatest handicap under which Sheridan laboured throughout his life was his Irish origin.[2] The verdict was no doubt correct. At the back of the minds of the English aristocrats with whom he associated, he was always something of an Irish adventurer, as Burke was too. In the hindsight of history a different conclusion is also possible. By his mother, a Chamberlaine, Sheridan was Anglo-Irish rather than Irish. This now almost extinct product of the Protestant ascendancy was a racial hybrid. It has been characterized above all by wit, charm, gaiety, and an enormous self-confidence. And it has given the English theatre most of its comic masterpieces for two or more centuries. Sheridan followed Goldsmith as Shaw followed Wilde. There are also the lesser figures—Farquhar, Arthur Murphy, O'Hara, Hugh Kelly, O'Keefe in the eighteenth century alone. Even Congreve, Sheridan's model and master, was to some extent Anglo-Irish. And this national uncertainty has also had its moral implications.

Sheridan's first marriage collapsed in a personal Anglo-Irish tragedy. In 1773 he had married Elizabeth Linley, a beautiful and very successful Bath soprano, after a romantic series of adventures

---

[1] The fullest account of the family is in Walter Sichel's *Sheridan*, 2 vols. (1909).
[2] Introduction to W. Fraser Rae's *Sheridan. A Biography*, 2 vols. (1896), p. x.

that included an escape to a French convent under his escort as well as two duels, in the second of which he was almost killed. But romance could not survive his persistent infidelities in the following years and in the end the despairing Elizabeth fell in love with one of the heroes in Ireland's long fight for total independence from England—Lord Edward Fitzgerald. She died shortly after giving birth to a daughter by Fitzgerald. That was in 1792. Three years later Sheridan married a nineteen-year-old daughter of the then dean of Winchester.

As a boy, like his later friend and admirer Byron, Sheridan went to Harrow, where the great Parr detected promise in his Latin while deploring his usual mischievousness. (Joseph Surface's 'sentiments' are certainly almost Ciceronian in their unctuousness.) A Harrovian contemporary, Nathaniel Brassey Halhed—who was later to be one of the founders of Sanskrit scholarship—introduced Sheridan into the fascinations of authorship by persuading him to collaborate in a versification (in the style of Pope and Prior) of some of the prose *Erotica* of the obscure Byzantine sophist Aristaenetus. They completed eighteen which were published in 1772 as *The Love Epistles of Aristaenetus*. The tepid indecencies of Byzantium would seem to have found few purchasers, but the epistles that are generally ascribed to Sheridan[3] have a promising combination of gaiety and polish. He was to go on writing occasional verse with fluency if not distinction for many years, but in the period of separation from Elizabeth that was imposed by his father from August 1772 to March 1773 prose occupied most of his attention, and it is likely that some of the witticisms and comic anecdotes scribbled on separate sheets that eventually found their way into *The School for Scandal* belong to this period.[4] Certainly the lively and witty letters that Halhed sent Sheridan[5] during their Aristaenetus collaboration—to which Sheridan's replies have not survived—have a decided flavour of that equally minor poet Sir Benjamin Backbite.

Sheridan enters English literature with *The Rivals*. The play was produced at Covent Garden Theatre in January 1775 and was so successful after a shaky first night—primarily due to the Sir Lucius O'Trigger being drunk—that Sheridan, instead of becoming a barrister, as his father would have liked, decided to turn dramatist. *The Duenna*, which followed at Covent Garden on 21 November 1776, was even more successful and more lucrative. The system was still

---

[3] The verses are most easily accessible in *The Plays and Poems*, ed. R. Crompton Rhodes, III (1928).
[4] For the 'jottings' see below, pp. xxxvi–xxxviii.
[5] *Letters to R. B. Sheridan*, ed. R. B. Sheridan junior [1872].

being followed of allowing the third, sixth, and ninth nights' profits to go to the author. *The Duenna* ran for 75 nights in the 1776–77 season alone, creating a theatrical record for that time. And, whereas Sheridan was thought lucky to have sold the copyright of *The Rivals* for £200, *The Duenna*'s copyright is believed to have brought him £500 only twelve months later.

But he was already a big spender. A less irregular and precarious source of theatrical income had become desirable. Fortunately for Sheridan, Garrick was about to retire from his long reign at Drury Lane Theatre. His half-share of the monopoly created by Charles II for two London theatres—which, by a complicated process of descent, had become Drury Lane and Covent Garden in the mid-eighteenth century, with a Haymarket Theatre for the summer months—was put up for sale for £35,000. With the help of Elizabeth's father, who contributed £10,000, a sleeping partner called Dr Ford, £1,300 in cash from Sheridan, and mortgages amounting to £8,700 assumed by him, the sum was found. The other moiety was acquired by a similar process in 1778, when by assuming its owner's mortgages Sheridan actually received £1,300 in cash. At twenty-six he found himself effectively the owner of the most famous theatre in England—and a mountain of debts which accumulated year by year. But except temporarily he had not had to disgorge a penny.

Sheridan's political career is not our concern. In 1780 he was elected Member for Stafford and his fortunes advanced and receded with Fox's. His most splendid moment was no doubt the speech on the Begums of Oude, when in moving the charge against Warren Hastings he spoke for nearly six hours (February 1787). He also held various ministerial posts, usually in association with Fox, from 1782 to 1807. With the loss of his seat in the House of Commons in 1812, however, he became liable to arrest for debt and was actually imprisoned for brief periods. He died in 1816, being given a splendid public funeral in Westminster Abbey. By that time he had reduced his debts to £5,300.

The biographies of Sheridan begin with Thomas Moore's *Memoirs of the Life of the Right Honourable Richard Brinsley Sheridan* (1825). Moore, though he moved in the same social circles, did not know Sheridan well, but the family allowed him access to all of Sheridan's private papers, some of which he seems to have mislaid or incorporated in the copy he sent the printers. A less well written but more detailed life is that by Walter Sichel (1909). Cecil Price has prefixed a short summary of Sheridan's life and character to his indispensable edition of the *Letters* (1966; abbreviated henceforth to *Letters*). The equally indispensable edition of the *Dramatic Works* (1973; henceforth abbreviated to *Price*) has a useful list of Some Dates in Sheridan's Life (p. xv).

SHERIDAN AT DRURY LANE

When the actors of His Majesty's Theatre in Drury Lane reassembled after the usual summer recess in September 1776, their feelings would have been mixed. Garrick, who had ruled their little kingdom for twenty-nine years, had abdicated, having made his last bow in the undemanding part of Don Felix in Susannah Centlivre's still popular comedy *The Wonder: A Woman Keeps a Secret* on 10 June. The Drury Lane 1775–76 season closed that night. The new manager-proprietor was, as the newspapers called him, 'the young Mr Sheridan'. That Sheridan, only twenty-five years old, was fully aware that he was almost indecently young to be stepping into the great Garrick's shoes, must be presumed from his allowing himself to be described as 'Acting Manager'. In fact, he was some twenty years younger than any of his principal actors and forty years younger than some. And even the actresses were considerably older than he was. Mrs Abington, the company's brightest star, who was to play the part of Lady Teazle, the young country wife in *The School for Scandal*, was not far off forty. But, as the actors were well aware, the young Mr Sheridan already had to his credit two successes at Covent Garden, and it would be natural to assume that something even more brilliant was on the way. Moreover, he had the help of his father, who was an experienced actor and theatrical manager. One of his first acts, indeed, on obtaining possession of the theatre had been to appoint his father as the Drury Lane manager for three years—hence perhaps the technical correctness of the label he had assumed of Acting Manager—but the arrangement was not a success. Thomas Sheridan proved 'unequal to his duties'.[6] No doubt old animosities still rankled. A more useful member of the family for Sheridan was his partner and father-in-law Thomas Linley, who was a successful musician and was to make 'Here's to the maiden of bashful fifteen' one of the hits of the century. Sheridan's wife kept the theatre accounts, neatly and accurately, and even undertook to read all the plays submitted to the theatre by aspiring dramatists.

[6] *Letters*, I, 341. His father, a strict disciplinarian, had greatly preferred the more docile elder brother, whom he wrongly thought the genius of the family.

Publicly the Sheridan era at His Majesty's Theatre in Drury Lane opened with a revival of *As You Like It* on 21 September 1776. As a Shakespeare play in which Garrick had not participated its selection was a prudent one, and the evening began—'punctually at six o'clock'—with a humorous prologue from Garrick himself on the theme 'The Stage is a Stage-Coach':

> Your late Old Coachman, tho' oft splash'd by dirt,
> And out in many a storm, retires unhurt.

This was included in a clever comic 'Prelude' by George Colman, who was in his last year as joint manager-proprietor of Covent Garden, the rival 'patent' theatre, and was shortly to take over the Little Theatre in the Haymarket. Colman's *New Brooms*, subtitled 'An Occasional Prelude', is a humorous warning from an old hand in the business of the perilous path the young manager was about to tread.[7] Let him beware, for example, of Catcall, the professional puffer, who writes as *'Dramaticus* in the Chronicle, the *Observer* in the Post, the *Elephant* in the Packet, the *Drury-Lane Mouse*, and *Covent-Garden Cricket'*,[8] a figure of fun who was to be amplified in Sheridan's own still unwritten *The Critic*.

The omens, then, for the new management, were distinctly favourable. Sheridan could not have had a more encouraging welcome from the old guard of the London stage, and there is no indication that the actors had their reservations. But it soon became apparent that he was a far from ideal manager. His one immediate innovation was to revive two of Congreve's comedies, which were no longer in the repertoire: *The Old Bachelor* (19 November), which ran for 10 nights, and *Love for Love* (29 November), which ran for 8 nights. Both had been announced as 'with Alterations', primarily of the verbal indecencies. An 'Occasional Prologue' by Sheridan (of which there is a MS in the Henry E. Huntington Library, California, that Sheridan editors would seem to have missed) preceded the revisions of Congreve on 16 November and ridiculed those spectators who complain that Congreve's wit is obscene:

> What! shall they lop and lop Will: Congreve's page,
> They'd better send him to the Opera Stage.

This was a curious under-estimation of the latent Puritanism of his time. That any changes that were made were trivial may be inferred

---

[7] Colman explains in an 'Advertisement' that 'The following little Piece was written at the request of Mr SHERIDAN'. He had been helped by a friend now 'in his retirement', who was clearly Garrick. (*The Poetical Works of David Garrick* (1785), II, 327, confirms the identification.)
[8] *New Brooms.* See *The Dramatic Works of George Colman*, IV (1777), 331.

from the comparatively short runs both revivals had, and from Sheridan's failure to submit either of them to the Lord Chamberlain to obtain the licence for their performance under Walpole's 'gagging' Act of 1737.

That his Drury Lane audience would not tolerate any but the mildest indecency in the play to which he was putting the final touches early in 1777 is an aspect of *The School for Scandal* which must not be overlooked. Sheridan wanted to write a Congrevian comedy, but his public would not tolerate a wholehearted comedy of sex, as it would have to be if it was to be in the Congreve tradition, except with *the teeth drawn*. Is a comedy of sex possible if the characters have first to be unsexed?

A Trip to Scarborough (first night 17 February 1777) was a decidedly 'lopped' version of Vanbrugh's *The Relapse*. Even so Edward Capell, the Shakespeare scholar then a deputy for the Lord Chamberlain's Examiner of Plays, complained that a sentence— which is in fact *verbatim* from Vanbrugh—'ought to be soften'd'.[*] In general, however, Sheridan did enough 'softening' for the play to become a stock piece. Vanbrugh's construction has been tidied up, but otherwise—apart from the title—Sheridan's own contribution is minimal except for much industrious deletion. Berinthia's sexuality is reduced to flirtatiousness, and only Hoyden, the uninhibited female animal, retains some of her original outrageous exuberance. (Hoyden was to provide such comic actresses as Mrs Abington and Mrs Jordan with a much-loved escape from the drawing-room parts to which they were generally condemned.)

By this time Sheridan, having learned how far it was safe to become the new Congreve, was completing his new play. The newspapers soon learned that a new comedy 'from the pen of the acting Manager', was in preparation. 'Each Actor in the Piece', the *Morning Chronicle* reported on 16 April, 'it is said, is already in possession of a fourth part of his character'. Garrick was optimistic of its success. 'A New Comedy', he wrote to Lady Spencer on 5 April 1777, 'is preparing at Drury Lane call'd the *School for Scandal* . . . I am told there is a great deal of wit'.[10] In due course he wrote a

[*] The sentence (in III. ii) was 'Look you Amanda, you may build Castles in the Air, and fume, and fret, and grow thin and lean, and pale, and ugly, if you please but I tell you *no Man worth having is true to his wife*, or ever will be so'. Berinthia was speaking. I have italicized the offensive clause.

[10] *Price*, p. 297 n. Garrick later attended the rehearsals. His one recorded advice to Sheridan was to bring the scandalmongers into the Auction scene, so as to avoid the flatness of having only one bidder (cit. *Price*, p. 299).

witty prologue for the play in which he stands up for 'our Young Bard'. The immediate success of *The School for Scandal* must have pleased him. Although not acted until 8 May—at the tail-end of the theatrical season—it ran for 20 nights to 7 June 1777, ran again in the 1777–78 season, and had altogether 261 performances at Drury Lane alone by the end of the 1799–1800 season. Though *The School for Scandal* is not by any means the best English comedy ever written, as Henry Irving surprisingly thought that it was, its unprecedented contemporary success is a historical fact that criticism must not forget.

Sheridan's gradual disengagement from and disenchantment with Drury Lane and its affairs can be summarized briefly. With the brilliant exception of *The Critic or A Tragedy Rehearsed* (first performance 30 October 1779)—whose first act Sheridan rightly considered of more value than any thing he ever wrote—his later plays and collaborations have little or no literary interest. *Pizarro* (24 May 1799), an adaptation from Kotzebue—a German playwright only remembered today because his *Lovers' Vows* was the play selected for the disastrous amateur theatricals in Jane Austen's *Mansfield Park*—had a *succés de scandale* because of its political allusions. Cecil Price has also included two 'improvisations', as he calls them, in his excellent edition of Sheridan's *Dramatic Works*. Although Sheridan's attendance to the claims of Drury Lane became more casual after 1780, when he was elected M.P. for Stafford, it remained an important source of income for him until the theatre was destroyed by fire in 1809.[11]

THE ORIGINAL CAST[12]

Charles Lamb's essay 'On the Artificial Comedy of the Last Century'[13] brings the modern reader closer than anything else I know to what it felt like seeing a performance of *The School for Scandal* as Sheridan intended it. Although Lamb had been to Drury Lane as a boy and had seen *The Way of the World* there in the 1781–82

[11] The depressing details of Sheridan's final decade at Drury Lane have been recorded by the indispensable Price in *Theatre Survey*, 17 (May 1976), 12–27.
[12] The late C. Deelman had a good essay on this topic in *RES* (1962), 257–66.
[13] As originally published in the *London Magazine* (April 1822) this was the second of three essays called 'The Old Actors'. The present title derives from the *Elia* collection (1823).

season, it was only in the 1789–90 season that he became an addicted playgoer. At that date many of the original cast of *The School for Scandal* still retained their old parts. The essay was written in 1822, but from the actors he specifies it is clear that he is writing from his earliest memories of the play.

The essay is often dismissed as a sophisticated defence of the immorality of Restoration comedy ('the utopia of gallantry', etc.), but this is to miss Lamb's central point—which is that *The School for Scandal*, which occupies Lamb for much of the essay, is essentially 'artificial', a play at the opposite extreme from the realism of Ibsen and his sentimental predecessors. The seduction scenes between Joseph and Lady Teazle are not the real article, just as the scandal-mongering of Mrs Candour, Crabtree, and Sir Benjamin cannot be taken seriously either. This satire has no bite. What Sheridan provides is 'good theatre'—with at its best moments premonitions of the 'nonsense' of Gilbert and Wilde, or even of Lear and Carroll. The characters are mere outlines—farcical types inviting the skilful actor to fill them out and give them flesh.

This, as Lamb put it, was a *'manager's comedy'*. Sheridan had inherited from Garrick some of the most skilful actors in Europe, and he knew exactly what each member of his company was capable of. This was true even of the beautiful 'Perdita' Robinson, not yet the prince of Wales's mistress, who could always be looked at with pleasure, but was often not heard at all, and who was therefore allotted the primarily decorative minor part of Maria. (Unfortunately Mrs Robinson became too obviously *enceinte* and the part had to go to the prompter's daughter Priscilla Hopkins, who had her youth to recommend her but little else.[14])

Lamb's most memorable comments in the essay are on the Joseph of John Palmer:

> When I remember the gay boldness, the graceful solemn plausibility, the measured step, the insinuating voice—to express it in a word—the downright *acted* villainy of the part, so different from the pressure of conscious actual wickedness,—the hypocritical assumption of hypocrisy,—which made Jack so deservedly a favourite in that character, I must needs conclude the present generation of play-goers more virtuous than myself, or more dense . . . The highly artificial manner of Palmer in this character counteracted every disagreeable impression which you might have received from the contrast, supposing them real, between the two brothers.

---

[14] The *London Magazine's* verdict (XLVI (1777), 232) was 'far from being striking'. She later married John Philip Kemble.

There is more, much more on Palmer, including a comparison with John Philip Kemble's Joseph, and also throwaway phrases like 'the pleasant old Teazle of *King*', and of Miss Pope (the original Mrs Candour) 'the perfect gentlewoman as distinguished from the fine lady of comedy'.

An actor's potential ability to turn his author's overt meaning almost upside-down—to re-create it, in fact—is recognized in Lamb's comment on the first scene of Act V:

> Charles [is] the real canting person of the scene—for the hypocrisy of Joseph has its legitimate ulterior ends, but his brother's professions of a good heart centre in downright self-satisfaction . . .

This is perhaps the basic weakness of the play. As compared with Congreve, Sheridan is not artificial enough. The contradiction is evident at a technical level on the confusion of the 'aside' and the soliloquy. The auction scene (IV. i) derives much of its humour from the 'asides' of Sir Oliver *in propria persona* contrasted with what he is compelled to say in his role as Mr Premium. This is acceptable because of the convention of the 'aside' as inaudible except to the audience. It is disconcerting therefore to have Lady Teazle entering Joseph's library two or three minutes later (IV. iii) with the words 'What, sentiment in soliloquy now!' The convention has become a reality. Lady Teazle has *overheard* what she correctly describes as a soliloquy, though it was only the sound of Joseph speaking that she has heard and not the gist of what he had said. But even the sound of his speaking should have been audible only to the audience.

Such potential abuses of an established convention made it easier for a clever actor to reinterpret a part. Reinterpretations of Shakespeare's plays in their own words by such actors as Garrick, Macklin, the Kemble family (which included Mrs Siddons), and Kean, differentiate the Sheridan epoch totally from the earlier adaptations, or rewritings, of the Restoration. *The eighteenth century was the period of actor-ascendancy*. For a play to succeed a certain thematic malleability had become above all necessary.

The about-turn in his character—from villain to semi-hero—that Palmer was able to effect for Joseph was repeated by Mrs Abington in the character of Lady Teazle. She retired from the stage in the year when Lamb's theatregoing began, and for her—as also for 'Gentleman' Smith, the original Charles Surface, and Thomas King, the Sir Peter (all three retired in 1790)—we must depend on critics less subtle and sensitive than Lamb.

James Boaden's lives of John Philip Kemble (1825) and Mrs

Siddons (1827) are mines of accurate information and comment, and Boaden being thirteen years older than Lamb, his memories of the Sheridan period go further back. On King, the first Sir Peter and the speaker of Garrick's prologue to *The School for Scandal*, his comment is that 'his peculiar sententious manner made him seek and require dialogue of the greatest point', which he combined with 'rapid utterance'.[15] Mrs Abington, too, who spoke the play's traditional comic epilogue (written by Colman) in the character of Lady Teazle, had, according to Boaden, 'a tartness in her pleasantry', that made her 'so fine a speaker of humour, like her friend Tom King . . . that they each lost nearly half their soul in separation'.[16] Another aspect of her performance, inevitably lost in the reading, is her long-distance sexual fascination for the original audience. She was fortyish when *The School for Scandal* was produced, and instead of the country girl revelling in London almost for the first time, as was apparently Sheridan's general intention, Mrs Abington exploited her riper charms and maturer knowledge of the love-game. Thus the *London Magazine* is provoked to comment on the scenes with Joseph that 'if there was any seduction at either side, it seemed to arise on that of the lady'. As Cecil Price reminds us, there was an inherent piquancy in the real-life parallel of the widely known fact that Mrs Abington was the mistress of the earl of Shelburne.

Real life added a similar further dimension to the character of Charles. William Smith, who monopolized the part until he retired, was not an actor *pretending* to be a gentleman. Educated at Eton and St John's College, Cambridge, and married in due course to the daughter of a peer, 'Gentleman' Smith *was* a gentleman, who had only to act his real self in the part.

Sheridan's inability or unwillingness to control the further evolution of his *dramatis personae* on the stage is evident even in such minor characters as Moses and Trip. Moses was acted by Robert Baddeley, a versatile character actor who had played Polonius and Petulant (in *The Way of the World*) the previous season. Sheridan's MSS and the editions with an authentic text make it clear that his part was intended to be rendered in correct English. But, according to *The Gazeteer* of 9 May 1777 he 'played the part . . . as a real Jew' in the original production, and this is confirmed by the text of the pirated 'Dublin' edition (1780) in II. iii, which has 'dat' for 'that' three times as well as examples of broken English ('Yes, dat

[15] James Boaden, *Memoirs of the Life of John Philip Kemble Esq.*, I, 59 (cit. *Price*, p. 304).
[16] ibid., I, 83 (cit. *Price*, p. 304).

is very great point', 'if you ask him no more as dat', 'he wants money very bad'). Trip, a similar case, was acted by Philip La Mash, who excelled as a gentleman's gentleman. Such parts are said to have 'fitted him like his clothes'[17] and he adorned them with a French accent, which is not once justified by Sheridan's text.

No doubt the usurpation of a dramatist's intentions or even his text by an actor or actress is a not uncommon phenomenon, but with *The School for Scandal* the process went much further and earlier than is usual. Sheridan's reaction—both with this play and with *The Critic*[18]—was not to correct an actor's interpretation but to provide what might be called a reading text, as in the 1781 edition of *The Critic*, side by side with the acting text used by Drury Lane Theatre. The details of the process are described in the following section.

That the discrepancy between authorial intention and theatrical tradition could be disconcerting for the actor is evident in the case of Charles Mathews, the brother of Wordsworth's early friend. Sheridan offered Mathews the part of Sir Peter and then read it aloud to him to make it clear how Sir Peter *ought* to be acted:

> Mr. Mathews had many misgivings on this subject, and most embarrassing it proved in the result; for so totally unlike was Mr. Sheridan's reading of the character from every other conception of it, that it was next to impossible for the actor to adopt any one of his suggestions . . . The consequence may be anticipated. Mr. Sheridan was dissatisfied with Mr. Mathews's performance when the night came, (as, it was said in the green-room, he had been with every previous representative of it, including King) . . .[19]

STAGING

That *The School for Scandal* acts better than it reads is no doubt still true. Horace Walpole's original enthusiasm on *seeing* it ('I have seen Sheridan's new comedy, and liked it much better than any I have seen since *The Provoked Husband*', i.e., by implication any of the stock plays continually revived), contrasts with his disappointment when *reading* a manuscript of the play: 'I have *read* the *School for Scandal*: it is rapid and lively, but is far from containing the

[17] J. Bernard, *Retrospections of the Stage*, I (1830), 319 (cit. *Price*, p. 310).
[18] I made the general point—with examples from *The Critic*—in a *TLS* letter of 9 May 1935.
[19] A. Mathews, *Memoirs of Charles Mathews, Comedian*, 2 vols. (1838–39), II, 6–7 (cit. *Price*, p. 304).

The collapse of the screen, IV. iii, 385. From an original print

wit I expected from seeing it acted'.[20] But Walpole was at least familiar with the physical conditions under which the play had been originally produced. The modern reader has not that advantage.

The stage at Drury Lane, for one thing, still projected some 12–14 feet into the auditorium. This 'apron' or 'forestage' was where the actors tended to cluster. A 1778 print of the screen scene (IV. iii) shows the screen itself approximately on the curtain-line, with Joseph level with the 'proscenium door' out of which he has just emerged; Sir Peter and Charles are on the curtain-line and only Lady Teazle is behind it, though she too is a long way from the back of the stage.

The advantages in greater audibility and closer intimacy with the audience are part of the reason why the forestage was retained. Its persistence made the 'aside' still effective. The comicality of the auction scene hinges on the ignorance of Charles and Careless of who 'Mr Premium' really is and the opportunities this gives Sir Oliver to share his true identity with the audience in a series of asides that fall hopelessly flat in a modern theatre. The surviving prints of this scene, both the unrealistic illustrations to the 1788 and 1793 pirated 'Dublin' editions and the more realistic one by Bunbury (April 1789), all show the actors bunched together; but by simply turning to the audience Sir Oliver was able to share the joke with them without it seeming totally implausible.

The projecting stage had its corollary in the two solid and traditional proscenium doors, each immediately adjoining the stage boxes. It was through these doors that Sheridan's actors made their entries and exits. As long as the doors remained in regular use the actors were compelled to have a forestage in order that their arrivals and departures should not be delayed by a long walk towards or from the area where the others were concentrated. It was not necessary apparently for the doors to be shut all the time. In the prompt-copy with '1778' on its cover in the British Library the preliminary note to II. ii (Lady Sneerwell's *soirée*) has 'the doors open', and so the characters do not have to be announced by a servant as they arrive; as they had been in I. i (Lady Sneerwell's dressing-room). *1778*, as it may be called, is probably the copy of a prompt-book rather than an actual prompt-book, but it has many details about the early production of *The School for Scandal* that have not hitherto been

[20] *Correspondence*, ed. W. S. Lewis, XXVIII (1955), 309 (16 May 1777); XXIX (1955), 35 (19 May 1780). Both to Mason. That it was not the pirated 'Dublin' edition of 1780 that disappointed Walpole is clear from the date of the second letter. The 'Dublin' edition was not being advertised until December 1780.

recorded. One is the regular incidence of 'discovery scenes'. The term is used by Sheridan himself in *The Critic* (III. i): [21]

Scene I—Before the Curtain
Enter Puff, Sneer *and* Dangle.

PUFF
    Well, we are ready. Now then for the Justices.
        Curtain rises; Justices, Constables, etc., *discovered.*
PUFF
    . . . What, gentlemen, do you mean to go at once to the discovery scene?

Naturally such technical terms do not enter into the dialogue of *The School for Scandal*, but they were evidently differentiated in the prompt-book with great care. Of the 14 scenes in the play, 4 are 'discovery scenes', one in each of the first four acts. These include the crucial IV. iii (Joseph's library)—a long scene on which the talented de Louther-bourg, the German-French painter who was in charge of the scenery at Drury Lane, lavished all his skill.[22] As the passage quoted from *The Critic* illustrates, the essence of a 'discovery' is that there should be characters already on the stage—as in I. i (Lady Sneerwell and Snake)—and that they should generally be seated when the curtain rises. In the 1778 engraving Joseph's library has what seem to be two enclaves on each side supported by elaborate pillars. De Loutherbourg had appar-ently converted the five 'wings'—in interiors normally painted to give the illusion of wallpaper—into something strange and new. (He may have felt justified by Joseph's insistence at the end of II. ii that Lady Teazle should honour her promise 'to give me your judgment on my library'.)

    The scenery, apart from 'wings', was normally a large back-flat

[21] The Buckinghamshire and the two Crewe MSS do have 'discover'd' for II. ii, as has *1778*. The term's presence cannot be taken as regularly distinguishing an acting version, though it will normally point to such an ultimate basis.
[22] Philippe Jacques de Loutherbourg, a German trained in Paris, joined the Drury Lane Theatre in 1771. In due course he became an R.A., and his value to Sheridan in 1777 is indicated by a salary of £500, which was as much as that of Thomas King, his principal actor and his stage-mana-ger (*Letters*, I, 114). De Loutherbourg's scenic triumphs were principally in tragedy or such romances as *The Tempest*. In addition to the Library his flat for Charles's Picture Room was much admired. Zoffany's portrait of Robert Baddeley (now in the Lady Leverhulme Collection and repro-duced in *Theatre Notebook*, VI (Oct.–Dec. 1951)) shows the skill with which de Loutherbourg introduced Charles's ancestral portraits into the scenery. (There is Deborah as a shepherdess, etc.)

held in 'grooves' on the stage and in the flies. Such flats were divided vertically in the middle, and the scene-shifting reduced itself to the two halves being joined in the right 'groove'. Sheridan's Drury Lane had five such grooves, the first being about 9 feet from the pro-scenium line and the four others about 5 feet apart from each other. As the depth of the scene depended entirely on the groove selected, this is a detail inserted at the head of each scene in the prompt-books. In *The School for Scandal* the shorter scenes generally demanded a second groove; Charles's drinking-party required a third groove and his picture room a fourth—as did Joseph's library.

As listed in the early prompt-books, the number of properties seems to have been minimal, and the same impression is given by such paintings as the Garrick Club screen scene (by David Roberts[23]) and Zoffany's Baddeley (as Moses), the illustrations in the 'Dublin' editions and the separate engravings. James Boaden's early memories of 'the miserable pairs of flats that used to clap together on even the stage trodden by Mr. Garrick; architecture without selection or propriety; a hall, a castle or a chamber; or a cut wood of which all the verdure seemed to have been washed away'[24] do not descend to the properties—perhaps because even Kemble, the principal re-former (he became Sheridan's manager at Drury Lane in 1788), left them alone. The surviving copies of the prompt-book repeat them-selves. IV. iii has a screen opposite the second wing, 3 chairs, a table and books (1778); James Fawcett's copy 'from the Promptor's Book, of the Theatre Royal, Drury Lane' (*c.* 1813) had the screen, two chairs in front of it and one behind, a table with a book on it; the Holl copy (*c.* 1840 at Harvard) also has the screen, the table, the two chairs 'and a seat behind it', and the one book.

The absence of all non-essential properties was a by-product of the use of two separate curtains. A green curtain had been in use since the Restoration, which 'rose' by being pulled up in three or four shallow festoons. This was a signal to the audience that the performance had begun and it did not fall until the farce which normally followed a five-act play had been completed. (*The School for Scandal* was followed on its first night by Samuel Foote's *The Mayor of Garratt*, perhaps the best of his satiric pieces, which had been originally produced at the Haymarket in 1769.) Behind the green curtain was a drop-curtain painted with a conventional design which was not introduced until *c.* 1750 when it was lowered at the

[23] Reproduced in *Theatre Notebook*, VI (Oct.–Dec. 1951). The Zoffany is also in the same issue.
[24] Boaden, *Kemble*, I, xxi.

end of each act. With a new play the prologue was spoken in front of it—as was the epilogue at the end of Act V of a five-act play.

The second or act-curtain was useful not only as a signal that the act was ended but as providing an opportunity for the scene-shifters to remove the flat and change the chairs and table, etc. of the last scene. The skilful dramatist usually saw to it that the penultimate scene had a flat in a groove nearer the audience than the last scene, so that the scene-shifters would not be unduly hurried.

A scene requiring changes of flats and properties within the act had to be made in full view of the audience. It was a more general requirement that each scene should begin with a different set of characters than those who had held the stage at the end of the preceding scene or act.

Sheridan was not particularly careful to carry out these conventions or conveniences. The flat was apparently in the second groove in I. i, but, according to Shargl, in the first in I. ii ('Sir Peter's Antique Chamber'). In II. i the 'scene continues'; in II. ii the groove is not specified, but as Holl demands 'Palace Arch Flats', it is presumably the fourth or fifth groove. In II. iii we return to Sir Peter's 'Antique Chamber' now, according to *Fawcett*, in the second groove, which cannot have allowed the flat to be installed in advance. In III. i the 'scene continues' in the second groove, though the 'Antique Chamber' is now described as striped; III. ii is a 'Drop' chamber in *1778, Fawcett,* and *Holl*, and was presumably independent of grooves, but III. iii (Charles's 'Antique Hall') is in the third groove and IV. i (the 'Picture Room') in the fourth groove (which would allow some advance preparation). IV. ii is again a 'Hall Drop', by the use of which time will have been provided for the Library scene (IV. iii). V. i calls for the Library once more, but with V. ii ('Antique Chamber') in second groove the audience must have seen the scene-shifting; but the Library flat can have remained undisturbed for 'Scene the last'.

Are there any conclusions to be drawn from the preceding analysis? One at least suggests itself, viz. that the earlier scenes—which carried over material from two juvenile sketches ('The Slanderers' and 'The Teazles')—are less expert than the second half of the play, most of which was probably written after Sheridan had installed himself in Drury Lane Theatre. The young would-be dramatist may well have been ignorant of the mysteries of grooves and scene-shifting; and he would almost certainly not have known that drop-scenes could be unrolled from the flies to supplement the flats. Such 'drops' had only been introduced apparently towards the end of Garrick's reign and were normally confined to scenes with the most conventional and uninteresting background. Two scenic innovations that are not recorded in *1778* (though they appear in Fawcett's copy of the Drury Lane prompt-book, and must therefore have received his at least tacit approval) are (i) the use of the gaps between the wings as a less obtrusive mode of exit than by the traditional proscenium doors, and (ii) the introduction of a central door in the flats themselves for the same purpose. Both devices were only used in the more crowded scenes. The second of these reforms—no doubt attributable to the innovating John Philip Kemble—is exemplified by the temporary absence of Joseph and Maria in II. ii. Lady Sneerwell suggests to Maria that she should 'sit down to piquet with Mr. Surface'. This is not followed by a stage direction in the early texts (including *1778*), but Fawcett's copy of the Drury Lane prompt-book adds 'Retires up with Lady Sneerwell and Surface M.D.', which becomes in the Holl prompt-book 'going into the next room through the door in the scene M.D.', the initials therefore standing for 'Middle Door', as opposed to P.S. (prompter's side) and O.P. (opposite prompter) which are regularly used for the proscenium doors.[25]

Stage Directions

The preceding example illustrates once again the gap between *The School for Scandal* as literature (good reading matter) and the play as a good theatrical performance. Like earlier English dramatists but at the opposite extreme from such early twentieth-century classics as Shaw and Barrie (who were the first to provide long and detailed stage directions), Sheridan assumed that his plays would act themselves for the reader from the dialogue alone. His method in preparing the manuscript presentation copies with which he honoured a few friends was to use theatrical copyists to prepare copies of the play from the current prompt-book and exclude all but the bare minimum of stage directions. These were adequate for the play's first critical reader—the Lord Chamberlain's Assistant Licenser of Plays. With rare exceptions, directions are limited to the entries and exits, and the place—very occasionally the time too—at which a scene occurred. It was assumed that the reader had already seen the plays acted, Sheridan's like Shakespeare's immediately becoming 'stock' plays.

---

[25] This section is indebted to Richard Southern's *Changeable Scenery: its Origin and Development in the British Theatre* (1952), which draws on the accumulated notes of W. J. Lawrence, one of the insufficiently recognized pioneers of English (and Irish) theatrical history. I have also found C. B. Hogan's introduction to the 1776–1800 vol. of *The London Stage* (Carbondale, Illinois, 1960–68) most helpful. They should be referred to for fuller treatment of this topic.

But were all Sheridan's closest friends and admirers theatregoers? The possibility, discussed elsewhere, that the manuscript known as the 'second' Crewe MS or *Crewe B* was originally a presentation copy to Mrs Crewe's mother Mrs Greville—now elderly but famous as poet, wit, and society hostess, and the dedicatee of *The Critic*— might explain why her manuscript has such an exceptionally large number of stage directions added in Sheridan's easily recognizable hand. Her daughter's manuscript, known as the 'first' Crewe MS or the Georgetown MS (it is now owned by that Washington university), has proportionately fewer directions.

The practice in the greater number of stage directions in the two Crewe manuscripts, the manuscript known as 'Spunge' (from the name given to Trip in the list of *dramatis personae* in it), and the Murray edition (1821 and 1823), which is textually comparable to these three manuscripts, is to insert 'Aside' in passages where the actors would have done so in a performance. But some other specimens of directions omitted by the copyists are of perhaps greater interest:

I. i, 30 *'They rise'*. *Spunge* (*'Get up'*, 1778 copy of prompt-book)
See below note, p. 8
I. i, 362ff. *'Going'* (4 times) followed by *'Returning'* or *'Returns'* (3 times).
Spunge (of Crabtree and Sir Benjamin)
III. i, 189 *'Kissing her hand'* (*Fawcett*)
IV. i, 20 *'Takes down a roll'* (*Georgetown*)
IV. iii, 260ff. *'Peeping'* (Lady Teazle, for third time; both Crewe MSS).

In this edition I have added from the prompt-books, or copies from them, the side of the stage from which entries and exits are made, 'left' and 'right' meaning facing the audience. The Banbury MS is, I believe, the only presentation copy to have this information, which is regularly noted in the prompt-copies. Movements across, up, or down the stage are not generally included in the notes.

Costumes

Unlike tragedy, for which Garrick had already taken the first steps to historically authentic costumes, comedy reflected the dress of the moment—but in its most expensive form. That Mrs Abington, the star of Drury Lane comedy, should have had in her contract with the theatre for 1781 £500 a year for her wardrobe as well as 'eighteen guineas a-week as an actress, together with a benefit' would make it credible that 'she never appears on the stage but in her own clothes'.[26] Her benefit night for 1777 was estimated by Sheridan to be worth £600.[27]

Zoffany's portrait of Baddeley as Moses,[28] makes the proper social distinction. He is wearing an elaborately curled black wig without powder. In other words he is rich but not a gentleman. The male Surfaces and Teazle demonstrate their gentility by refusing to wear a wig but covering their hair with white powder. Their ladies, on the other hand, have tall and elaborate headdresses. Roberts's painting[29] of the screen-scene shows Sir Peter, Joseph, and Charles, all wearing almost identical contemporary suits, sumptuously plain but with their heads white with powder, and Lady Teazle looking rather absurd underneath her enormous headdress. The picture nicely confirms Charles's epigram in the auction scene (it is addressed to Moses):

> Here now are two that were a sort of cousins of theirs. You see, Moses, these pictures were done some time ago, when beaux wore wigs, and the ladies their own hair. (IV. i, 53–6)

The School for Scandal on the eighteenth-century stage: certainties and possibilities

The kind of prompt-book detail which, as we see from this section of the introduction and from the commentary notes, survives for *The School for Scandal*, allows us to construct with fair accuracy an account of the staging of an early performance of the play, and so to bring it alive as the theatrical triumph it was from the very beginning.

The green curtain rises to signal the beginning of the performance, but the drop-curtain behind it is still in place behind him as Tom King comes out on to the forestage, dressed as he will be to play the part of Sir Peter Teazle. The audience are not in darkness; Tom King, like Sir Peter, is a modern man in contemporary dress; the time is the present. What is powerfully suggested is that real people, like King or anyone in the audience, play their parts in plays like the one that is to be seen. That sense of immediate possibility and credibility is the foundation of the link between *The School for Scandal* and its contemporary audience. It was not an eighteenth-century costume piece for them, and it was the real world which furnished them in this play with their sense of the extraordinary.

---

[26] *A Picture of England.* Translated from the German of Wide Archenholtz (1797), p. 110.
[27] *Letters,* I, 113.
[28] Now in the Lady Leverhulme Collection, Port Sunlight. Reproduced in *Theatre Notebook,* VI (Oct.–Dec. 1951).
[29] In the Garrick Club, London.

In the prologue, written by Garrick and spoken by King on the forestage, the whole relationship between stage and audience is played out. The prologue has stage directions incorporated (*sips*), and there can be little doubt that King came on stage with a cup of tea and a newspaper, entering probably through the left proscenium door, as Sir Peter does at his first entrance, in I. ii.

So Tom King, dressed as Sir Peter, enters with Lady Wormwood's tea and newspaper, and reaches her direct speech at line 9. Lady Wormwood then, by reading aloud from the newspaper, returns upon the audience's most everyday experience. The veils of fiction, each of them no more than a filmily thin separation from real life, lead through a sequence that comes to rest in everyday reality. The theatrical metaphor of line 17 ensures that the audience's present position as spectators in a theatre is also caught in the sequence. The play extends itself a little as King begins to speak the manservant's words as well, before it reaches a brief climax and disappears to leave King once again speaking in his own person to the audience. All these fictional manoeuvres have altered nothing, have left undisturbed the relationship between player and spectators. The imaginative extension is not in depth, to worlds beyond worlds, but is horizontal; and so, as the play proper begins, we should be prepared for a use of the depth of the inner stage not to give us another world, an exotic or imagined world, as sometimes it did in the eighteenth-century theatre, but to give extension to a world already established on the forestage. The inner stage functions in this play, then, as a version of the rooms and houses outside the theatre from which the audience has come to the play, and not as a world they can never hope to visit, even though that familiar world is itself subdivided into the more and the less sympathetic.

At the beginning of the play proper, the drop-curtain rises to reveal the discovery scene of Lady Sneerwell's dressing room. Lady Sneerwell sitting to the right and Snake sitting to the left must in the audience's mind be a kind of Lady Wormwood and Lisp now brought dramatically to life as they introduce the scandalmongering society they live in. The inner stage is not very deep here, so that when Lady Sneerwell rises at line 30 she would need only two or three steps to bring her to the place where the prologue was spoken, and perhaps it is here, at a point on the stage which is in more intimate relationship with the spectators, that for the first time she directly addresses the audience and not Snake or her own dressing table as she confesses in terms that a little arouse our sympathy what motives drive her (lines 31–6).

After an exposition of the basic intrigue involving Charles and Joseph Surface, Lady Sneerwell and Maria, Joseph enters by the left proscenium door, through which all Lady Sneerwell's visitors arrive, announced by a servant in formal fashion, but leaving the door open behind him. As a consequence, after Snake's exit, right, into the less public part of Lady Sneerwell's house at line 123, Maria can come in abruptly and unannounced at line 133. Both at her entrance here and throughout her time on stage in this scene, Maria is not part of the formal, mannered world in which scandal flourishes. When Mrs Candour comes in, again stage left, as the next visitor, formally announced, Lady Sneerwell and Mr Surface are, as it were, socially visible to her immediately, but only after a moment or two does she say, 'Ah, Maria, child!' (line 185). Both Maria's speech here in the exchange with Mrs Candour, her silence after the formal arrival of Crabtree and Sir Benjamin, and no doubt her obscure and unflamboyant position on stage, contribute to the audience's sense of her singularity amid the other characters. Maria's position, of course, is not one of weakness but of strength, and her exit, left (away from Lady Sneerwell's), at line 350 is not formally negotiated with the group of characters on stage but is enabled by a private word to the audience: 'Their malice is intolerable.'

Maria's exit, abrupt, determined and principled, contrasts with the rest of I. i, which is full of 'dishonest' exits and half-exits, if there can be such things. There is a finality about the fact of a character leaving the stage which could have been explored by the players here either (as with Maria) to leave with the audience a sense of simple and honest decision, or to leave an impression of murky double-dealing.

At the beginning of the next scene, Sir Peter has to come on left because Lady Sneerwell has just exited right with Joseph; but coming through the left proscenium door on to the forestage he also reminds us of Tom King speaking the prologue, especially since his first speech is alone to the audience. There begins to develop as the pattern of the play unfolds a distinction between the ceremonious, socially formal world of the scandalmongers (which appropriately the audience, as it were, overhears) and the more relaxed and direct relationship with the audience that we have seen by now both with Maria and Sir Peter.

The scene with Sir Peter and Lady Teazle at the beginning of Act II follows a little awkwardly the division between the acts. The curtain has dropped and rises again to reveal the same scene and Sir Peter coming on by the door through which he has just exited. However the exchange between him and his young wife allows the discovery scene at II. ii to be set up behind the first groove flats. This scene is to take place further back on the inner stage but is as yet concealed by the scene in progress at II. i. There is thus a sharply dramatic contrast between Sir Peter speaking direct to the audience at the end of II. i, and Lady Sneerwell merely overheard and more remote from the audience at the beginning of II. ii, as Sir Peter exits and the flats are drawn aside to reveal the scene behind at a much greater depth of stage (fourth or fifth groove).

Much of II. ii does not so much advance the plot as show the scandal world flourishing under Lady Sneerwell's patronage. As they rise to cards at line 183, Sir Peter tries to exit, to extricate himself, 'unperceived', with a lack of ceremony that reminds one of Maria at I. i, 350, but Maria herself this time is less fortunate and is entangled with Joseph and Lady Teazle before she escapes through the middle door in the back flat of the inner stage, which is an escape of a kind, but only to a yet more intimate room in Lady Sneerwell's house where the cards are to be played, card playing being a good image for scandalmongering conversations – 'Child, you are wanted in the next room' (line 224).

The company on stage have all gone out by exits in the inner stage at the end of II. ii, and Sir Peter's house assembles itself in front of the blocked-off scene at Lady Sneerwell's at the beginning of II. iii. Again the end of act curtain comes down on Sir Peter's house and rises upon it, with what by now seems less like awkwardness and more like deliberation, a feeling for the punctuating effects of the curtain.

Act III works its way steadily inwards, from Sir Peter's house in III. i where the expedition to Charles Surface's house is planned, to an outer chamber of Charles' house in III. ii, and the discovery scene in III. iii where the moneylenders meet Charles in the intimate interior of his house, debt invading the ruined man. Though not in formal terms a discovery scene, IV. i uses the rising curtain to reveal the picture room in Charles' house emptily awaiting the despoilers. This is not where Charles lives and drinks his wine, this is not III. iii; it is as it were the shrine he should venerate, the place of his household gods. But Charles is not a venerator.

The picture room of IV. i was one of the grand new scenes advertised in the playbills as created especially for *The School for Scandal*. In this formal holy of holies, Charles' informal manner (with the significantly close relationship with the audience that that encourages) contrasts memorably with Lady Sneerwell's formality of manner in her supposedly intimate dressing room at the beginning of the play. We may suppose that an eighteenth-century audience would react more vividly than we to these contrasts, aware as they would be of the difference of manner various different parts of a large house would normally evoke.

Charles knocking down his ancestors is a deal better than the scandalmongers tearing apart their 'friends', and the contrast is no doubt intended, especially since Charles will not part with the picture of his benefactor at IV. ix. i, 104. By way of that valuing of real human friendship we return at IV. ii to the scene as at III. ii, the tour of Charles' inner self, his real motives and allegiances complete. The discovery scene at IV. iii begins the investigation of Joseph's inner self, again, as with IV. i, a new scene created specially for the play. The complex tangle of deception which constitutes Joseph's inner life is vividly enacted in the desperate hidings and accidental discoveries of this set piece of farcical stagecraft in IV. iii. We reach the moment in the play where the physical movement and positioning of characters on the stage most vividly picture psychological and moral reality. And no doubt the enormously energetic response of the contemporary audience to the screen scene (see page xlvii) was because of their recognition that here Sheridan had come to the point where the *trompe l'œil* apparatus of the stage, all its sliding flats and moving curtains, was indeed the natural language in which to describe the society of his day.

Act V opens more quietly, after the hectic activity of IV. iii, with the scene as before when the curtain rises. The quietening sense of nothing new complements the irresistibly continuing process of Joseph's unmasking. Villainy is in retreat. By V. ii, where a scene assembles itself that in some ways reminds one of I. i, but now at Sir Peter's house and not on Lady Sneerwell's more promising territory, the audience would be aware perhaps that the scandalmongering world, nearing the end of its power, can no longer effectually manipulate the language of social formality. The maid at the beginning of the scene does not introduce Mrs Candour but refuses her. The other tittle-tattlers come in unannounced (and perhaps evidently somewhat ill at ease about this). The informal, good-hearted world now controls the scene, as it did not when Maria entered in I. i.

The plot unravels rapidly in the last scene of the play, the scandalmongers caught in its simplifying momentum, less and less able to maintain a world of formal intrigue and complexity. At V. iii, 58 Joseph even calls for a servant who is not to hand, and must instead try to do the servant's dirty work himself. We may imagine the movement and gesture on the stage becoming more and more natural, in marked contrast to a redundancy of manner that surely characterised the first scene of the play where scandalous words are the only real action and no restless or urgent physical activity is needed to maintain the scandalous world. After Sir Oliver is revealed in his true character, Joseph tries feebly to do what he may with words once more, at line 121, but can do nothing; Charles by contrast, who has tried to help his brother thrust out Stanley/Premium, makes no attempt at verbal self-justification at line 128 and so is able to speak genuine and natural words at lines 139–45. But this is a play where in the last analysis it is not even good words which are the most potent enemies of tittle-tattle, where it is the unforced simplicity of movement of one character to another which seems the most genuine human communication. Maria who was largely silent and still in the witty, worldly, play-acting context of the first scene of the play, accepts Charles' love at the end of the play with a silence whose genuineness cannot be gainsaid, even by her – 'she has looked *yes*' (line 236). The play ends by leaving the artificial stage, and advising the audience to do likewise.

> No more in vice or error to engage
> Or play the fool at large on life's great stage.

Epilogue, lines 49–50

THE SEQUENCE OF TEXTS

The establishment of a sound text of *The School for Scandal* is a matter of exceptional complexity. In the *embarras de richesse* created by the survival of at least 20 contemporary manuscripts (several still in private collections) and 45 or more editions, many of considerable rarity, all copied or published before 1830, a first step is necessarily to sift those with some degree of authenticity from the 40 or more unauthorized texts that may be compared to the 'bad quartos' of Shakespeare's plays. Sheridan refused to allow his play to be printed for two good reasons: (i) with the author's text available in the bookshops, as *The Rivals*, *The Duenna*, and *The Critic* all soon became, a rival company in London or touring the provinces (or indeed in the United States or the West Indies) would be able to compete on equal terms with his own Drury Lane company; (ii) Sheridan immediately realized that there were minor imperfections in the version used on the first night—it was too long for one thing —and kept on tinkering with his text in the hope of ultimately achieving the verbal concentration that Congreve and Pope had also obtained by continuous revision.

The counter-strategy adopted by touring companies needing a text of this popular play is described in entertaining detail in the editions of R. Crompton Rhodes[30] and Cecil Price.[31] There were two possibilities—either the use of 'traitor actors' from Drury Lane, or else of note-takers, perhaps using shorthand, in the audience. Some of the manuscripts—for example, the Lowell MS now at Harvard—suggest a conflation of both methods.

Two of these piratical texts were soon printed, one allegedly in Dublin (to by-pass English copyright law) in 1780, of which there were at least 40 editions by 1830, the second in New York in 1786 (with reprints in Philadelphia and Washington). Although greatly superior to such Elizabethan piracies as *Hamlet* Q1, an examination of their texts immediately betrays their corrupt origin. An example,

---

[30] *The Plays and Poems*, II (1928), 162–4.
[31] *Price*, pp. 324–8.

selected at random from I. i, is Lady Sneerwell's response to the maid announcing Mrs Candour's call:

> Desire her to walk up. (*Exit* SERVANT) Now, Maria, here's a character to your taste, though Mrs Candour is a little talkative, yet everybody allows she is the best-natured sort of woman in the world. (*1780.*)

Authorized texts:

> Beg her to walk in. (*Exit* SERVANT) Now, Maria, however, here is a character to your taste; for though Mrs Candour is a little talkative, everybody allows her to be the best natured and best sort of woman.

The note-taker is not able to keep up with the actor's speed of speech—or alternatively (but improbably) the actor was not word-perfect. The American piracy is a little better than the 'Dublin' one, but they are both of only occasional textual interest. Their principal importance is in the stage directions they supply, which often being based upon the evidence of the eye sometimes provide details Sheridan thought superfluous in the Drury Lane prompt-book.

The authorized text—Sheridan's own words and stage directions—begins with what Cecil Price has called the 'jottings'. A sheet that Moore records in his Life of Sheridan, which was based on Sheridan's own very miscellaneous papers lent to him by the family, has not survived (perhaps Moore failed to return it?), but it is worth a mention as the ultimate *fons et origo* of the play.

This sheet's jokes are more improper than might have been expected. 'She is a constant attendant at church', for example, 'and very frequently takes Dr. M'Brawn home with her'[32] is hardly worthy of Congreve. But 'she was inclined to be a little too plump before she went' which survives in Mrs Candour's account of the widow in the next street, who 'got rid of her dropsy and recovered her shape in a most surprising manner' (I. i) is not much subtler. The sheet is headed in *Moore* 'THE SLANDERERS—A Pump-Room Scene', on which he comments 'that it was his original intention to satirize some of the gossips in Bath',[33] and may be presumed to be correct. The date would then be shortly after the duels, probably in 1772.

A second sheet of jottings has survived and is now in Robert H. Taylor's remarkable collection. Its epigrams and snatches of dialogue seem to be later and were many of them incorporated into the play. They include on a separate line, almost as if it was a summary of

---

[32] *Moore*, I (1825), 210.
[33] ibid.

Sheridan's satiric thinking, the four words 'The School for Scandal'.[34] The second stratum in the play's evolution need only be summarized.[35] It is represented by two long extant drafts, also in Robert H. Taylor's collection, one of which (called by Moore 'The Slanderers') expands and dramatizes the scandalmongering satire of the jottings; it introduces Mrs/Lady Sneerwell, Maria, Mrs Candour, and Sir Benjamin, and puts into their mouths such anecdotes as the misunderstanding about the Nova Scotia sheep's twin lambs (here assigned not to Backbite but to Spatter, a prototype of Snake).[36] The other draft, now generally called 'The Teazles', is concerned with Sir Peter and his wife, and an embryonic Charles (here called Frank Pliant) and Joseph (here Young Pliant).[37]

The two drafts give the impression of being originally intended to be sketches for two separate plays. One or other of them may well be the mysterious 'two act comedy for Covent Garden', which Sheridan, now married and a father, wrote to his father-in-law about on 31 December 1775.[38] If this should be so, the first painful conjunction of the two sketches into what was to be *The School for Scandal* must have been almost simultaneous with Sheridan's acquisition of Drury Lane Theatre—probably indeed an immediate consequence of it. The new partner-manager was certainly expected by his partners and actors to give Drury Lane a play not less successful than *The Rivals* and *The Duenna* had been at Covent Garden.

That Sheridan more than exceeded such expectations was effected by a decidedly melodramatic plot. Lady Sneerwell in addition to leading the scandalmongers of 'The Slanderers' has also to be secretly in love with Charles and prepared to go to any lengths to get her man. Charles (Frank Pliant of 'The Slanderers'), though wholly ignorant of this infatuation, has to be in love with Maria (who appears in both sketches). His wicked brother now has to make love to her for her fortune without ceasing in his attempts to seduce the Lady Teazle of 'The Teazles'.

The earliest extant manuscript incorporating the fusion of the two sketches is *Frampton Court*—so called because it was retained by the Sheridan family at their Dorset mansion until 1929; it is now

---

[34] *Price*, p. 289. The words are ringed in the MS (possibly by Moore), as if to call special attention to them.
[35] *Price* (pp. 293–5) provides a tabulation of the material in the drafts 'wherever it bears some relationship to the version produced in the opening performances'.
[36] *Moore*, I, 212.
[37] There is also a Maria in 'The Teazles' whose role is similar to that of the Maria of 'The Slanderers'.
[38] *Letters*, I, 95.

also in Robert H. Taylor's possession but on loan to Princeton University Library. This manuscript is the first to give the play more or less in its completed form; it lacks the auction scene and there are many minor omissions and some superfluities, but it has the great virtue of being throughout in the handwriting of Sheridan himself.

A few later manuscripts do sometimes contain corrections or additions—or more often subtractions—by Sheridan in his own spidery handwriting. The crucial early manuscript, however, that of the text of the play submitted to the Licenser of Plays on 7 May 1777 asking for his approval of the play's performance the following day, is in the hands of William Hopkins, the Drury Lane prompter, and his assistant copyists.[39] This is now at Yale.

One other pre-performance manuscript survives. It only contains Act I, but its text has many corrections in Sheridan's hand of considerable interest. As this manuscript has not been available to earlier editors—it is now in the British Library—it is discussed in more detail in the Textual Appendix.[40] Briefly, it has a copyist base derived from a revision by Sheridan (presumably) of *Frampton Court*, which is here transformed in his own hand almost but not quite to the textual state of the Licenser's copy (*Lord Chamberlain*, as it is called in *Price*, as he was the Court official ultimately responsible).[41] When sold at Sotheby's, the cataloguer called this fragment the 'Shargl' MS from a misreading of 'Spangle' in the *Dramatis Personae*, a name Sheridan at one time gave Charles's footman. Since Price uses the strange word, I have retained it.

The only 'good' printed edition of the play to be published in Sheridan's lifetime—that of Dublin, 1799—is textually similar to but not identical with *Lord Chamberlain*. It had been printed from a manuscript Sheridan had given his sister Alicia, who sold it to the

---

[39] William Van Lennep (*Theatre Notebook*, VI (Oct.–Dec. 1951)) attributes the prologue, *dramatis personae*, and Acts I, III, IV, and V to Hopkins, II being in another hand, the epilogue in a third. A fourth hand has added some lines on a blank page. Three inserted sheets are treated in *Price* (pp. 337–8) as a separate MS. It is more likely that Sheridan had *Frampton Court* by his side when preparing the Licenser's copy and the prompt-book in April 1777. The 'doxology' (Moore's term)—'Thank God! R.B.S.—Amen! W. Hopkins'—at the end of *Frampton Court* (now detached, but found by Price in Library of Congress—see his letter in *TLS*, 4 May 1962) vividly re-creates the rush with which the first performance was achieved. A fire at the 19th-century bindery unfortunately damaged many of the leaves' outer edges. See *Price*, p. 337.

[40] See below, p. 140.

[41] *Price* prefers this short title.

manager of Dublin's Smock Alley Theatre, Thomas Ryder. Variants from it are recorded in *Nettleton*.

That Sheridan was not satisfied with some details in the play as presented on 8 May 1777 is clear from the early manuscripts. The first datable post-performance one is that acquired recently (with *Shargl*) by the British Library at the Clare Sheridan sale (Sotheby, 29 November 1971), which has '1778' in a contemporary hand on its cover. The reference is to the 1778–79 season as is clear from one apparent difference from the original cast: instead of Maria being taken by 'Miss P. Hopkins', the part is now assigned to Mrs 'Broughton', an error of the copyist for Brereton, Priscilla Hopkins's married name, which first appears on the play bills for 1778–79. This text derives from a prompt-copy and has instructions on the properties needed for each scene, cues, etc. Textually it is of interest in spite of much carelessness because it represents a state intermediate between the first performance one and that of the earliest of the presentation manuscripts—that to the countess of Buckinghamshire.[42] Both *1778*, as it will be convenient to call the manuscript, and *Buckinghamshire* have a Sir Harry singing 'Here's to the maiden of bashful fifteen', whereas *Lord Chamberlain* has Careless singing it. There are minor variants, such as 'tolerable' for 'tolerably' early in the first scene, only found in *1778* and *Buckinghamshire*, which confirm the latter's apparent priority to the two Crewe MSS.

There was once a third Crewe MS. Its existence is implicit in the title of Sheridan's verses 'A Portrait Address'd to a Lady with the Comedy of the School for Scandal', which are prefixed to the Tickell MS of the play as well as to its text in the 1821 *Works*. (The lady portrayed was Frances Anne Crewe.) There are several references to the poem in the correspondence of the period from which it appears that it was in existence in July 1777.[43] Sheridan mentioned it in a letter to his second wife on 15 October 1814 when an unidentified newspaper printed part of the poem: 'They were sent with a M.S. copy of the Play finely bound etc.' Neither of the extant Crewe MSS is 'finely bound' now, and both their texts are so much more advanced than *1778*, for example, or even *Buckinghamshire* (which I would date 1779 at the earliest), that it is quite impossible to believe one of them accompanied 'A Portrait' to Mrs Crewe in or about July 1777—only two and a half months at most after the play's first performance.

<hr>

[42] *Price* has collations of this MS (which now is at Yale). The prologue has the words 'Written by Mr. Garrick' in Sheridan's hand, and the attribution of the epilogue to Colman is also in Sheridan's hand. There is no evidence that he looked at the text of the play, which is in an unidentified hand.

If the lost first Crewe MS should ever turn up, it will only have a curiosity value. The two extant Crewe MSS are greatly superior to what it must have been, considered as literature, and they have the additional interest of having corrections and additions in Sheridan's own hand. Much of the new autograph material consists of stage directions, which may be considered the reader's compensation for the absence of actors and scenery; but the actual writing is also improved in a greater stylistic precision and by the excision of melodrama.

It is not unreasonable to connect the superiority of the two Crewe MSS as literature—rather than as 'theatre'—to the influence of two remarkable women. Mrs Crewe—beautiful, clever, enigmatic, immoral—to whom the manuscript now at Georgetown University, Washington, D.C., was inscribed by Sheridan ('To Mrs. Crewe. From the Author') was the daughter of Frances Greville, and it seems possible that the other Crewe MS, which has the same bookplate with a coronet superimposed (her husband was raised to the peerage in 1806), had originally been presented to her and ultimately bequeathed to Mrs Crewe.

Mrs Greville's 'Ode to Indifference' is one of the best short poems written in English between Pope and Cowper, achieving in its central stanzas a really remarkable tragic intensity. That Sheridan admired both the poem and its author is clear from the terms in which he dedicated *The Critic* (1781) to her. Mrs Crewe had by this time included Sheridan among her 'favoured' lovers.[44] 'A Portrait', on

[43] 'A Portrait' can be dated with some precision. On 11 August 1777 Lord Camden thanked Garrick for the loan of a copy of the poem which he had shown to Fox (who admired it), and his own 'Girls' had taken a copy of it. As the poem runs to 136 lines of polished Popian couplets and Garrick's copy, now at Harvard, had been seen by at least half a dozen of Sheridan's admirers by August it cannot have been written later than July 1777. The copy of *The School for Scandal* referred to in it will therefore almost certainly be that with a text identical with or close to that of the first performance, that of 8 May. The Drury Lane 1776–77 season terminated on 10 June. 'A Portrait' 's first lines appeared in a newspaper in 1814 (see *Letters*, III), but the complete poem was only published in the Murray, Wilkie, Ridgway edition of Sheridan's *Works* (1821).

[44] Sheridan's letters to Mrs Crewe have been preserved by her descendants, but they would not allow Price to include them in the *Letters*. The most explicit reference to the 'affair' is in Elizabeth Sheridan's letter of 27 November 1788 to their elder sister Alicia Lefanu, now married in distant Dublin, and unaware of recent London happenings: 'You know also that Mrs Crewe among other lovers (favour'd ones I mean) had had our brother in her train . . . [But] her charms have diminished, and passion [is] no longer the tie between them' (Betsy Sheridan's *Journal*, cit. *Sichel*, II, 100).

the other hand, gives the impression of a distant admirer making only tentative amorous approaches to Mrs Crewe.

The preceding considerations suggest a date for both Crewe MSS *c.* 1780. That Sheridan considered the play in its then condition *publishable*, likely to attract the general reading public as it had already attracted the theatregoing public in London and in the provinces, is confirmed as probable by two advertisements that have hitherto escaped notice. In its issue of 20–22 June 1781 *Lloyd's Evening Post* carried the following notice:

> In a few days will be published, The School for Scandal . . . By R. B. Sheridan . . . for J. Murray, No. 32, Fleet Street.

J. Murray was the founder of the great publishing house of John Murray. But nothing came of this and it was not until 1823 that John Murray II, Byron's publisher and Moore's, was able to bring out a separate Murray edition of *The School for Scandal.* (It was in fact a mere reprint of the play from the *Works* of 1821.) On 25 October 1781, however, a second advertisement followed. The publisher this time was Thomas Beckett, who had just brought out *The Critic* ('Corrected and Revised by the Author'). A third edition of *The Critic* was announced in the *Morning Herald and Daily Advertiser*, 25 October, by Beckett 'By whom will be speedily published The School for Scandal . . . by R. B. Sheridan'. This promise too was not kept.

The version of the play which Sheridan dangled successively before Murray and Beckett, perhaps obtaining an advance from each, is likely to have been of the *Georgetown* type. This manuscript is certainly an advance upon all earlier texts. The numerous exclusions—especially of the more melodramatic passages—and the general refinement of the diction make the play decidedly less clumsy, more *readable.* The reader is also assisted by the increasingly specific stage directions, many inserted in Sheridan's own hand, as some had already been inserted in *Crewe B.* What Sheridan had left to the actors in the theatrical texts—gestures, movements, modulations of the voice—are now described, so that the reader might enact them internally to himself as he passed from one sentence or speech to the next.

In the end, however, Sheridan must have decided that more revision was still necessary. Nothing more is heard of publication until 1799 when James Ridgway, the publisher of Sheridan's *Pizarro*, inserted the following announcement in the fifteenth edition of that successful melodrama:

SCHOOL FOR SCANDAL
A genuine Edition from the Original Copy
By R. B. SHERIDAN, Esq.
Is in the Press, and will be published on *Monday*,
30th Sept. instant, 1799.
JAMES RIDGWAY having purchased the Copyright of the
above celebrated comedy, gives Notice, that the Venders of the
Spurious Copies which have been attempted to be imposed on
the Public, will be prosecuted as the Law directs.[45]

But Monday, 30 September 1799 came and went—and Sheridan's
'genuine' revision proved still unobtainable. According to Moore,
who ₁asked him about it in 1823, Ridgway 'expostulated pretty
strongly' over this delay. Sheridan's impudent but no doubt honest
answer was, 'The fact is, Mr. R., I have been nineteen years
endeavouring to satisfy my own taste in this play, and have not yet
succeeded'. Moore has recorded Ridgway's recollection of this
curious conversation in his *Journal*,[46] and he repeats its gist in the
Memoirs.[47]

The conversation rings true. But why *nineteen* years? The figure
is curiously specific—and the interval that divides the negotiations
with Murray and Beckett and those with Ridgway *was* exactly nineteen years. The implication then of Sheridan's excuse is that throughout all those nineteen years he had continually returned to *The
School for Scandal* in the hope that he could at last give it an
ultimate polish—and that he was still at it.

At least three other revisions seem to belong to Sheridan's later
life. One is the incomplete 'Spunge' MS[48] which is unique in the
number of new readings it introduces in Sheridan's own hand, though

---

[45] The reference is to the 'Dublin' piracies, some of which had not even
pretended to be published in Ireland.
[46] 5 May 1819. *Memoirs, Journal and Correspondence*, 8 vols. (1853–56),
ed. Lord John Russell.
[47] *Moore*, I, 260.
[48] 'Spunge' because this is the name given to Trip in the list of *dramatis
personae*. It is deleted but is still clearly visible. *Price*, whom I follow in
calling it the 'Spunge' MS, has listed the principal variant readings (pp.
837, 850–1). Most of the variants are not found in any other MS or
edition. Most of them are in Act I, but there is a long insertion in IV. iii
(carried over verbatim from *Frampton Court*) in which Joseph elaborates
his arguments for Lady Teazle's seduction. It is of considerable interest. Cecil Price has printed the more legible part in *Theatre Notebook*
XXI (1967). Like *Shargl* and *1778* the British Library acquired *Spunge*
at the Clare Sheridan sale in 1971.

not all of them can be considered changes for the better.[49] The Powell MS of *c.* 1809 (now at Harvard) is more conservative, but its Act I introduces a number of new readings that seem to be authentic. A third manuscript is the important Tickell MS (described more fully below). All three have a far better claim than the Crewe MSS to constitute Sheridan's last revision of his comedy.

In addition to the manuscripts there is one early edition of un-doubted authenticity. This is the Dublin edition of 1799, which has already been referred to. Moore collated a copy of it with *George-town*, then still owned by Mrs Crewe, and found them in general agreement—as they are. But he added that 'the copy given by Mr. Sheridan to Lady Crewe' was 'the last, I believe, ever revised by himself . . .' And he found it 'with the few exceptions already men-tioned, correct throughout'.[50] His conclusion has misled recent editors of Sheridan. No evidence is provided, but as the collated copy of *1799* (now, as W. J. Lawrence discovered, in the Royal Irish Academy, Dublin) includes readings cited from *Crewe B* as well as *Georgetown*, his informant may have been Lady Crewe herself. Whoever it was, he or she was mistaken. At least three manuscripts —*Powell* of Act I (*c.* 1809), *Tickell* (*c.* 1812, paper watermarked 1808), and *Fawcett* (*c.* 1813)[51]—embody later revisions. *Spunge* too is almost certainly later. And there is the text in the 1821 edition of the *Works*. The excuse offered to Ridgway can also bear no other meaning. Moore had a grievance against Murray. Sheridan's modern editors should not have allowed themselves to be misled. He had certainly been promised the editing of the *Works*, but his prolonged absence in France to avoid his creditors had made it necessary for Murray to proceed without him. Sheridan had died in July 1816 and the demand for an authoritative text of *The School for Scandal* was pressing. Moreover, a fact unknown to Moore, a final revision of the play by Sheridan was found to be in existence.

This is the text preserved in *Tickell* and with minor differences in the 1821 edition of Sheridan's *Works* published by Murray (who may have inherited rights from his father), Ridgway, who had bought the copyright of *The School for Scandal* in 1799 and had

[49] A notice in *The World* (15 Oct. 1787, cit. *Price*, p. 323), while acknow-ledging the play's general excellence, 'perhaps in all but tendency, the best in the language', deplores some recent changes in it 'not for the better'. Was this the *Spunge* version?

[50] *Moore*, I, 260.

[51] 'Scott' in *Price*, but this copy of the Drury Lane prompt-book of *c.* 1813 was made for the actor James Fawcett; Clifford Scott, the Victorian literary critic, only acquired it in 1881. I therefore call it 'Fawcett'.

published *Pizarro*, and Thomas Wilkie, whose father had published *The Rivals*.

The special importance of *Tickell* is that it authenticates the 1821 text of the play. The manuscript was originally the property of Elizabeth Ann Tickell, whose father Richard Tickell had been one of Sheridan's closest friends and had married Mary Linley, sister of Sheridan's first wife. The parents had both died in the 1790s, but Elizabeth Ann's uncle (Charles William Ward) became the secretary of the Managers of Drury Lane Theatre in September 1808, and he would have been able to get a copy of the prompt-book made for her without difficulty. There are, however, no signs of a theatrical origin in the manuscript, and its most remarkable feature, 'A Portrait',[52] complete and in an excellent text, points to some family source.

Moore consistently disparages *Murray*, and even the judicious Price refuses to accept its authority. But the evidence supplied by *Tickell*, now in the Bodleian Library, Oxford, together with the excellence of most of its revisions, is overwhelming. It is the only manuscript to prefix 'A Portrait', and the text is identical with that of *Murray*. The text of the play is in general the same in both *Tickell* and *Murray*, and some of the readings they share are brilliant innovations. Here are two.

(i) I. i, 274–6: 'when you shall see them on a beautiful quarto page, where a neat rivulet of text shall meander through a meadow of margin'. [*Tickell: meander*; all earlier MSS *murmur*. Fawcett reads *murmur through a meander*.] The image Sir Benjamin presents of his 'love elegies' is visual ('you shall see'). Unlike James Hammond's *Love Elegies* (1743) they must be assumed to follow the pattern of Gray's 'Elegy' (and most eighteenth-century elegies), rhyming ABAB and with the second and fourth lines indented. By an extension of this visual image Backbite's lines *meander* like the Phrygian river whose winding course has given us the English word.

(ii) IV. iii, 15–16: 'My opposite neighbour is a maiden lady of so anxious a temper'. [*Tickell: anxious*; all other MSS *curious*.]
Joseph is explaining to his manservant why he wants the screen put in front of the window. This virgin, presumably middle-aged and wealthy to be living in such an expensive neighbourhood, is more than inquisitive ('curious'). She is also disturbed and excited, not only because she fears

---

[52] This spirited but essentially irrelevant *pièce d'occasion* is often prefixed to *The School for Scandal*. It was written a month or two after the play's triumphant *début* and makes no direct reference to it. That Sheridan used the play as a card with which to trump more aristocratic competitors for Mrs Crewe's heart—and bed—is a fact of his personal life with no direct literary consequence, except perhaps in *Georgetown*. It is not included in this edition.

the worst for Lady Teazle, but because she has become an unconscious co-conspirator with her neighbour Joseph against the Teazle's chastity. Either way she is on tenterhooks—anxious.

It is true *Murray* has sporadic divergences from the *Tickell* text of the play, which is puzzling. Some specimen readings follow.

I. i, 90 rallying *for* arraigning (all other texts)
I. i. 342 the synagogues *for* the Synagogue (all other texts)
II. ii, 74–5 as it were thus, *How do you do, madam?—Yes, madam* (only found elsewhere in *1778*)
III. ii, 42 I'll insure my place *for* Insure my place (4 presentation MSS)
III. iii, 119–20 wants to borrow money *for* wants money to borrow (all MSS)

These readings all seem to me decidedly superior—each considered on its local merits—to those in *Tickell* or its authentic predecessors. It is embarrassing therefore to find them, with at least twice as many obviously inferior readings, *all* in the hopelessly corrupt 'Dublin' edition of 1780. The two or three non-*Tickell* readings that are not in *1780* may turn up in one of its numerous reprints.

The 'Prefatory Note' in *Rae* includes the following item:

I am indebted to Mr. John Murray [= John Murray IV] for information gathered from the books of his firm to the effect that his grandfather paid Tom Moore and Mr. Wilkie for their labours with regard to preparing Sheridan's plays for the press. I assume, then, that Mr. Wilkie acted as editor.

Wilkie was the son of the original publisher of *The Rivals* and as such he appears on the title-page of the 1821 *Works* alongside Ridgway, publisher of *Pizarro* and copyright-holder of *The School for Scandal*. Murray himself had perhaps inherited similar rights from his father. If, as seems likely, the Murray text derives from a lost copy or duplicate of *Tickell*, an 'editor' would certainly have been needed to tidy up the stage directions, especially to add where necessary '*Aside*'. It might have been tempting for Wilkie (or an employee of his) to 'improve' the text by comparing it with one already in the bookshops and borrowing readings from it. Wilkie certainly modernized a *Tickell*-type manuscript. Thus *an humbler* (II. i, 31) becomes *a humbler*; *an humbled* (V. iii, 257) becomes *a humbled*. Sir Peter's characteristic *miserablest* is twice corrected to *most miserable*. But it *is* always possible that the modernizer was Sheridan himself in his drunken and decrepit old age.

THE CRITICAL VERDICT

The literary status of *The School for Scandal* is not as high as it
once was. That must be immediately admitted. It is an obvious fact
of cultural history that reputations rise and fall as one generation
of readers succeeds another. E. E. Kellett's *The Whirligig of Taste*
(1929) is an instructive examination of the phenomenon. For
Matthew Arnold, Pope's poetry hardly existed at all *as poetry*,[53] and
he shows little or no interest in William Blake, who is now generally
considered one of the greatest of English poets. The literature of
the eighteenth century has been particularly susceptible to these
mutations of critical esteem. Blake was our first great Romantic;
Sheridan, who was born only six years before Blake, is a part of
the great uncommitted trough between Neo-Classicism ('Augustan-
ism') and Romanticism in which few of us today can take much
interest. The 'Georgian' literature of the early twentieth century has
something of the same half-and-half quality and it may not be an
accident that a scholarly interest in Sheridan's play only began in
the 1920s—like calling, as it were, to like, the uninteresting to the
uninteresting.

Although Sheridan's plays were a great theatrical success when
originally produced, their popularity probably reached its zenith in
the mid-Victorian period. In 1888 the *Dramatic Review* organized a
referendum among the English dramatic critics of the time, who
were asked to name the English comedy—excluding Shakespeare's
and translation from the French, etc.—that they considered on the
whole the 'best'.[54] The verdict surprised me: *The School for Scandal*
won with an overwhelming vote. I don't suppose it would today.
By an ironical coincidence *The Importance of Being Earnest*, which
I consider a decidedly better play, was only a few years away in
1888. (It was first produced at the St James's Theatre in February
1895.) Wilde subtitled his play 'a trivial comedy for serious people'.
The critical case against *The School for Scandal*, which I do not
intend to pursue here, is that it is essentially a serious comedy for
trivial people—only just saved from total banality by a brilliant style
and its excellent moments of farce.

Sheridan's contemporaries, if one could cross-examine them today,

[53] Arnold's selection of the typical Pope couplet in 'The Study of Poetry'
is almost comically perverse:

> To Hounslow Heath I point, and Banstead Down;
> Thence comes your mutton, and these chicks my own!

[54] For details see Arthur C. Sprague, 'In Defence of a Masterpiece',
English Studies Today, 3rd ser. (1964), pp. 125–35.

would no doubt reply that it is a false distinction to separate Sheridan's words from the actors for whom they were originally intended. Let Boaden be their spokesman on *The School for Scandal*:

> I think his comedy was better *spoken*, in all its parts, than any play that I have witnessed upon the stage. [Every change of actors has caused] a sensible diminution of the original effect. The lingered sentiment of Palmer—the jovial smartness of Smith—the caustic shyness of King—the brilliant loquacity of Abington,—however congenial to the play, have long been silent. [But] the first actors of the School for Scandal were imitated throughout the country, and some portion of *their* [performance] must reach a distant age.[55]

But has it? An enormous obstacle that Boaden overlooked is the 'fancy dress' a modern producer is likely to insist on. An eighteenth-century costume—with the men's powdered hair and the ladies' tall headdresses—at once falsifies the dramatic effect. Performances in fashionable modern dress would always be preferable. Even so, the element of surprise that T. S. Eliot has rightly demanded in all great literature can never be recovered from the 'strong' scenes, notably the screen scene (IV. iii). Frederick Reynolds remembered that when he was making his way home from Westminster School aged about fifteen one May he 'heard such a tremendous noise over my head' as he passed through the Pit passage behind Drury Lane Theatre that he ran for his life, but 'found, the next morning, that the noise did not arise from the *falling* of the house, but from the *falling* of the screen, in the fourth act; so violent, and so tumultuous were the applause and laughter'.[56]

Does the screen scene evoke any similar response today? It is admittedly 'good theatre', but is not the theatricality much too contrived? That 'closet' into which Sir Peter is unceremoniously bundled and in due course extricated from can only have been the right-hand proscenium door, temporarily suspended from its normal function of providing an entry or exit. The most cursory examination of the reliable 1778 engraving of the scene allows no other possibility. And in that case Sir Peter could hardly have failed to see who the little milliner really was. The screen, all the illustrations agree, was not four-sided. There is also in several texts (not *Tickell*) the little matter of Lady Sneerwell's demanding an immediate audience with Joseph downstairs. Our knowledge of her conspiratorial relationship with Joseph makes it utterly implausible for him to desert the dangerous situation in which he found himself to satisfy some whim of hers.

[55] James Boaden, *Memoirs of Mrs. Siddons* (1827), I, 111–12.
[56] *The Life and Times of Frederick Reynolds, written by himself*, 2 vols. (1826), I, 110.

But Joseph's temporary absence was *theatrically* necessary.

The School for Scandal survives, then, as a classic of English literature in spite of its plot—to which the modern reader will be well advised to turn a deaf ear. It survives because of the continuous liveliness of the dialogue. Its supreme moment for me is not the casuistical episode at the beginning of Act IV, when for once Joseph's insistence on a small slip from chastity as a preservative of a lady's reputation has Sheridan entering into competition with Congreve's comedy of sex. In a way indeed this is the most 'serious' moment in the play. But Sheridan's *forte* is not really comedy but a kind of sublime farce comparable to Molière's *Les Fourberies de Scapin*. Act V of *The School for Scandal* is ruined by the relentless exposure of melodramatic villainy, but it has one moment that is perhaps almost the funniest in the whole of English literature (V. ii, 65–93). Sir Benjamin, it will be remembered, has been giving details of the fictitious duel between Sir Peter and Charles. It was, he says, with swords, when his uncle Crabtree rushes in:

> With pistols, nephew—pistols. I have it from undoubted authority.

And after a little wrangling Crabtree is allowed to proceed:

> A pair of pistols lay on the bureau (for Mr Surface, it seems, had come home the night before late from Salthill, where he had been to see the Montem with a friend, who has a son at Eton). So, unluckily, the pistols were left charged . . . Sir Peter forced Charles to take one, and they fired, it seems, pretty nearly together. Charles's shot took effect, as I told you, and Sir Peter's missed; but, what is very extraordinary, the ball struck against a little bronze Pliny that stood over the fireplace, grazed out of the window at a right angle, and wounded the postman, who was just coming to the door with a double letter from Northamptonshire.

Not one word of this, of course, is true. But the 'circumstantiality', which even Sir Benjamin concedes, creates the absurdity. This is a *parody* of the irrelevant complexity of social reality. And throughout the play there are similar intimations of a reckless, almost Falstaffian irreverence of the probable and the familiar, which continue to delight and reassure the doubting reader. If such defiances are farcical rather than comic, in the strict or Meredithian[57] sense

---

[57] *An Essay on Comedy* (1897) has a single disparaging reference to Sheridan (p. 39). For Meredith *Le Misanthrope* was comedy's zenith. For us the best of Sheridan is more appropriately compared with his contemporary Foote's classic impromptu which begins: 'So she went into the garden to cut a cabbage-leaf—to make an apple-pie. And at the same time a great she-bear, coming up the street, pops its head into the shop. "What no soap?" So he died, and she very imprudently married the barber . . .'

of the word, some farce must still be taken seriously—as some light
verse can be great poetry.

THE PRESENT TEXT

Text and Notes
It is usual in New Mermaid editions to present textual notes
separately from those notes that gloss a meaning or explain an
allusion. In the case of *The School for Scandal*, however, it is
impossible to make this division because the variants are almost
always authorial. If an editor is not to adopt the parallel-text solu-
tion—in this case there would have to be some ten parallel texts
—the logic of his dilemma compels him to be a sort of umpire.
In other and more technical words, a scholarly edition of *The
School for Scandal* must be textually eclectic. But the eclecticism
must be a responsible one, in which a note justifies the reading adopted. (Trivial corrections by Sheridan himself are sometimes
ignored.)

This is a hard gospel, and no previous edition of *The School for
Scandal* has exemplified it. W. Fraser Rae plumped for the pre-
performance Frampton Court MS, which he reproduced erratically
in *Sheridan's Plays now printed as he wrote them* (1902). This text
was also followed by G. H. Nettleton (1906). All other editions of
that period—including Joseph Knight's Oxford one (1906)—followed
(often blindly) the text in the edition of Sheridan's *Works* (1821).
A dramatic change followed the discovery by W. J. Lawrence of
Thomas Moore's collation of the Crewe MS in a copy of the Dublin
edition of 1799. It was then remembered that Moore in his *Memoirs
of Sheridan* (I, 260) had described the Crewe MS as 'the last, I
believe, ever revised by himself', and I. A. Williams and R. Crompton Rhodes (1926 and 1928 respectively) did their imperfect best,
with the help of Moore's collation, to reproduce this Crewe text.
The discovery of the manuscript itself ('To Mrs. Crewe, From the
Author'), now at Georgetown University, enabled Nettleton to
include its text in a collection of plays co-edited with A. E. Case
(1939). Its publication demonstrated that Moore's collation, though
accurate as far as it went, was very far from complete.

Modern editions, except Price's (1973), have had the fatal defect
of confinement to a single text. The texts that various editors have
selected have all had their merits, but none of them had a Highest
Common Denominator of the best readings. Price's text is superior
to any of them because he is not continuously committed to a single

text, though the Crewe Georgetown version is very decidedly his favourite. (In Act IV, for example, there are only 10 exceptions, none of them important, when its readings are rejected, and 7 of the 10 are from a second Crewe MS (*Crewe B*), the other 3 from *Buckinghamshire*.) Price's criteria for a reading's inclusion in his very useful collations are, however, eccentric. Unless a manuscript is 'in Sheridan's handwriting', or can be shown to 'bear some traces of it' (e.g., *Buckinghamshire* by his prefixing Colman's name to the epilogue), it is not eligible. This ruling excludes both the 1799 edition which Moore had pronounced 'perfectly correct', except for a few 'unimportant omissions and verbal differences',[58] and the apparently official *Works* of 1821, the superiority of some of whose readings has been discussed above (p. xlv), as well as such Drury Lane prompt-copy texts as *1778*, *Fawcett*, *Cumberland*, etc. It was a nineteenth-century habit of most printers to burn their 'copy' once a book had been printed, and this was no doubt the fate of the 1821 MS, which may well nevertheless have had insertions in Sheridan's hand.

The editorial moral seems clear: the ultimate test of a text's authenticity is the superior quality of its readings. Murray's 1821 text of *The School for Scandal* is by that test unquestionably authentic, however dependent on *Tickell* and with its share of Wilkie insertions—though like the Crewe MSS and all other manuscripts and editions it too has its share of errors. In this edition I have tried to present the best of Sheridan's text, utilizing the whole range of manuscripts and editions from 1777 on that can plausibly claim to be authoritative.

Spelling and Punctuation

Somewhat similar considerations underlie the modernization of spelling, punctuation, and the use of capitals or italics. Here, however, the criterion is not which is 'best', but which convention will be immediately intelligible to the twentieth-century reader. These 'accidentals', as W. W. Greg endearingly if misleadingly called them, were the creation of the printing-houses, and many authors, Sheridan among them, have found them difficult to master. Moreover, there has been a continuous evolution in their uses comparable to and partly reflecting changes in the spoken language—particularly in the pronunciation of the upper and middle classes. It would be an absurd

---

[58] *Moore*, I, 260. Price also includes among the MSS he collates that sent to the Lord Chamberlain for a licence, though its text is entirely the work of Hopkins, the prompter, and assistant copyists. Its authenticity is not, of course, in doubt.

affectation for a modern actor to drop the -g in present participles just because Sheridan and his actors will have done so.

In any case, the original punctuation of *The School for Scandal*— and some of its other accidentals too—inevitably does Sheridan less than justice. The only manuscript of the play that can be described as a holograph, i.e., entirely in his hand, is the pre-performance Frampton Court one. This manuscript was obviously copied out by Sheridan in a tremendous hurry, and its inconsistencies, often excusable enough in themselves, have no critical interest. Thus, as photocopied by Princeton University from the original, now in the possession of Robert H. Taylor, a typical extract from III. i runs as follows. Sir Peter is soliloquizing:

> What this Fellow has confess'd may be true—, —and my suspicions of Lady Teazle and Charles unjust but I'll no be too credulous—I have never yet open'd my mind on this subject to my—Friend Joseph. —I am determined I will do it—[deleted] He will give me his opinion sincerely.—

The inconsistencies of spelling (*confess'd*, *open'd* but *determined*), the erratic distribution of initial capitals, the slip of *no* for *not*—all of these point to haste. The punctuation—especially the use of dashes, long and short, with or without a full stop—is especially slapdash.

Cecil Price has adopted *Frampton Court*'s accidentals, wherever possible, he tells us, because they give us an accurate idea of Sheridan's rather wayward use of the conventions of his day. The punctuation, he adds, 'certainly suggests the way in which he intended the play to be spoken'. Both of these propositions are doubtful, or at best half-truths.

Price has himself sensibly but extensively modified the manuscript's eccentricities in his own text, as the following passage, a typical one, sufficiently illustrates:

> Well go bring me this Snake, [*20 words added here*] I should be glad to be convinced, my Suspicions of Lady Teazle and Charles were unjust —I have never yet open'd my mind on this subject to my—Friend Joseph—I'm determined I will do it—He will give me his Opinion Sincerely.—

Little seems to be gained by such half-way normalization. The initial capitals in 'Suspicions', 'Opinion', and 'Sincerely' are a reversion to an earlier convention and are occasionally due to Price's misreading of the original. The dashes are simplified uncritically. It is possible that the dash before 'Friend Joseph' *may* be an instruction to an actor to pause here, but such a pause would have no dramatic justification at this point in the play, when Sir Peter was still convinced that Joseph was his friend.

A sobering comment on such 'copy-text' fantasies is provided by the same passage as transcribed by William Hopkins, the Drury Lane prompter whom Sheridan inherited from Garrick—an educated man with a long experience of copying out plays correctly—in the Banbury MS of *c*. 1780:

> Well, go bring me this Snake; [same 20 words omitted] I should be glad to be convinc'd, my suspicions of Lady Teazle and Charles were unjust. I have never yet open'd my mind on this subject to my Friend Joseph; I am determined. I will do it, he will give me his Opinion Sincerely.

In spite of some inconsistencies this is a great improvement on Sheridan's accidentals in the Frampton Court version. What is especially noticeable is the complete absence of dashes—a punctuation mark Sheridan abused grossly—in it. In the Murray texts (1821 and 1823), in which there are many excellent substantive revisions, as well as some errors, both spelling and punctuation approximate to modern usage. In the specimen passage that I have used there are only two dashes ('—I am determined I will do it—'), and more generally between the accidentals in *Murray* and those of a leading article in *The Times* today the difference is no greater than that between educated speech then and now—a dip, as it were, between hillocks rather than a chasm between mountains. Sheridan may well have had a small share in the creation of modern English; his spelling and punctuation have had no influence at all. In any case, to put the issue bluntly, is there any *necessary* connection between the ability to write good plays and either faultless spelling or correct pointing? The accidentals in Shakespeare's scene now recognized to be in his own hand in *Sir Thomas More* are atrocious.

The textual base has been taken to be the Lord Chamberlain's MS, which was that submitted to the Chamberlain's 'Licenser of Plays' on 7 May 1777. Since the first performance of the play was on 8 May, it must be assumed that the Lord Chamberlain's copy—which has few stage directions—was the text used. The absence of readings from it either dropped or changed in either manuscripts copied from prompt-copies or the various presentation copies is recorded, but passages that have survived unrevised in all the texts are naturally not included. Pre-performance texts, notably *Frampton Court*, are ignored unless their readings are of special interest, e.g., when there are reversions to such early readings. Completely trivial

variations in later manuscripts are also ignored: the test for inclusion is the meaningfulness of the variant.

There is considerable variation in the early texts in the use of such
abbreviated forms as *I'll*, *I'm*, *'Tis*, *'Twas*, *you'd*, *you'll*, *can't*, *don't*,
ma'am. Unless there are considerations of emphasis or formality (or
even stylistic variety) determining otherwise, I follow the *Tickell/
Murray* text in such textually neutral matters on the ground that
Sheridan seems to have taken more trouble in them than in any
earlier text except perhaps the Crewe (Georgetown) MS. I have
also followed *Tickell/Murray* where the balance of preferability as
between theirs and an earlier reading seemed about equal. (See
Textual Appendix, below, p. 140.)

Stage directions have been normalized and the prompter's behind-
scene notes are ignored, except as to the sides of the stage from
which an entry or exit is to be made. 'Left' and 'right', as already
explained, are the actors' left and right and not the audience's. How
far the complicated pattern of the actors' movements across or up/
down the stage is Sheridan's is not clear.[59] Whatever information on
this, as on the scenery, seems to reflect the state of affairs in the
earlier performances is summarized either in square brackets in the
stage directions or in the notes.

[59] Ellen Terry's anecdote (reported *Price*, p. 393) of Sheridan's correcting
Mrs Abington's performance of III. i, 235ff. at a rehearsal is not confirmed
by the prompt copies. In this account—derived from Charles Reade's
mother—when Sir Peter had said 'No, no, madam, the fault's in your
own temper', Mrs Abington as Lady Teazle had replied without sufficient spirit. Sheridan stopped her, 'No, no, that won't do at all. It
mustn't be *pettish*. That's shallow—shallow. You must go up stage with,
"You are just what my cousin Sophy said you would be", and then turn
and sweep down on him like a volcano. "You are a great bear to abuse
my relations! How *dare* you abuse my relations!"' The earlier copies
from prompt-books, such as even Fawcett's detailed one, have no directions at this point. The Holl copy at Harvard has at 'your own temper'
the instruction 'both retire up' and at 'You are just' 'down again'.

FURTHER READING

This list is intended to supplement the bibliography on pp. xii-xv, and the works mentioned in the introduction. Hence it mainly covers books and essays published since the New Mermaid edition first appeared in 1979, but some interesting earlier work is included.

Editions

The Rivals, The Critic, The School for Scandal, ed. Eric S. Rump (Penguin, 1988). A scholarly edition with a general introduction.

Books

Auburn, Mark S., *Sheridan's Comedies* (Nebraska University Press, 1977).
Ayling, Stanley, *A Portrait of Sheridan* (Constable, 1986), Biography.
Bevis, Richard, *The Laughing Tradition* (Georgia University Press, 1979; Prior, 1981). Sheridan's plays in their theatrical context.
Brooks, Cleanth, and R. B. Heilman (eds.) *Understanding Drama* (Harrap, 1946). Includes a text and critical commentary on *The School for Scandal.*
Davison, Peter (ed.). *Sheridan's Comedies: A Casebook* (Macmillan, 1986). Excellent anthology of critical essays.
Durant, Jack D., *Richard Brinsley Sheridan* (Twayne's English Authors, 1975). Short biography; critical studies of the plays.
Hume, Robert D., *The Rakish Stage* (South Illinois University Press, 1983). Chapter on 'Goldsmith and Sheridan and the Supposed Revolution of "Laughing" against "Sentimental" Comedy."
Kelly, Linda, *Richard Brinsley Sheridan, A Life* (London, 1997).
Loftis, John, *Sheridan and the Drama of Georgian England* (Blackwell, 1976).
McMillin, Scott, (ed.) *Restoration and Eighteenth-Century Comedy* (New York, 1997).
Morwood, James, *The Life and Works of Richard Brinsley Sheridan* (Scottish Academic Press, 1985). Biographical and critical study.

lix

Morwood, James, and David Crane (eds.), *Sheridan Studies* (Cambridge University Press, 1995). Collection of essays by various hands on all aspects of Sheridan's life and writing.

Ranger, Paul, *The School for Scandal* (Macmillan Master Guides, 1986). Sedulous student guide.

Redford, Bruce, *The Origins of 'The School for Scandal'* (Princeton University Library, 1986).

Essays

Durant, Jack D., 'The Sheridanesque: Sheridan and the Laughing Tradition', *Southern Humanities Review*, vol. 16 (1982) 287-301.

Durant, Jack D., 'Sheridan's Picture Auction Scene', *Eighteenth Century Life*, vol. 11 no. 3 (1987) 34-47.

Hayman, Ronald, 'Surface Impressions', TLS (1983) 58. On John Barton's production of *The School for Scandal*.

Hess-Lüttich, Ernest W. B., 'Maxims of Maliciousness: Sheridan's School for Conversion', *Poetics*, vol, 11 (1982) 419-47.

Jackson, J. R. de J., 'The Importance of Witty Dialogue in *The School for Scandal*', *Modern Language Notes*, vol. 76 (1961) 601-7. Also in Davison above.

Morwood, James, 'Sheridan, Molière and the Idea of the School in *The School for Scandal*', *Sheridan Studies*, eds. James Morwood and David Crane (Cambridge University Press, 1995) 71-86.

Murray, Geraldine, 'A Sheridan Emendation', *Notes and Queries*, vol. 234 (1989) 482-3. Interestingly supports 'our friend Teazle' at *School for Scandal* V. ii, 28-9; see p. 116 below.

Rump, Eric, 'Sheridan, Congreve and *The School for Scandal*', *Sheridan Studies*, eds. James Morwood and David Crane (Cambridge University Press 1995) 58-70.

Schiller, Andrew, *'The School for Scandal:* The Restoration Unrestored', *Publications of the Modern Language Association of America*, vol. 71 (1956) 694-704. Also in Davison above.

Wiesenthal, Christine S., 'Representation and Experimentation in the Major Comedies of Richard Brinsley Sheridan', *Eighteenth-Century Studies*, vol. 25, no. 3 (1992) 309-30.

Reference

Durant, Jack D., *Richard Brinsley Sheridan: A Reference Guide* (G. K. Hall, 1981.

Audio Cassette

The School for Scandal. Listen for Pleasure, mono TC-LEP 80055/6. Dame Edith Evans as Lady Sneerwell, Claire Bloom as Lady Teazle, Cecil Parker as Sir Peter.

Title-page. From the Tickell MS (*c.* 1812), which embodies Sheridan's final revision of the play.

Title of play. The four words occur by themselves in an early jotting (above, p. xxxvii) which also has witticisms and anecdotes ultimately used in the text of the play. Molière's *L'Ecole des femmes* (1662) had set a fashion for such titles. Of the dozen or more such late 18th-century plays Hugh Kelly's *The School for Wives* (produced Drury Lane, December 1773) must have been known to Sheridan. It was produced anonymously and actually attributed in two periodicals 'to the younger Mr. Sheridan' (see *Price*, p. 290). The error suggests Sheridan's play was already known to be in preparation.

That Sheridan may at one time have considered *The School for Slander* as a preferable title is suggested by Harlan W. Hamilton (see *Price*, p. 351n), who has noticed references to Sheridan's play under this title in the *Morning Post*, 25 February, 31 March 1777. But the malicious gossip of Mrs Candour, Crabtree, and Backbite is not criminal, and the complicated alliteration of *School* and *Scandal* was too memorable to lose. By April, when rehearsals had begun, the newspapers are already referring to the play by its final title.

THE

SCHOOL FOR SCANDAL

COMEDY

In Five Acts

by

the Right Honourable

Richard Brinsley Sheridan.

DRAMATIS PERSONAE: The earliest list is in *Frampton Court*. Joseph is there called Young Surface, 'Charles his Brother' takes the place of 'Frank' (deleted); 'Rowland' is corrected to 'Rowley'. The names not surviving had been carried over from the early drafts ('The Slanderers' and 'The Teazles'). Trip is here called 'Spangle'. The actors taking the seven leading parts are as in the final version. No actors' names appear opposite 'Spangle', Moses, Snake, Careless (and 'other companions to Charles'), or any of the women, whose names remained unchanged, though 'Miss Verjuice' is added to the list. Against Lady Teazle 'Abington' seems to be written, though it is deleted so as to be almost illegible.

Text here is from *Tickell*. The original playbill gives the actors' names but not those of their parts. They add three names—R. Palmer, Norris, Chaplin—for the 'Gentlemen' in III. iii. *Tickell* is alone in assigning to a Mrs Smith the 'Maid', who was presumably employed by both Lady Sneerwell and Lady Teazle in announcing their guests. Who took the part of Joseph's servant William is not known.

The 'New Scenes and Dresses' of the playbills continue to be announced throughout the first season. Each playbill also announces the farce that was to follow *The School for Scandal*. This varied, almost from night to night, that on 8 May 1777 being an old favourite—Samuel Foote's *The Mayor of Garratt*.

2

DRAMATIS PERSONAE

[As play was originally acted at Drury Lane Theatre, 8 May 1777]

Men

SIR PETER TEAZLE	*Mr King* [1730–1805]
SIR OLIVER SURFACE	*Mr Yates* [1706?–96]
JOSEPH SURFACE	*Mr Palmer* [1742–98]
CHARLES SURFACE	*Mr Smith* [1730–1819]
CRABTREE	*Mr Parsons* [1736–95]
SIR BENJAMIN BACKBITE	*Mr Dodd* [1740?–96]
ROWLEY	*Mr Aickin* [d. 1803]
MOSES	*Mr Baddeley* [1733–94]
TRIP	*Mr La Mash* [d. 1800]
SNAKE	*Mr Packer* [1729–1806]
CARELESS	*Mr Farren* [1725–95]
SIR HARRY [*later* TOBY] BUMPER	*Mr Gaudry* [fl. 1776–86]

Women

LADY TEAZLE	*Mrs Abington* [1737–1815]
MARIA	*Miss P. Hopkins* [1756–1845]
LADY SNEERWELL	*Miss Sherry* [d. 1782]
MRS CANDOUR	*Miss Pope* [1742–1818]

3

PROLOGUE

A School for Scandal! Tell me, I beseech you,
Needs there a school this modish art to teach you?
No need of lessons *now*, the knowing think;
We might as well be taught to eat and drink.
Caused by a dearth of scandal, should the vapours   5
Distress our fair ones—let them read the papers.
Their powerful mixtures such disorders hit;
Crave what you will—there's *quantum sufficit.*
'Lord!' cries my Lady Wormwood (who loves tattle,
And puts much salt and pepper in her prattle),   10
Just risen at noon, all night at cards when threshing,
Strong tea and scandal—'Bless me, how refreshing!
Give me the papers, Lisp—how bold and free! (*sips*)
Last night Lord L. (sips) was caught with Lady D.
For aching heads what charming sal volatile! (sips)   15
If Mrs B. will still continue flirting,
We hope she'll draw, or we'll undraw the curtain.
Fine satire, poz—in public all abuse it,
But, by ourselves, (*sips*) our praise we can't refuse it.
Now, Lisp, read you—there, at that dash and star'.   20

Prologue. By Garrick (whose talent for light verse has been overshadowed by his genius as an actor). His prologues and epilogues are collected in his *Poetical Works,* ed. G. Kemsley, 2 vols. (1785). It was spoken by Thomas King—on the fore-stage, in front of the secondary, or painted, curtain when the orchestra had completed its 'Third Music' and the green curtain had been drawn. King would be in the same suit in which he was to appear as Sir Peter in I. ii. Text followed here is that supplied (by Garrick himself?) to *London Chronicle,* 19–21 June; *Gazetteer,* 21 June; *Gentleman's Magazine, London Magazine* (both July 1777). *Price* records variants—some apparently by Sheridan—in MSS of the play.

For early version in Folger Library, Washington, D.C., see *Price,* pp. 355–6.
    8 *quantum sufficit.* As much as needed (Latin jargon in medical prescriptions).
   13 *Lisp.* Type-name for lady's maid (cf. Lippet in early drafts of I. i).
   17 *draw, or we'll undraw the curtain.* The metaphor from the green curtain only drawn at the beginning and end of the 18th-century play suggests the theatrical exposures popularized by Samuel Foote at the Haymarket Theatre.
   18 *poz.* Fashionable (especially feminine) slang abbreviation of *positively.*

5

'Yes, ma'am: *A certain lord had best beware,*
Who lives not twenty miles from Grosvenor Square;
For should he Lady W. find willing,
Wormwood is bitter'—'Oh! that's me, the villain!
Throw it behind the fire and never more   25
Let that vile paper come within my door'.
Thus at our friends we laugh, who feel the dart;
To reach our feelings, we ourselves must smart.
Is our young bard so young to think that he
Can stop the full spring-tide of calumny?   30
Knows he the world so little, and its trade?
Alas! the devil's sooner raised than laid.
So strong, so swift, the monster there's no gagging;
Cut Scandal's head off, still the tongue is wagging.
Proud of your smiles once lavishly bestowed,   35
Again our young Don Quixote takes the road;
To show his gratitude he draws his pen
And seeks this hydra Scandal in his den.
For your applause all perils he would through—
He'll fight—that's write—a cavalliero true,   40
Till every drop of blood—that's ink—is spilt for you.

---

22 *Grosvenor Square.* One of London's most exclusively aristocratic neigh-
    bourhoods; its building had only begun *c.* 1695.
35 *The Rivals* (Covent Garden 1775) and *The Duenna* (Covent Garden
    1776), though very successful, were not strictly attacks on scandal.
36 *young Don Quixote.* Sheridan was only 25. His earlier plays and
    adaptations show little interest in the scandal theme.

s.d. The scenes are all in London's West End, the 'Town' as distinct from the still Puritan 'City'. This, like II. ii, III. iii, IV. iii, was a 'discovery scene', i.e., at raising of painted curtain characters are already on stage, often seated (as here). All other scenes begin with entries through two proscenium doors. Prompt-copies describe this scene's scenery as 'new' (later 'blue'— the wall-paper?)—on flats in second of the five 'grooves' (= 14 feet behind curtain-line).

s.d. I. i, *at toilet*. Substituted in Sheridan's hand in *Spunge* for other texts' *at the dressing table* (suggesting Drury Lane's property-room had only one!). *The Way of the World*, Sheridan's principal model, has for its III. i 'A Room in Lady Wishfort's House, Lady Wishfort at her Toilet, Peg waiting'. An equivalent to Peg in *Frampton Court* and *Shargl* is a silent 'Lappet' (deleted in *Shargl* and not found in later texts). Apart from the precedent in Congreve, 'at her toilet' has the great theatrical merit of giving Lady Sneerwell something to do. When she rises at 1.30 the toilet has been completed and she can confide to Snake the secrets of her heart. The direction ('*They rise*') is in Sheridan's hand in *Spunge*. Dressing-room scenes were popular in Restoration comedy. *A Trip to Scarborough*, Sheridan's adaptation of Vanbrugh's *The Relapse* (Drury Lane, 24 February 1777), has three such scenes. Snake's chocolate, the fashionable morning beverage, is therefore appropriate. (Maria wishes Sneerwell 'good morning' at the scene's end, l. 350.)

8

THE SCHOOL FOR SCANDAL

Act 1, Scene i

A dressing-room in LADY SNEERWELL's *house.* LADY SNEERWELL
[*on right*] *at her toilet;* SNAKE [*left*] *drinking chocolate*

LADY SNEERWELL
The paragraphs, you say, Mr Snake, were all inserted?
SNAKE
They were, madam, and as I copied them myself in a feigned
hand, there can be no suspicion whence they came.
LADY SNEERWELL
Did you circulate the report of Lady Brittle's intrigue with
Captain Boastall?   5

1 *paragraphs.* Items of news—especially in such scandalous dailies as the
Morning Post.
   Sneerwell's first sentence was originally (in 'The Slanderers') 'The
paragraphs you say were all inserted', which is repeated verbatim in
Frampton Court and by the copyist responsible for base of *Shargl.* In
Shargl, however, Sheridan has h imself corrected this (i) to 'And Snake
you say got both the paragraphs inserted', (ii) to 'The paragraphs you
say, Mr. Snake, were all inserted'. Originally Lady Sneerwell was
addressing Spatter; in *Frampton Court* it was Miss Verjuice, who is
retained in the first two levels of *Shargl,* Snake being at this stage
external to the play. With his final revision in *Shargl* Sheridan has
made Snake a *dramatis persona,* who replaces Verjuice. Whereas she
had been a mere 'poor relation', a 'cousin'; Snake, on the other hand,
is 'a writer and a critic', known as such to Sir Peter (V. iii, 227–8).
That the change was a last-minute one is evident from the transference
of all Verjuice's other speeches to Snake without alteration. Sneerwell,
while here calling him 'Mr. Snake', reduces him elsewhere to 'Snake'
without any apparent reason. Even in *Lord Chamberlain* the speech-
headings were still 'Verjuice', which had to be crossed out and 'Snake'
substituted.
   Mr Snake. That Snake was a last-minute inspiration makes it
improbable that Sheridan had any particular contemporary in mind.
R. C. Rhodes (*Harlequin Sheridan* (1933), pp. 71–2) reports a
theatrical tradition to dress Snake in black, and a letter in the *General
Advertiser,* 12 May 1777, refers to Henry Bate (1745–1824), the
'fighting parson' who was the scurrilous first editor of the *Morning
Post,* as 'the Revd. Mr. Snake'. That Sheridan may also have had
William Jackson (1737?–95), an even more objectionable clerical
journalist, in mind is also possible. Jackson had figured as 'the Revd.
Dr. Viper' in Foote's *The Capuchin* (acted Haymarket Theatre,
August 1776). Grub Street had several such reptiles at the time.
4 *report.* So 'The Slanderers', *Frampton Court, Shargl, Crewe B,
Powell, Tickell, Murray; reports Lord Chamberlain, Buckingham-
shire, Georgetown, Banbury, Spunge, Fawcett,* etc. A trivial variant

9

SNAKE

That's in as fine a train as your ladyship could wish. In the
common course of things I think it must reach Mrs Clackitt's
ears within four and twenty hours—and then, you know, the
business is as good as done.

LADY SNEERWELL

Why truly Mrs Clackitt has a very pretty talent—and a great   10
deal of industry.

SNAKE

True, madam, and has been tolerably successful in her day.
To my knowledge she has been the cause of six matches
being broken off and three sons disinherited, of four forced
elopements, and as many close confinements, nine separate   15
maintenances, and two divorces. Nay, I have more than once
traced her causing a *tête-à-tête* in the *Town and Country
Magazine*, when the parties perhaps had never seen each
other's face before in the course of their lives.

LADY SNEERWELL

She certainly has talents, but her *manner is gross*.   20

SNAKE

'Tis very true. She generally designs well, has a free tongue,

---

but of interest as indicating the superiority of the copyist's MS underlying *Tickell, Murray*.

7 *Mrs Clackitt.* Dr Johnson glosses the verb 'to clack' as 'to let the
tongue run'.

17-18 *Town and Country Magazine.* A monthly (January 1769–December 1796) publication, with usual miscellaneous contents, but notori-
ous for the *'Tête-à-Tête'* in each issue, in which a sexual scandal in
high society is exposed with engravings of guilty parties under easily
identifiable aliases ('Baron Otranto', I, 617=Horace Walpole, etc.).
Horace Bleackley's articles, *N&Q* (23 September–30 December 1905),
demonstrated that most of the parties had certainly 'seen each other's
face'. Stephen Beaufort (d. 10 May 1786) was 'author of most of the
tête-à-tête' pieces (*European Magazine and London Review* (1786),
382); a certain Count Caracioli is also mentioned by Bleackley and
E. H. W. Meyerstein, *A Life of Thomas Chatterton* (1930), p. 404.
For the editor's defiant comment on Sheridan's aspersion see *Rhodes*,
II, 15.

18-19 *each other's face.* So *Tickell, Murray* and typical of their greater
linguistic precision. Other MSS have the more colloquial *each other's
faces*. But one face can only see a single face in such a context at
the same time.

21-4 *designs . . . mellowness.* Semi-technical terms from artistic criticism.
Sheridan will have been familiar with Pope's 'To a Lady' (*Moral
Essays*, II, esp. ll. 17–20), where such terms differentiate types of
feminine prettiness. Some of the compliments he pays the beautiful
Mrs Crewe in 'A Portrait' (written July 1777?) are in this genre.

and a bold invention; but her colouring is too dark and her
outlines often extravagant. She wants that delicacy of hint
and mellowness of sneer which distinguishes your ladyship's
scandal.   25

LADY SNEERWELL

You are partial, Snake.

SNAKE

Not in the least. Everybody allows that Lady Sneerwell can
do more with a word or a look than many can with the most
laboured detail, even when they happen to have a little truth
on their side to support it.   *They rise*   30

LADY SNEERWELL

Yes, my dear Snake, and I am no hypocrite to deny the
satisfaction I reap from the success of my efforts. Wounded
myself in the early part of my life by the envenomed tongue
of slander, I confess I have since known no pleasure equal
to the reducing others to the level of my own injured   35
reputation.

SNAKE

Nothing can be more natural. But, Lady Sneerwell, there is
one affair in which you have lately employed me wherein, I
confess, I am at a loss to guess your motives.

LADY SNEERWELL

I conceive you mean with respect to my neighbour Sir Peter   40
Teazle and his family?

SNAKE

I do. Here are two young men, to whom Sir Peter has acted
as a kind of guardian since their father's death—the elder
possessing the most amiable character and universally well
spoken of, the other the most dissipated and extravagant   45
young fellow in the kingdom, without friends or character—

33-4 *envenomed tongue of slander*. The phrase survives from the earliest
   draft (called by Moore 'The Slanderers'). This is the one justification
   Sneerwell provides for the campaign of malice she wages against
   lovers luckier than herself. The background and details are never
   filled in. Instead the impression she creates later in the scene and in
   II. ii is of a good hostess, considerate to Maria, and by no means the
   'fury' and 'malicious creature' she is revealed to be in V. iii. Historically she descends from the 'strong plots' of Restoration comedy
   which demanded a villainess, but she is an embarrassment to the
   modern reader.
43-5 *the elder . . . the other*. Corrected in Sheridan's hand in *Spunge*
   from the colloquial *eldest* (*or oldest*) and *youngest* of all other texts,
   except *Georgetown* (*elder . . . youngest*).

the former an avowed admirer of your ladyship and apparently your favourite; the latter attached to Maria, Sir Peter's
ward—and confessedly beloved by her. Now on the face of
these circumstances it is utterly unaccountable to me why   50
you, the widow of a City knight with a good jointure, should
not close with the addresses of a man of such character and
expectations as Mr Surface—and more so why you should
be so uncommonly earnest to destroy the mutual attachment
subsisting between his brother Charles and Maria.   55
LADY SNEERWELL

Then at once to unravel this mystery I must inform you that
love has no share whatever in the intercourse between Mr
Surface and me.
SNAKE

No!
LADY SNEERWELL

His real attachment is to Maria—or her fortune. But finding   60
in his brother a favoured rival he has been obliged to mask
his pretensions and profit by my assistance.
SNAKE

Yet still I am more puzzled why you should interest yourself
in his success.
LADY SNEERWELL

How dull you are! Cannot you surmise the weakness which   65
I hitherto through shame have concealed even from you?

51 *a City knight.* Possibly a City merchant who had been knighted. To
those who lived outside the walls of medieval London, such a knight
would still be a 'cit' and unacceptable in fashionable circles. Sneerwell, a woman of breeding and brains, had perhaps been compelled
to marry such a vulgarian because of her tarnished reputation, but
the possibility is not explored. In *Spunge* Sheridan has corrected this
himself to 'your own mistress and independent in your fortune'.
Presumably he decided the City knight was an irrelevance, but it
seems worth preserving as a faint hint justifying Sneerwell's malice.
All the other texts have the knight.
52 *addresses.* So *Spunge* alone, in Sheridan's hand (which at least recog-
nizes the vulgarity of the *passion* found in the other texts). In
Congreve's *The Double-Dealer*, I. i, Mellefont is plagued by his
aunt's 'violent passion' *and* 'addresses'.
55 *subsisting.* The unnecessary and pretentious word is found in all the
best texts—but not in *1799, Fawcett,* or the American piracies.
57 *intercourse.* The word had not yet acquired its modern sexual sense.
65 *How . . . are!* So *Tickell, Murray.* Earlier texts all prefix 'Heavn's',
but the irritation the exclamation presumes is out of character with
the glacial self-control Sneerwell maintains elsewhere until her final
exposure (V. iii, 182, 188, 197–8).

Must I confess that Charles, that libertine, that extravagant,
that bankrupt in fortune and reputation, that he it is for
whom I am thus anxious and malicious—and to gain whom
I would sacrifice everything?   70

SNAKE

Now, indeed, your conduct appears consistent; but how
came you and Mr Surface so confidential?

LADY SNEERWELL

For our mutual interest. I have found him out a long time
since. I know him to be artful, selfish, and malicious—in
short, a sentimental knave, while with Sir Peter, and indeed   75
with all his acquaintance, he passes for a youthful miracle
of prudence, good sense, and benevolence.

SNAKE

Yes, yet Sir Peter vows he has not his equal in England; and
above all, he praises him as a Man of Sentiment.

LADY SNEERWELL

True; and with the assistance of his sentiment and hypocrisy   80
he has brought Sir Peter entirely into his interest with regard
to Maria, while poor Charles has no friend in the house,
though I fear he has a powerful one in Maria's heart, against
whom we must direct our schemes.

75 *a sentimental knave.* The paradox depends upon the two conflicting
   contemporary senses of the word *sentimental* (a term not recorded
   until the later 1740s): (i) as the English adjective of Fr. *sentiment*
   (= aphoristic moral generalization of some special moral issue); (ii)
   as the primarily English shorthand for the *enjoyment* of private
   emotion for its own sake (primitive form of romanticism), as in
   parts of Sterne's *Sentimental Journey* (1776). Sheridan was responsible
   for modern figurative sense ('the true sentimental and nothing
   ridiculous in it', *The Critic,* I. i).
78 *Yes, yet Sir Peter.* So *Tickell, Murray;* 'Yes, yes, I know' *Lord
   Chamberlain;* 'Yes, I know', *Crewe B;* 'Yet, Sir Peter' *Georgetown,*
   etc.
79 *Man of Sentiment.* Plays with such titles were popular—Goldsmith's
   The Good Natur'd Man (Covent Garden, January 1768), Colman's
   The Man of Business (Covent Garden, January 1744), Kelly's *The
   Man of Reason* (Covent Garden, February 1776). Sheridan's realiza-
   tion of Joseph's comic possibilities as a sententious aphorist, perhaps
   the most original element in the play, was only reached in the final
   stage of its composition (February 1777?). A friendly hit at Covent
   Garden from no-nonsense Drury Lane is perhaps intended. Erik
   Erämetsä's *Study of the Word 'Sentimental'* (Helsinki, 1951) is useful.
82–4 *while poor Charles . . . our schemes.* Om. *Georgetown* alone;
   though deplorably melodramatic, Snake's involvement is necessary
   to plot. See ll. 90–3.
84 s.d. Sneerwell's visitors all enter and leave through the left-hand

Enter SERVANT [*left*]

SERVANT

Mr Surface.   85

LADY SNEERWELL

Show him up. He generally calls about this time. I don't
wonder at people's giving him to me for a lover.

Exit SERVANT [*left*]

Enter JOSEPH SURFACE [*left*]

JOSEPH

My dear Lady Sneerwell, how do you do today? Mr Snake,
your most obedient.

LADY SNEERWELL

Snake has just been arraigning me on our mutual attach-   90
ment; but I have informed him of our real views. You know
how useful he has been to us, and, believe me, the confidence
is not ill placed.

JOSEPH

Madam, it is impossible for me to suspect a man of Mr
Snake's sensibility and discernment.   95

LADY SNEERWELL

Well, well, no compliments now; but tell me when you saw
your mistress, Maria—or what is more material to me, your
brother.

JOSEPH

I have not seen either since I left you; but I can inform you
that they never meet. Some of your stories have taken a good 100
effect on Maria.

---

proscenium door. This is to be taken as the way in from the street.
The other door, communicating with the rest of the house, is only used
by Snake, and then by Joseph and herself at the end of this scene.

86-7 *He generally . . . lover.* The sentences fill the awkward interval in
which the servant has to go downstairs from the dressing-room and
admit Joseph—to which must be added the time it will take Joseph
to ascend there. Their omission in *Tickell* and *Murray* may be due
to the former's copyist having reached bottom of page. All earlier
texts include them. Sheridan's comic sense comes to our rescue. He
did not in fact utilize the sentiment in IV. iii where it might well
have been appropriate.

89 *most obedient. Spunge* adds in Sheridan's hand 'and most faithful'—
theatrically an effective addition; faith was *not* a characteristic of
Joseph's.

90 *arraigning.* So all texts except *Murray* (which has 'rallying' from a
'Dublin' edition; above, p. xlv).

LADY SNEERWELL

Ah, my dear Snake, the merit of this belongs to you. But do
your brother's distresses increase?

JOSEPH

Every hour. I am told he has had another execution in the
house yesterday. In short, his dissipation and extravagance   105
exceed anything I have ever heard of.

LADY SNEERWELL

Poor Charles!

JOSEPH

True, madam, notwithstanding his vices, one can't help feeling for him. Poor Charles! I'm sure I wish it were in my
power to be of any essential service to him, for the man who   110
does not share in the distresses of a brother, even though
merited by his own misconduct, deserves—

LADY SNEERWELL

O lud, you are going to be moral and forget that you are
among friends.   *(ie putting on an act)*

JOSEPH

Egad, that's true. I'll keep that sentiment till I see Sir Peter. 115
However, it is certainly a charity to rescue Maria from such
a libertine, who, if he is to be reclaimed, can be so only by a
person of your ladyship's superior accomplishments and
understanding.

SNAKE

I believe, Lady Sneerwell, here's company coming. I'll go and   120
copy the letter I mentioned to you. Mr Surface, your most
obedient.

JOSEPH

Sir, your very devoted.   *Exit* SNAKE [*right*]
Lady Sneerwell, I am very sorry you have put any further
confidence in that fellow.   125

LADY SNEERWELL

Why so?   *can — even
                                        trust servant.*

JOSEPH

I have lately detected him in frequent conference with old
Rowley, who was formerly my father's steward and has
never, you know, been a friend of mine.

LADY SNEERWELL

And do you think he would betray us?   130

104 *execution.* Seizure of goods for non-payment of debt.

JOSEPH

Nothing more likely. Take my word for 't, Lady Sneerwell, that fellow hasn't virtue enough to be faithful even to his own villainy. Hah, Maria!

Enter MARIA *[left]*

LADY SNEERWELL

Maria, my dear, how do you do? What's the matter?

MARIA

Oh, there's that disagreeable lover of mine, Sir Benjamin 135
Backbite, has just called at my guardian's with his odious uncle Crabtree. So I slipped out and have run hither to avoid them.

LADY SNEERWELL

Is that all?

JOSEPH

If my brother Charles had been of the party, ma'am, perhaps 140
you would not have been so much alarmed.

LADY SNEERWELL

Nay, now you are ill-natured; for I dare swear the truth of the matter is, Maria heard you were here. But, my dear, what has Sir Benjamin done that you should avoid him so?

MARIA

Oh, he has *done* nothing; but 'tis for what he has said. His 145
conversation is a perpetual libel on all his acquaintance.

JOSEPH

Aye, and the worst of it is there is no advantage in not knowing him, for he'll abuse a stranger just as soon as his best friend—and his uncle's as bad.

LADY SNEERWELL

Nay, but we should make allowance. Sir Benjamin is a wit 150
and a poet.

---

133 s.d. Entry from *left,* i.e., the street. She is able to enter unannounced because of her intimacy with Sneerwell. Entries and exits to right are into Sneerwell's private apartments.
142 *ill-natured.* Correction in Sheridan's hand in *Spunge* for 'severe' of other texts. Joseph's comment was unkind rather than censorious.
146 *libel. OED* cites this passage as example of 'popular use'; 'slander' would be the *correct* term.
149 *uncle's as bad.* So earlier MSS, *Tickell, Murray;* 'uncle Crabtree's as bad' *Fawcett.*

MARIA

For my part, I confess, madam, wit loses its respect with me
when I see it in company with malice. What do you think,
Mr Surface?

JOSEPH

Certainly, madam. To smile at the jest which plants a thorn   155
in another's breast is to become a principal in the mischief.

LADY SNEERWELL

Pshaw, there's no possibility of being witty without a little
ill nature. The malice of a good thing is the barb that makes
it stick. What's your opinion, Mr Surface?

JOSEPH

To be sure, madam, that conversation where the spirit of   160
raillery is suppressed will ever appear tedious and insipid.

MARIA

Well, I'll not debate how far scandal may be allowable; but
in a man, I am sure, it is always contemptible. We have
pride, envy, rivalship, and a thousand motives to depreciate
each other; but the male slanderer must have the cowardice   165
of a woman before he can traduce one.

Enter SERVANT *[left]*

SERVANT

Madam, Mrs Candour is below and, if your ladyship's at
leisure, will leave her carriage.

LADY SNEERWELL

Beg her to walk in.   *Exit* SERVANT *[left]*
Now, Maria, however, here is a character to your taste, for   170
though Mrs Candour is a little talkative, everybody allows
her to be the best-natured and best sort of woman.

MARIA

Yes, with a very gross affectation of good nature and benevolence, she does more mischief than the direct malice of old
Crabtree.   175

JOSEPH

I' faith that's true, Lady Sneerwell. Whenever I hear the

152 *confess.* 'Own' in the texts before *Tickell, Murray; confess* is ironi-
cally (sarcastically) apologetic; Maria does not want to be thought a
philistine, but she is not ashamed of her convictions.
158–9 *The malice . . . stick.* Word for word from 'The Slanderers'
(above, p. xxxvii).
169 *Beg her to walk in.* Sheridan deletes this in his own hand in *Spunge*
and substitutes 'I shall be happy to see her'. The change is not found
in later texts and does not seem an obvious improvement.

current running against the characters of my friends, I never
think them in such danger as when Candour undertakes their
defence.

LADY SNEERWELL

Hush! Here she is.   180

Enter MRS CANDOUR [*left*]

MRS CANDOUR

My dear Lady Sneerwell, how have you been this century?
Mr Surface, what news do you hear? Though indeed it is no
matter, for I think one hears nothing else but scandal.

JOSEPH

Just so, indeed, ma'am.

MRS CANDOUR

Ah, Maria, child! What, is the whole affair off between you   185
and Charles? His extravagance, I presume? The town talks
of nothing else.

MARIA

Indeed! I am very sorry, ma'am, the town is not better
employed.

MRS CANDOUR

True, true, child; but there's no stopping people's tongues. I   190
own I was hurt to hear it, as indeed I was to learn from the
same quarter that your guardian, Sir Peter, and Lady Teazle
have not agreed lately as well as could be wished.

MARIA

'Tis strangely impertinent for people to busy themselves so.

MRS CANDOUR

Very true, child, but what's to be done? People *will* talk;   195

178–9 *when Candour undertakes their defence.* The moral status of *candour* changed drastically in the 18th century in both English and French. In Johnson's *Dictionary* (1755) it is still a virtue; cf. Voltaire's *Candide* (1759). By the 1770s it was approaching the malicious sense celebrated by Canning: 'but of all the plagues good Heav'n, thy wrath can send, / Save, save, oh, save me from the Candid Friend' ('The New Morality', *Anti-Jacobin*, 1798). See the acute discussion by Donald Davie, *PN Review*, 4 (1977), which, however, overlooks the cant-value satirized in Mrs Candour.

188–9 *is not better employed.* Earlier texts have 'has so little to do', a milder rebuke; the amended reading is in *Spunge, Tickell,* and *Murray.* The whole passage from 'I am very sorry' to 'as could be wished' is inserted in the preceding blank page in *Lord Chamberlain,* though it was in *Frampton Court.* Perhaps simply a careless copyist's omission being restored? W. Van Lennep, *Theatre Notebook,* VI (October–December 1951), 12 decides that, 'as the scene reads well without' them, Sheridan 'decided at the last moment to restore them'.

there's no preventing it. Why it was but yesterday I was told
that Miss Gadabout had eloped with Sir Filigree Flirt. But,
Lord, there's no minding what one hears—though to be sure I
had this from very good authority.

MARIA

Such reports are highly scandalous.   200

MRS CANDOUR

So they are, child—shameful, shameful! But the world is so
censorious, no character escapes. Lord, now who would have
suspected your friend Miss Prim of an indiscretion? Yet such
is the ill nature of people that they say her uncle stopped her
last week just as she was stepping into the York diligence   205
with her dancing-master.

MARIA

I'll answer for't there are no grounds for that report.

MRS CANDOUR

Oh, no foundation in the world, I dare swear. No more
probably than for the story circulated last month of Mrs
Festino's affair with Colonel Cassino—though to be sure that   210
matter was never rightly cleared up.

JOSEPH

The licence of invention some people take is monstrous
indeed.

MARIA

'Tis so—but in my opinion those who report such things are
equally culpable.   215

MRS CANDOUR

To be sure they are. Tale-bearers are as bad as the tale-
makers—'tis an old observation, and a very true one. But
what's to be done, as I said before? How will you prevent
people from talking? Today Mrs Clackitt assured me Mr
and Mrs Honeymoon were at last become mere man and   220
wife like the rest of their acquaintance. She likewise hinted
that a certain widow in the next street had got rid of her
dropsy and recovered her shape in a most surprising manner.
And at the same time Miss Tattle, who was by, affirmed that

205 *York diligence.* The faster and more expensive stage-coach to York;
    'a postchaise' in *Shargl, 1778, Spunge.*
208 *Oh, no foundation.* Sheridan's use of the exclamations 'Ah', 'Hah',
    'Oh', etc. is confused and contradictory, varying in texts and parallel
    situations even in the same texts. Some modernization seems per-
    missible. In general, 'Oh' indicates an intellectual response (as of
    agreement or surprise); 'Ah' is more emotional (as of sympathy).

Lord Buffalo had discovered his lady at a house of no extra-   225
ordinary fame—and that Sir Harry Bouquet and Tom
Saunter were to measure swords on a similar provocation.
But, Lord, do you think I would report these things? No, no,
tale-bearers, as I said before, are just as bad as the tale-
makers.   230

JOSEPH

Ah, Mrs Candour, if everybody had your forbearance and
good nature!

MRS CANDOUR

I confess, Mr Surface, I cannot bear to hear people attacked
behind their backs, and when ugly circumstances come out
against one's acquaintance, I own I always love to think the   235
best. By the bye, I hope 'tis not true your brother is absolutely ruined?

JOSEPH

I am afraid his circumstances are very bad indeed, ma'am.

MRS CANDOUR

Ah, I heard so—but you must tell him to keep up his spirits.
Everybody almost is in the same way—Lord Spindle, Sir   240
Thomas Splint, Captain Quinze, and Mr Nickit. All up, I
hear, within this week. So if Charles is undone, he'll find half
his friends and acquaintance ruined too, and that, you know,
is a consolation.

JOSEPH

Doubtless, ma'am, a very great one.   245

Enter SERVANT [*left*]

SERVANT

Mr Crabtree and Sir Benjamin Backbite. *Exit* SERVANT [*left*]

LADY SNEERWELL

So, Maria, you see your lover pursues you; positively you
shan't escape.

Enter CRABTREE *and* SIR BENJAMIN BACKBITE [*left*]

CRABTREE

Lady Sneerwell, I kiss your hand. Mrs Candour, I don't
believe you are acquainted with my nephew, Sir Benjamin   250

241 *Nickit.* A nick was a winning throw at dice. *Spunge* is alone in
    reading 'Pharo', a popular gambling game—usual spelling 'faro'—in
    which one of the original cards is said to have portrayed Pharaoh.
243 *friends and.* Sheridan's insertion in *Spunge.* It would be less of a
    consolation if the bankrupts were only 'acquaintance' (as in other
    texts).

Backbite? Egad! ma'am, he has a pretty wit—and is a pretty
poet too, isn't he, Lady Sneerwell?

SIR BENJAMIN

Oh, fie, uncle!

CRABTREE

Nay, egad, it's true. I back him at a rebus or a charade
against the best rhymer in the kingdom. Has your ladyship   255
heard the epigram he wrote last week on Lady Frizzle's
feather catching fire? Do, Benjamin, repeat it—or the
charade you made last night extempore at Mrs Drowzie's
conversazione. Come now: your first is the name of a fish,
your second a great naval commander, and—   260

SIR BENJAMIN

Uncle, now, prithee—

CRABTREE

I' faith, ma'am, 'twould surprise you to hear how ready he
is at all these fine sort of things.

LADY SNEERWELL

I wonder, Sir Benjamin, you never publish anything.

SIR BENJAMIN → Sheridan?

To say truth, ma'am, 'tis very vulgar to print. And as my   265
little productions are mostly satires and lampoons on particular people, I find they circulate more by giving copies in
confidence to the friends of the parties. However, I have
some love elegies, which, when favoured with this lady's
smiles, I mean to give the public.   270

CRABTREE

'Fore Heaven, ma'am, they'll immortalize you! You will be
handed down to posterity, like Petrarch's Laura, or Waller's
Sacharissa.

254 *rebus.* 'Enigmatical representation of name, word, or phrase' by a
    pun on each syllable (*OED*).
    charade. 'Riddle, in which each syllable of the word to be guessed
    . . . is described enigmatically' (*OED*, first example 1776).
        Sir Benjamin added the grace of rhyme to his enigmas. Addison
    had condemned the original pictorial rebus as 'false wit' (*Spectator,*
    8 May 1722).
259 *conversazione.* A social assembly ('At Home') introduced from Italy
    into England in the 18th century; it was devoted to elegant discourse
    on cultural topics, with occasional musical entertainment.
265 *'tis very vulgar to print.* Sir Benjamin was out of date with his convenient
    excuse. See J. W. Saunders, *The Profession of English Letters* (1964).
    The stigma of print was already an extinct snobbery.
273 *Waller's Sacharissa.* Millamant in *The Way of the World* quotes
    several fragments from Waller, including the love poems to Lady

SIR BENJAMIN

Yes, madam, I think you will like them when you shall see
them on a beautiful quarto page, where a neat rivulet of text   275
shall meander through a meadow of margin. 'Fore Gad, they
will be the most elegant things of their kind!

CRABTREE

But, ladies, that's true. Have you heard the news?

MRS CANDOUR

What, sir, do you mean the report of—

CRABTREE

No, ma'am, that's not it. Miss Nicely is going to be married   280
to her own footman!

MRS CANDOUR

Impossible!

CRABTREE

Ask Sir Benjamin.

SIR BENJAMIN

'Tis very true, ma'am. Everything is fixed and the wedding
liveries bespoke.   285

CRABTREE

Yes, and they do say there were *pressing* reasons for it.

LADY SNEERWELL

Why, I have heard something of this before.

MRS CANDOUR

It can't be. And I wonder anyone should believe such a story
of so prudent a lady as Miss Nicely.

SIR BENJAMIN

O lud, ma'am, that's the very reason 'twas believed at once.   290
She has always been so cautious and so reserved that everybody was sure there was some reason for it at bottom.

MRS CANDOUR

Why, to be sure, a tale of scandal is as fatal to the credit of

---

Dorothy Sidney under this name. Crabtree was behind the times in
his admiration of Waller. See comments by Samuel Johnson, *The
Lives of the Poets* (1781). The conjunction with Petrarch was a Grub
Street commonplace.

276 *meander*. So *Tickell, Murray* (and *Fawcett*?); all other texts have
'murmur'. The change is discussed above, pp. xliv–xlv.

286 *pressing*. The *double entendre* (from the earliest page of jottings,
Price, p. 288) is untypical. Was Crabtree's sense of humour a survival
from Pope's (d. 1744) or Sheridan's own schoolboy days?

293 *Why, to be sure*. Substituted in Sheridan's hand in *Shargl* for 'Yes'.
The speech was originally assigned to Sneerwell. The whole passage
is in parts from the early draft ('The Slanderers') and much is in

a prudent lady of her stamp as a fever is generally to those
of the strongest constitutions. But there is a sort of puny,   295
sickly reputation that is always ailing, yet will outlive the
robuster characters of a hundred prudes.

SIR BENJAMIN

True, madam, there are valetudinarians in reputation as well
as in constitution, who, being conscious of their weak part,
avoid the least breath of air and supply their want of stamina   300
by care and circumspection.

MRS CANDOUR

Well, but this may be all a mistake. You know, Sir Benjamin,
very trifling circumstances often give rise to the most in-
jurious tales.

CRABTREE

That they do, I'll be sworn, ma'am. Did you ever hear how   305
Miss Piper came to lose her lover and her character last
summer at Tunbridge? Sir Benjamin, you remember it?

SIR BENJAMIN

Oh, to be sure—the most whimsical circumstance.

LADY SNEERWELL

How was it, pray?

CRABTREE

Why, one evening at Mrs Ponto's assembly the conversation   310
happened to turn on the breeding Nova Scotia sheep in this
country. Says a young lady in company, 'I have known
instances of it, for Miss Letitia Piper, a first cousin of mine,
had a Nova Scotia sheep that produced her twins'. 'What',

---

the still earlier second page of jottings that begins 'Dodsley's Grey's
Elegy'. See *Price*, p. 289.

302-6 *Well, but . . . her lover.* Sheridan deletes whole passage, then
changes his mind ('Stet') in *Shargl*. Miss Piper's lover does seem
dispensable.

307 *Tunbridge.* Tunbridge Wells was still a fashionable watering-place,
though it lost ground rapidly to Bath in the later 18th century.
Another indication that Crabtree was no longer in touch with fashion.

311 *breeding Nova Scotia sheep.* So *Tickell, Murray*; earlier texts, including *Georgetown* and *1799*, have 'difficulty of breeding Nova Scotia
sheep', which may be logically necessary but delays the point of the
anecdote unnecessarily.
   The anecdote appears in 'The Slanderers', but the owner of the
Nova Scotia sheep is there Miss Shepherd of Ramsgate. 'Shepherd'
becomes 'Piper' in post-performance texts, and Ramsgate was not
repeated in other pre-performance versions. Sheridan had been
criticized for the puns in *The Rivals*; they were generally avoided
by the English Augustans.

cries the Lady Dowager Dundizzy, who you know is as deaf   315
as a post, 'has Miss Piper had twins?' This mistake, as you
may imagine, threw the whole company into a fit of laughter.
However, 'twas next morning everywhere reported—and in a
few days believed by the whole town—that Miss Letitia Piper
had actually been brought to bed of a fine boy and a girl.   320
And in less than a week there were some people who could
name the father and the farm-house where the babies were
put to nurse.

LADY SNEERWELL

Strange indeed!

CRABTREE

Matter of fact, I assure you. O lud, Mr Surface, pray is it   325
true that your uncle Sir Oliver is coming home?

JOSEPH

Not that I know of, indeed, sir.

CRABTREE

He has been in the East Indies a long time. You can scarcely
remember him, I believe? Sad comfort, whenever he returns,
to hear how your brother has gone on.   330

JOSEPH

Charles has been imprudent, sir, to be sure; but I hope no
busy people have already prejudiced Sir Oliver against him.
He may reform.

SIR BENJAMIN

To be sure, he may. For my part I never believed him to be
so utterly void of principle as people say, and, though he has   335
lost all his friends, I am told nobody is better spoken of by
the Jews.

CRABTREE

That's true, egad, nephew. If the Old Jewry was a ward, I
believe Charles would be an alderman. No man is more
popular there, 'fore Gad! I hear he pays as many annuities as   340
the Irish tontine—and that whenever he is sick they have

---

325 *Matter of fact . . . assure you.* Deleted in *Shargl*, but restored in
     later texts to damage of grammar.
338 *Old Jewry . . . a ward.* As today, Old Jewry was then only a short
     street and would never qualify as a ward. Before Edward I's expul-
     sion of the Jews in 1290 the area *was* a Jewry, and when Cromwell
     permitted their return, it was in this part of the City that they
     settled.
341 *Irish tontine.* A form of lottery invented by Lorenzo Tonti of Naples
     c. 1653, in which contributors to a loan were paid annuities as long

prayers for the recovery of his health in the Synagogue.

SIR BENJAMIN

Yet no man lives in greater splendour. They tell me when he
entertains his friends he will sit down to dinner with a dozen
of his own securities, have a score of tradesmen waiting in   345
the antechamber, and an officer behind every guest's chair.

JOSEPH

This may be entertainment to you, gentlemen, but you pay
very little regard to the feelings of a brother.

MARIA

Their malice is intolerable. Lady Sneerwell, I must wish you
a good morning. I'm not very well.   *Exit* MARIA [*left*]   350

MRS CANDOUR

Oh dear, she changes colour very much.

LADY SNEERWELL

Do, Mrs Candour, follow her: she may want assistance.

MRS CANDOUR

That I will, with all my soul, ma'am. Poor dear girl, who
knows what her situation may be?   *Exit* MRS CANDOUR [*left*]

LADY SNEERWELL

'Twas nothing but that she could not bear to hear Charles   355
reflected on, notwithstanding their difference.

SIR BENJAMIN

The young lady's *penchant* is obvious.

CRABTREE

But, Benjamin, you must not give up the pursuit for that.—
Follow her, and put her into good humour. Repeat her some
of your own verses. Come, I'll assist you.   360

SIR BENJAMIN

Mr Surface, I did not mean to hurt you; but depend on't
your brother is utterly undone.   *Going*

_____

as they lived, the sum increasing as each contributor died. The Irish
Parliament set up a successful tontine to pay off government debts.
An English one followed in 1765.

342 *Synagogue.* So all texts except *Murray* (derived from a 'Dublin'
piracy? See above, p. xlv).

346 *officer.* Bailiff. As in Goldsmith's *The Good-Natur'd Man* (January
1768), III.

355 *'Twas nothing.* Preceded in *Fawcett* by the stage direction 'Looks at
them a little'. Possibly an actor's 'business' and not due to Sheridan.

362 ff. s.d. *Going . . . Returning.* Half departures and returns added in
Spunge (in Sheridan's hand); *Georgetown* has *Going* (6 times).
Tickell has *Going* twice, early MSS *Going* only once, except *Shargl*,
4 times. All other MSS *Going* only.

CRABTREE

O lud, aye! Undone as ever man was. Can't raise a guinea!

Going

SIR BENJAMIN

And everything sold, I'm told, that was movable.

Returning

CRABTREE

I have seen one that was at his house. Not a thing left but 365
some empty bottles that were overlooked—and the family
pictures, which I believe are framed in the wainscots. *Going*

SIR BENJAMIN

And I'm very sorry, also, to hear some bad stories against
him.   *Returning*

CRABTREE

Oh, he has done many mean things, that's certain.   *Going* 370

SIR BENJAMIN

But, however, as he's your brother—   *Returning*

CRABTREE

We'll tell you all another opportunity.

Exeunt CRABTREE *and* SIR BENJAMIN *[left]*

LADY SNEERWELL

Ha, ha! 'tis very hard for them to leave a subject they have
not quite run down.

JOSEPH

And I believe the abuse was no more acceptable to your 375
ladyship than Maria.

LADY SNEERWELL

I doubt her affections are farther engaged than we imagined.
But the family are to be here this evening, so you may as
well dine where you are, and we shall have an opportunity
of observing farther. In the meantime I'll go and plot mis- 380
chief—and you shall study sentiment.   *Exeunt [right]*

378 *evening. 1780* (unauthorized text) has 'afternoon'. Even high society
often dined about 4 o'clock. Drury Lane's playbills announce opening of 'Doors' (to seats) at 'Half after Five'.
381 *sentiment.* So *Tickell, Murray*; 'sentiments' *1799, Georgetown.* The
plural suggests an application to the sentiments of others, e.g., Samuel
Richardson; *sentiment* means Joseph's concoction of his own moral
aphorisms.

Act I, Scene ii

SIR PETER TEAZLE'*s house*

Enter SIR PETER [*left*]

SIR PETER

When an old bachelor marries a young wife, what is he to
expect? 'Tis now six months since Lady Teazle made me the
happiest of men—and I have been the miserablest dog ever
since. We tifted a little going to church, and fairly quarrelled
before the bells had done ringing. I was more than once   5
nearly choked with gall during the honeymoon, and had lost
all comfort in life before my friends had done wishing me
joy. Yet I chose with caution—a girl bred wholly in the
country, who never knew luxury beyond one silk gown, nor
dissipation above the annual gala of a race ball. Yet now she   10
plays her part in all the extravagant fopperies of the fashion
and the town, with as ready a grace as if she had never seen
a bush nor a grass plat out of Grosvenor Square. I am
sneered at by all my acquaintance and paragraphed in the
newspapers. She dissipates my fortune and contradicts all   15
my humours. Yet the worst of it is, I doubt I love her, or I
should never bear all this. However, I'll never be weak
enough to own it.

Enter ROWLEY [*right*]

---

s.d. I. ii. Prompter's note (*Shargl*): 'striped chamber, 1st groove', i.e. flats
    well behind curtain-line, with striped wallpaper; Sir Peter enters
    through left proscenium door, Rowley through right.
  1 *marries.* So *Tickell. Murray* reverts unnecessarily to 'takes' of earlier
    MSS—no doubt because *wife* implies marriage. But Sir Peter's mode
    of speech is essentially repetitive.
  3 *miserablest dog. Lord Chamberlain, Georgetown* add 'that ever com-
    mitted wedlock' (*Spunge* and *Tickell*: 'matrimony'); *Shargl, Spunge*
    add, then delete, apparently in Sheridan's hand; all other texts omit
    phrase. This humorous variant on 'committed murder' is out of
    character (Sir Peter is not a wag or punster), and immediate repeti-
    tion of 'ever' is clumsy.
  4 *tifted.* Had a tiff, quarrelled.
    fairly quarrelled (Murray); 'came to a quarrell', *Lord Chamberlain,
    1799, Tickell, Georgetown, Fawcett.*
 13 *plat.* So all MSS, a dialectal variant of 'plot'.
 16 *I doubt.* I fear.

ROWLEY

Oh, Sir Peter, your servant. How is it with you, sir?

SIR PETER

Very bad, Master Rowley, very bad. I meet with nothing but   20
crosses and vexations.

ROWLEY

What can have happened to trouble you since yesterday?

SIR PETER

A good question to a married man!

ROWLEY

Nay, I'm sure your lady, Sir Peter, can't be the cause of your
uneasiness.   25

SIR PETER

Why, has anybody told you she was dead?

ROWLEY

Come, come, Sir Peter, you love her, notwithstanding your
tempers don't exactly agree.

SIR PETER

But the fault is entirely hers, Master Rowley, I am myself
the sweetest-tempered man alive and hate a teasing temper   30
—and so I tell her a hundred times a day.

ROWLEY

Indeed!

SIR PETER

Aye—and what is very extraordinary in all our disputes she
is always in the wrong. But Lady Sneerwell and the set she
meets at her house encourage the perverseness of her dis-   35
position. Then, to complete my vexations, Maria, my ward,
whom I ought to have the power of a father over, is determined to turn rebel too, and absolutely refuses the man
whom I have long resolved on for her husband;—meaning,
I suppose, to bestow herself on his profligate brother.   40

ROWLEY

You know, Sir Peter, I have always taken the liberty to differ
with you on the subject of these two young gentlemen. I
only wish you may not be deceived in your opinion of the
elder. For Charles (my life on't!), he will retrieve his errors
yet. Their worthy father, once my honoured master, was at   45

19 *Oh, Sir Peter.* The *Oh* (first added by *Shargl*) suggests encounter is
   accidental, not by appointment.
26 *anybody. Georgetown* only text to prefer 'anyone'.
33 *Aye.* Beginning to have an old-fashioned flavour. In I. i it is only
   used by the elderly Crabtree.

his years nearly as wild a spark; yet, when he died, he did
not leave a more benevolent heart to lament his loss.

SIR PETER

You are wrong, Master Rowley, you are wrong. On their
father's death, you know, I acted as a kind of guardian to
them both, till their uncle Sir Oliver's eastern liberality gave   50
them an early independence. Of course, no person could have
more opportunities of judging of their hearts, and I was
never mistaken in my life. Joseph is indeed a model for the
young men of the age. He is a Man of Sentiment, and acts
up to the sentiments he professes; but for the other, take my   55
word for't, if he had any grain of virtue by descent, he has
dissipated it with the rest of his inheritance. Ah, my old
friend Sir Oliver will be deeply mortified when he finds how
part of his bounty has been misapplied.

ROWLEY

I am sorry to find you so violent against the young man,   60
because this may be the most critical period of his fortune.
I came hither with news that will surprise you.

SIR PETER

What? Let me hear.

ROWLEY

Sir Oliver *is* arrived and at this moment in town.

SIR PETER

How? You astonish me. I thought you did not expect him   65
this month.

ROWLEY

I did not; but his passage has been remarkably quick.

SIR PETER

Egad, I shall rejoice to see my old friend. 'Tis fifteen years
since we met. We have had many a day together. But does
he still enjoin us not to inform his nephews of his arrival?   70

---

48 *you are wrong.* The repetition of the phrase is only found (in Sheridan's handwriting?) in *Spunge.* But it is too characteristic of Sir
Peter's bluster to lose.

54 *Man of Sentiment.* See note to I. i, 79. Not to be confused with the
sentimentalists of the *comédie larmoyante* or its English equivalent in
the plays of Richard Cumberland.

68 *fifteen. Tickell, Murray* alone in this reading; Sheridan may have
wished to make Sir Oliver's vitality more plausible by reducing the
period of his exposure to the Indian climate from 16 years while still
keeping him unrecognizable by his nephews. Actors may also have
complained of the sibilant, in 'sixteen'.

ROWLEY

Most strictly. He means, before it is known, to make some
trial of their dispositions.

SIR PETER

Ah, there needs no art to discover their merits; however, he
shall have his way. But pray does he know I am married?

ROWLEY

Yes, and will soon wish you joy.   75

SIR PETER

What, as we drink health to a friend in a consumption? Ah,
Oliver will laugh at me. We used to rail at matrimony
together, and he has been steady to his text. Well, he must
be soon at my house, though. I'll instantly give orders for his
reception. But, Master Rowley, don't drop a word that Lady   80
Teazle and I ever disagree.

ROWLEY

By no means.

SIR PETER

For I should never be able to stand Noll's jokes. So I'd have
him think, Lord forgive me, that we are a very happy couple.

ROWLEY

I understand you. But then you must be very careful not to   85
differ while he is in the house with you.

SIR PETER

Egad, and so we must—and that's impossible. Ah, Master
Rowley, when an old bachelor marries a young wife, he
deserves—no, the crime carries its punishment along with it.
                    Exeunt [SIR PETER *left and* ROWLEY *right*]

---

78 *together. Spunge* adds 'hours of rough mirth and jolly scrapes which
   I dare swear he has not forgot' (in Sheridan's hand). He must later
   have forgotten or rejected the addition.

79 *at my house.* Sir Peter meant 'here'; but at Drury Lane with its
   'apron' or 'forestage' the clumsy locution must have seemed necessary.

89 *its punishment.* Sheridan wavered between the more colloquial *its*
   (Lord Chamberlain, 1778, Crewe B, Banbury, Tickell, Murray), and
   the more elegant but artificial 'the' *(Shargl, Buckinghamshire, George-*
   town, Fawcett). Spunge corrects 'the' to *its* (not in Sheridan's hand).

Act II, Scene i

SIR PETER TEAZLE's *house*

Enter SIR PETER *and* LADY TEAZLE [*left*]

SIR PETER
Lady Teazle, Lady Teazle, I'll not bear it!
LADY TEAZLE
Sir Peter, Sir Peter, you may bear it or not as you please;
but I ought to have my own way in everything—and what's
more I will too. What, though I was educated in the country,
I know very well that women of fashion in London are   5
accountable to nobody after they are married.
SIR PETER
Very well, ma'am, very well. So a husband is to have no
influence, no authority?
LADY TEAZLE
Authority? No, to be sure. If you wanted authority over me,
you should have adopted me and not married me. I am sure   10
you were old enough.
SIR PETER
Old enough! Aye—there it is. Well, well, Lady Teazle,
though my life may be made unhappy by your temper, I'll
not be ruined by your extravagance.
LADY TEAZLE
My extravagance! I'm sure I'm not more extravagant than a   15
woman of fashion ought to be.
SIR PETER
No, no, madam, you shall throw away no more sums on
such unmeaning luxury. 'Slife, to spend as much to furnish
your dressing-room with flowers in winter as would suffice

---

s.d. II. i. *1778* describes the scene as 'striped chamber' and 'continuous',
    i.e., the end-of-act (painted) curtain rises to reveal the same scenery
    as in I. ii. See above, pp. xxxi–xxxii. The Teazles enter together left
    by left proscenium door. By 1813 *(Fawcett)* the entry is made from a
    wing on the left—'Lady Teazle 1st, Sir Peter following'. Time of day
    apparently continuous afternoon and evening Acts II to IV (see
    I. i, 378).
  2 *Sir Peter, Sir Peter*. Here and often in rest of scene Lady Teazle is
    mimicking her husband's repetitiveness.

to turn the Pantheon into a greenhouse and give a *fête*   20
champêtre at Christmas!

LADY TEAZLE

Lord, Sir Peter, am I to blame because flowers are dear in
cold weather? You should find fault with the climate and
not with me. For my part, I'm sure I wish it was spring all
the year round and that roses grew under one's feet!   25

SIR PETER

Oons, madam, if you had been born to this, I shouldn't
wonder at your talking thus. But you forget what your situation was when I married you.

LADY TEAZLE

No, no, I don't. 'Twas a very disagreeable one, or I should
never have married you.   30

SIR PETER

Yes, yes, madam, you were then in somewhat an humbler
style—the daughter of a plain country squire. Recollect, Lady
Teazle, when I saw you first, sitting at your tambour in a
pretty figured linen gown with a bunch of keys by your side,
your hair combed smooth over a roll, and your apartment   35
hung round with fruits in worsted of your own working.

LADY TEAZLE

Oh, yes! I remember it very well, and a curious life I led—
my daily occupation to inspect the dairy, superintend the

---

20 *Pantheon*. In Oxford Street, opened 1772; the largest non-ecclesias-
   tical public building in London; an imitation of the Pantheon in
   Rome, much used for large fashionable gatherings.
20–1 *fête champêtre*. Large High Society picnic: such affairs were a
   favourite subject for 18th-century French painters. Climate often
   impelled their taking place indoors. *Price* (p. 374n) cites Robert
   Adams's conversion of supper-room at 'The Oaks' into an imitation
   fête champêtre.
26 *Oons*. An archaic abbreviation from 'God's wounds'. 'Zounds' was
   the more usual form.
31 *an humbler*. In all earlier texts, 'a humbler' confined to *Murray*;
   the loss of 'h' in pronunciation (standard in similar words of French
   origin until 19th century, *OED*) became confused with the cockney
   vulgarism. To avoid any suspicion of 'dropping the aitch', as by
   Dickens's Squeers, the modern form gradually became standard in
   London English. If this is Sheridan's, it may show the sensitiveness
   of Sheridan's ear to living speech, but it is more likely to be a
   reading Thomas Wilkie retained from a late 'Dublin' edition.
33 *tambour*. 'A circular frame formed of one hoop fitting within
   another, in which silk, muslin, or other material is stretched for
   embroidering' *(OED)*.

poultry, make extracts from the family receipt-book, and
comb my aunt Deborah's lap-dog.   40

SIR PETER

Yes, yes, ma'am, 'twas so indeed.

LADY TEAZLE

And then, you know, my evening amusements—to play
Pope Joan with the curate; to read a sermon to my aunt; or
to be stuck down to an old spinet to strum my father to
sleep after a fox-chase.   45

SIR PETER

I am glad you have so good a memory. Yes, madam, these
were the recreations I took you from; but now you must
have your coach—*vis-à-vis*—and three powdered footmen
before your chair, and in the summer a pair of white cats
to draw you to Kensington Gardens. No recollection, I   50
suppose, when you were content to ride double behind the
butler on a docked coach-horse.

LADY TEAZLE

No—I swear I never did that. I deny the butler and the
coach-horse.

SIR PETER

This, madam, *was* your situation; and what have I done for   55

40 *Deborah.* Already dying out as a Christian name in polite society.
In 17th century a popular name in Puritan circles; Milton's youngest
grand-daughter was a Deborah. Here the name adds to the absurdity
of the portrait.

43 *Pope Joan.* A game played by three or more persons with a pack of
cards from which the eight of diamonds had been removed. The
name seems to derive from the fabulous female pope, Joan, but cf.
the French name, *nain jaune* (yellow dwarf). Perhaps Lady Teazle's
aunt made up the card-party—or maybe the want of a third player
indicates the depths of the boredom.
sermon. Georgetown substitutes 'novel' (found elsewhere only in
Banbury and *Fawcett*); but the change is not for the better. See
F. W. Bateson, in *Evidence in Literary Scholarship: Essays, in
memory of James Marshall Osborn* (1979), for detailed discussion.

48 *vis-à-vis.* With the two occupants sitting face to face.

49 *chair.* Sedan (cf. Bath-chairs).
cats. So all texts, except the precursor of the passage (*Moore*, I,
229) in 'The Slanderers' (which has 'dogs'). *Price* suggests short for
'cattle'—and more plausibly quotes from Colman's prologue to
Garrick's *Bon Ton* (1775) as examples of Society's luxuries:

> A rose, when half a guinea is the price;
> A set of bays, scarce bigger than six mice.

It seems best to retain the *cats* at their absurd face value. Cf. Lady
Betty Curricle's 'duodecimo phaeton' (see note to II. ii, 9). The 'cobs'
in *Rae* is a misreading of *Frampton Court.*

you? I have made you a woman of fashion, of fortune, of
rank—in short, I have made you my wife.

LADY TEAZLE

Well, then—and there is but one thing more you can make
me to add to the obligation, and that is—

SIR PETER

My widow, I suppose?   60

LADY TEAZLE

Hem! Hem!

SIR PETER

Thank you, madam. But don't flatter yourself; for, though
your ill conduct may disturb my peace, it shall never break
my heart, I promise you. However, I am equally obliged to
you for the hint.   65

LADY TEAZLE

Then why will you endeavour to make yourself so disagreeable to me and thwart me in every little elegant expense?

SIR PETER

'Slife, madam, I say—had you any of these little elegant
expenses when you married me?

LADY TEAZLE

Lud, Sir Peter, would you have me be out of the fashion?   70

SIR PETER

The fashion, indeed! What had you to do with the fashion
before you married me?

LADY TEAZLE

For my part, I should think you would like to have your
wife thought a woman of taste.

SIR PETER

Aye! There again! Taste! Zounds, madam, you had no taste   75
when you married me.

LADY TEAZLE

That's very true, indeed, Sir Peter; and after having married
you I should never pretend to taste again, I allow. But now,

78 *I allow.* Sheridan amends from 'I am sure' (earlier in sentence) in
his own hand in *Georgetown*. The improvement is not obvious and
is not found in any other text (including *Frampton Court*). *Moore*
(I, 260-1n) gives the reading as an example of Sheridan's retentive
memory. He had also found it in 'all his earlier manuscripts of the
play'. No such manuscripts have survived. Moore's collation of
Georgetown (now in the Royal Irish Academy) confirms that Sheridan's emendation to 'I allow' was as above—'as it is in the other
MS copies'. The early draft Moore was referring to may have been
among the material described in *Price* (p. 23), some of which was
apparently lost in a wreck in the Mediterranean.

Sir Peter, if we have finished our daily jangle, I presume I
may go to my engagement at Lady Sneerwell's.   80

SIR PETER

Aye, there's another precious circumstance. A charming set
of acquaintance you have made there!

LADY TEAZLE

Nay, Sir Peter, they are all people of rank and fortune, and
remarkably tenacious of reputation.

SIR PETER

Yes, egad, they are tenacious of reputation with a vengeance;   85
for they don't choose anybody should have a character but
themselves. Such a crew! Ah, many a wretch has rid on a
hurdle who has done less mischief than these utterers of
forged tales, coiners of scandal, and clippers of reputation.

LADY TEAZLE

What, would you restrain the freedom of speech?   90

SIR PETER

Oh, they have made you just as bad as any one of the society.

LADY TEAZLE

Why, I believe I do bear a part with a tolerable grace. But I
vow I bear no malice against the people I abuse. When I say
an ill-natured thing, 'tis out of pure good humour, and I
take it for granted they deal exactly in the same manner   95
with me. But, Sir Peter, you know you promised to come to
Lady Sneerwell's too.

SIR PETER

Well, well, I'll call in just to look after my own character.

81–3 *Aye . . . Nay.* Lady Teazle parodies Sir Peter's affirmative archaism
   with an archaic negative.
87–8 *rid on a hurdle.* Traitors (including those who defaced the king's
   coins) were dragged to the place of execution on a hurdle instead
   of riding in a cart like other criminals.
88 *these. Crewe B* and *Georgetown* have 'those', a copyist's error
   Sheridan must have missed. *Crewe* MSS are of interest textually as
   demonstrating the same copyist's base.
88–9 *utterers . . . coiners . . . clippers.* Three separate abusers of mone-
   tary system—those who put forged coins into circulation, those
   responsible for the actual forgery, those who debased currency
   values by cutting away coins' outer rim.
92 *a tolerable grace. Fawcett* alone permits Sir Peter to interrupt 'Grace
   indeed!' (But the pirated 'Dublin' editions have it. An actor's gag?)

LADY TEAZLE

Then, indeed, you must make haste after me, or you'll be too
late. So good-bye to ye!   *Exit [right]*   100

SIR PETER

So I have gained much by my intended expostulation. Yet
with what a charming air she contradicts everything I say—
and how pleasingly she shows her contempt for my authority.
Well, though I can't make her love me, there is great satisfaction in quarrelling with her. And I think she never appears   105
to such advantage as when she is doing everything in her
power to plague me.   *Exit [through proscenium door left]*

Act II, Scene ii

At LADY SNEERWELL'S

LADY SNEERWELL, MRS CANDOUR, CRABTREE, SIR BENJAMIN BACKBITE,
and JOSEPH SURFACE

LADY SNEERWELL

Nay, positively, we *will* hear it.

JOSEPH SURFACE

Yes, yes, the epigram, by all means.

ALL

Yes, the epigram if you please.

100 *ye.* This unstressed objective form of *you* was still in use in a few
    phrases.
100 s.d. *Exit.* Earliest prompt-copy *(1778)* has both Teazles coming in
    and leaving by right proscenium door. Later *(Fawcett)* they enter
    right through wings with Lady Teazle leading; she crosses to right
    —no doubt under Sheridan's instruction—at *fox-chase* (l. 45) and
    goes out right through wings. Sir Peter goes out through the left
    wings.

s.d. II. ii. A 'discovery' scene. *1778* describes the scenery as 'New' and
    the (proscenium) 'doors' as 'open'. Only property specified is a 'card
    table'. *Fawcett* has: 'Pembroke Table on, and tea-things . . . Servant
    attending the company with tea; card-table, six striped chairs before
    the scene' (=back-flat). It is clearly late afternoon of same day as I. i.
  3 ALL. *Yes . . . if you please.* Reading only found in T. H. Lacy's ed.
    (1840?) which claims to be 'Collated from the Author's own Copy'
    (it has Covent Garden cast of 1836). If authentic, it must have been
    very late addition by Sheridan. But the sense certainly requires some-
    thing of the sort.

SIR BENJAMIN

Oh, plague on't, uncle! Tis mere nonsense.

CRABTREE

No, no. 'Fore Gad, very clever for an extempore.   5

SIR BENJAMIN

But, ladies, you should be acquainted with the circumstance.
You must know that one day last week as Lady Betty
Curricle was taking the dust in Hyde Park in a sort of
duodecimo phaeton, she desired me to write some verses on
her ponies, upon which I took out my pocket-book and in   10
one moment produced the following:

Sure never were seen two such beautiful ponies;

Other horses are clowns, but these macaronis.

To give 'em this title I'm sure isn't wrong,

Their legs are so slim and their tails are so long.   15

CRABTREE

There, ladies, done in the smack of a whip and on horseback,
too.

JOSEPH SURFACE

A very Phoebus mounted. Indeed, Sir Benjamin!

SIR BENJAMIN

Oh, dear sir! Trifles, trifles.

Enter [left] LADY TEAZLE *and* MARIA

MRS CANDOUR

I must have a copy.   20

LADY SNEERWELL

Lady Teazle! I hope we shall see Sir Peter?

LADY TEAZLE

I believe he'll wait on your ladyship presently.

LADY SNEERWELL

Maria, my love, you look grave. Come, you shall sit down to
piquet with Mr Surface.

4 *Oh, plague. Georgetown* only text to omit *Oh*, which is clearly
    necessary to maintain Backbite's affected reluctance.
9 *duodecimo phaeton.* 'Small' 4-wheeled open carriage.
12ff. The epigram has been detached from Sheridan's longer *jeu
    d'esprit* called in *Rhodes* 'Lines by a Lady of Fashion' (III, 241–42),
    first unearthed by *Moore* (I, 239–40). Rhodes suggests 'the end of
    1776' as the probable date of composition. Sheridan utilized two
    other phrases from them in this scene—'take the dust in High Park'
    (l. 8) and 'My hair . . . like a cornet's, tuck'd under my hat' (cf. l.
    95). *macaronis.* Fops who had toured Europe—from the Marconi
    Club, which provided members with foreign dishes (from *c.* 1760).
    See *Town and County Magazine*, IV (1772), 243 (*Price*, p. 377n).

MARIA

I take very little pleasure in cards; however, I'll do as your   25
ladyship pleases.

LADY TEAZLE (*Aside*)

I am surprised Mr Surface should sit down with her; I
thought he would have embraced this opportunity of speaking to me before Sir Peter came.

MRS CANDOUR

Now, I'll die; but you are so scandalous I'll forswear your   30
society.

LADY TEAZLE

What's the matter, Mrs Candour?

MRS CANDOUR

They'll not allow our friend Miss Vermilion to be handsome.

LADY SNEERWELL

Oh, surely she is a pretty woman.

CRABTREE

I am very glad you think so, ma'am.   35

MRS CANDOUR

She has a charming fresh colour.

LADY TEAZLE

Yes, when it is fresh put on.

MRS CANDOUR

Oh, fie! I'll swear her colour is natural. I have seen it come
and go.

LADY TEAZLE

I daresay you have, ma'am: it goes off at night and comes   40
again in the morning.

SIR BENJAMIN

True, Lady Teazle, it not only comes and goes, but, what's
more, egad—her maid can fetch and carry it.

MRS CANDOUR

Ha, ha, ha! How I hate to hear you talk so. But surely now,
her sister is—or *was*—very handsome.   45

---

25 *in cards.* Sheridan has crossed out *piquet* and inserted 'cards' in his
own hand in the two Crewe MSS. This suggests that piquet—a card-
game for two using only 32 cards and as such appropriate here—
had become unfashionable by *c.* 1780. A hint perhaps from Mrs
Crewe or Mrs Greville. Pope testifies to its being played a generation before in the highest social circles (*Epistle to Cobham,* l. 55).

42–3 *True, Lady Teazle . . . carry it. 1799* reading and clearly correct.
Earlier texts have 'Uncle' for *Lady Teazle*; *Tickell* and *Murray* have
'ma'am' (Lady Teazle and Lady Sneerwell are both occasionally
addressed as 'madam' in spite of their titles.)

CRABTREE

Who—Mrs Evergreen? Oh, Lord, she's six and fifty if she's
an hour.

MRS CANDOUR

Now *positively* you wrong her. Fifty-two or fifty-three is the
utmost—and I don't think she looks more.

SIR BENJAMIN

Ah, there is no judging by her looks unless one could see her   50
face.

LADY SNEERWELL

Well, well, if Mrs Evergreen *does* take some pains to repair
the ravages of time, you must allow she effects it with great
ingenuity; and surely that's better than the careless manner
in which the widow Ochre caulks her wrinkles.   55

SIR BENJAMIN

Nay, now, Lady Sneerwell, you are severe upon the widow.
Come, come, it is not that she paints so ill—but, when she
has finished her face, she joins it on so badly to her neck
that she looks like a mended statue, in which the connoisseur
sees at once that the head's modern, though the trunk's   60
antique.

CRABTREE

Ha, ha, ha! Well said, nephew!

MRS CANDOUR

Ha, ha, ha! Well, you make me laugh, but I vow I hate you
for it. What do you think of Miss Simper?

SIR BENJAMIN

Why, she has very pretty teeth.   65

LADY TEAZLE

Yes; and on that account, when she is neither speaking nor
laughing (which very seldom happens), she never absolutely
shuts her mouth, but leaves it always on a jar, as it were
thus.   [*Shows her teeth*]

MRS CANDOUR

How can you be so ill-natured?   70

LADY TEAZLE

Nay, I allow even that's better than the pains Mrs Prim takes
to conceal her losses in front. She draws her mouth till it
positively resembles the aperture of a poor's-box and all her

59–60 *the connoisseur sees*. So Lord *Chamberlain, Banbury, Tickell,
Murray*; 'may see' (*Georgetown, Fawcett*). Discussed by Price in
Papers of the Bibliographical Society of America, LXI (1967), p. 356.

words appear to slide out edgewise, as it were thus, *How do
you do, madam?—Yes, madam.*   75

LADY SNEERWELL

Very well, Lady Teazle; I see you can be a little severe.

LADY TEAZLE

In defence of a friend it is but justice. But here comes Sir
Peter to spoil our pleasantry.

Enter SIR PETER TEAZLE [*left proscenium door*]

SIR PETER

Ladies, your most obedient.
(*Aside*) Mercy on me, here is the whole set. A character dead   80
at every word, I suppose.

MRS CANDOUR

I am rejoiced you are come, Sir Peter. They have been *so*
censorious—and Lady Teazle as bad as anyone.

SIR PETER

It must be very distressing to *you*, Mrs Candour, I dare
swear.   85

MRS CANDOUR

Oh, they will allow good qualities to nobody—not even good
nature to our friend Mrs Pursy.

LADY TEAZLE

What, the fat dowager who was at Mrs Codille's last night?

MRS CANDOUR

Nay, her bulk is her misfortune; and when she takes such
pains to get rid of it, you ought not to reflect on her.   90

LADY SNEERWELL

That's very true, indeed.

LADY TEAZLE

Yes, I know she almost lives on acids and small whey; laces
herself by pulleys; and often in the hottest noon of summer,

74–5 Lady Teazle's imitative examples (*How do you do, madam?—Yes,
    madam)* are not found in any of the authorized texts except *Murray.*
    But they are in the 'Dublin' piracies (from *1780*), from one of which
    Thomas Wilkie may have obtained them for *Murray.*
80 *character dead at every word.* An echo of Pope's *The Rape of the
    Lock,* III, 16 ('At every word a reputation dies').
83–6 *and Lady . . . Oh.* Om. in presentation copies—presumably to
    abbreviate the scene. Sir Peter's involvement in the conversation is,
    however, clearly necessary.

you may see her on a little squat pony, with her hair
plaited up behind like a drummer's, and puffing round the   95
Ring on a full trot.

MRS CANDOUR

I thank you, Lady Teazle, for defending her.

SIR PETER

Yes, a good defence truly.

MRS CANDOUR

But Sir Benjamin is as censorious as Miss Sallow.

CRABTREE

Yes, and she is a curious being to pretend to be censorious   100
—an awkward gawky without any one good point under
Heaven!

MRS CANDOUR

Positively you shall not be so very severe. Miss Sallow is a
near relation of mine by marriage, and as for her person
great allowance is to be made; for let me tell you a woman   105
labours under many disadvantages who tries to pass for a
girl at six and thirty.

LADY SNEERWELL

Though surely she is handsome still and for the weakness
in her eyes, considering how much she reads by candlelight it
is not to be wondered at.   110

MRS CANDOUR

True, and then as to her manner—upon my word I think it
is particularly graceful considering she never had the least
education. For you know her mother was a Welsh milliner
and her father a sugar-baker at Bristol.

SIR BENJAMIN

Ah, you are both of you too good-natured.   115

SIR PETER (*Aside*)

Yes, damned good-natured! This their own relation! Mercy
on me!

94–5 *hair plaited . . . a drummer's.* A condensed rewording of Sheridan's
    opening couplet in the earlier fragment (see l. 12):

> Then, behind, all my hair is done up in a plat,
> And so, like a cornet's, tuck'd under my hat.

96 *the Ring.* 'Fashionable drive in Hyde Park, shut in by railings and
    fine trees' (*Price*, p. 379n). Created by Charles I.

MRS CANDOUR

For my part I own I cannot bear to hear a friend ill spoken
of.

SIR PETER

No, to be sure!   120

SIR BENJAMIN

Oh, you are of a moral turn. Mrs Candour and I can sit for
an hour and hear Lady Stucco talk sentiment.

LADY TEAZLE

Nay, I vow Lady Stucco is very well with the dessert after
dinner; for she's just like the French fruit one cracks for
mottoes—made up of paint and proverb.   125

MRS CANDOUR

Well, I never will join in ridiculing a friend—and so I
constantly tell my cousin Ogle, and you all know what
pretensions *she* has to be critical in beauty.

CRABTREE

Oh, to be sure. She has herself the oddest countenance that
ever was seen. 'Tis a collection of features from all the   130
different countries of the globe.

SIR BENJAMIN

So she has indeed. An Irish front . . .

CRABTREE

Caledonian locks . . .

SIR BENJAMIN

Dutch nose . . .

CRABTREE

Austrian lip . . .   135

SIR BENJAMIN

Complexion of a Spaniard . . .

118–22 *For my part . . . Lady Stucco.* So *Lord Chamberlain, Tickell,
Murray;* presentation MSS abbreviate (without any special advantage?) to: 'SIR BENJAMIN. And Mrs. Candour is of so moral a turn.
She can sit for an hour to hear Lady Stucco talk sentiments'.
132 *Irish front.* Forehead. 'A Portrait', addressed to Mrs Crewe with a
copy of the play, has 'wrinkled front' (l. 16), but the attribution of
any such feature to the Irish seems fanciful.
133 *Caledonian locks.* Long hair like a Highlander's.
134 *Dutch nose.* Flat or snub-nosed.
135 *Austrian lip.* Protrusion of lower lip characteristic of the Habsburg
(Imperial) family.
136 *Complexion of a Spaniard.* Dark-skinned (from infusion of Moorish
blood).

CRABTREE

And teeth à la Chinoise!

SIR BENJAMIN

In short, her face resembles a *table d'hôte* at Spa, where no
two guests are of a nation—

CRABTREE

Or a Congress at the close of a general war—wherein all the   140
members, even to her eyes, appear to have a different
interest, and her nose and chin are the only parties likely to
join issue.

MRS CANDOUR

Ha, ha, ha!

SIR PETER (*Aside*)

Mercy on my life—a person they dine with twice a week!   145

LADY SNEERWELL

Go, go; you are a couple of provoking toads.

MRS CANDOUR

Nay, but I vow you shall not carry the laugh off so. For give
me leave to say that Mrs Ogle—

SIR PETER

Madam, madam, I beg your pardon. There's no stopping
these good gentlemen's tongues. But when I tell *you*, Mrs   150
Candour, that the lady they are abusing is a particular
friend of mine, I hope you'll not take her part.

LADY SNEERWELL

Ha, ha, ha! Well said, Sir Peter! But you are a cruel creature,
too phlegmatic yourself for a jest, and too peevish to allow wit
in others.   155

SIR PETER

Ah, madam, true wit is more nearly allied to good nature
than your ladyship is aware of.

LADY TEAZLE

True, Sir Peter. I believe they are so near akin that they can
never be united.

137 *à la Chinoise.* Crabtree's knowledge of Chinese dentistry cannot have
      been profound, but *chinoiserie* was a fad of the French court which
      spread to England. See A. O. Lovejoy in *Essays in the History of
      Ideas* (1948).
138 *Spa.* The watering-place in Belgium, much patronized for its curative
      mineral springs.
146 *a couple of provoking toads.* So *Lord Chamberlain, Tickell, Murray,*
      but om. *1778, 1799,* and the presentation copies. One of the 'jottings'
      'go you scandalous toad' (*Price,* p. 289).

SIR BENJAMIN

Or rather, madam, suppose them to be man and wife, 160
because one seldom sees them together.

LADY TEAZLE

But Sir Peter is such an enemy to scandal I believe he would
have it put down by Parliament.

SIR PETER

'Fore Heaven, madam, if they were to consider the sporting
with reputation of as much importance as poaching on 165
manors and pass an Act for the Preservation of Fame, I
believe there are many would thank them for the Bill.

LADY SNEERWELL

O lud, Sir Peter, would you deprive us of our privileges?

SIR PETER

Aye, madam; and then no person should be permitted to kill
characters or run down reputations, but qualified old maids 170
and disappointed widows.

LADY SNEERWELL

Go, you monster!

MRS CANDOUR

But sure you would not be quite so severe on those who only
report what they hear?

SIR PETER

Yes, madam, I would have law merchant for them too; and 175
in all cases of slander currency, whenever the drawer of the
lie was not to be found, the injured parties should have a
right to come on any of the endorsers.

CRABTREE

Well, for my part I believe there never was a scandalous
tale without some foundation. 180

SIR PETER

Oh, nine out of ten of the malicious inventions are founded
on some ridiculous misrepresentation.

166 *manors.* The Lord of the Manor as owner, possessor of the newest
shot-gun, and Justice of the Peace was particularly involved. The
most savage game-laws and man-traps belong to this period.

175 *merchant.* Cater. Many editors treat 'merchant' as a noun and compare
the Law of the Staple, Forest Law, etc., but this seems unnecessary
and would not be understood by an 18th-century audience.

181–2 *Oh, nine out of ten . . . ridiculous misrepresentation.* So *Lord
Chamberlain, Tickell, Murray;* om. *Georgetown, 1799, Banbury,
Fawcett.*

LADY SNEERWELL

Come, ladies, shall we sit down to cards in the next room?

Enter a SERVANT *[left], who whispers* SIR PETER

SIR PETER

I'll be with them directly.   [*Exit* SERVANT]

[*Aside*] I'll get away unperceived.   185

LADY SNEERWELL

Sir Peter, you are not leaving us?

SIR PETER

Your ladyship must excuse me; I'm called away by particular
business. But I leave my character behind me.

Exit SIR PETER *[left]*

SIR BENJAMIN

Well, certainly, Lady Teazle, that lord of yours is a strange
being. I could tell you some stories of him would make you   190
laugh heartily if he were not your husband.

LADY TEAZLE

Oh, pray don't mind that. Come, do let's hear them.
They join the rest of the company, all talking as they are
going into the next room [i.e., *upper end stage*]

JOSEPH (*Rising with* MARIA)

Maria, I see you have no satisfaction in this society.

MARIA

How is it possible I should? If to raise malicious smiles at
the infirmities or misfortunes of those who have never   195
injured us be the province of wit or humour, Heaven grant
me a double portion of dullness!

JOSEPH

Yet they appear more ill-natured than they are. They have
no malice at heart.

MARIA

Then is their conduct still more contemptible, for, in my   200

190 *I could tell you some stories. Fawcett* alone allows Lady Teazle a
   'Why don't you?'
192 s.d. *the next room. Fawcett* adds 'M.D.' (middle door in back flat?);
   Holl is more specific ('through the door in the scene').

opinion, nothing could excuse the intemperance of their
tongues but a natural and ungovernable bitterness of mind.

JOSEPH

Undoubtedly, madam; and it has always been a sentiment of
mine that to propagate a malicious truth wantonly is more
despicable than to falsify from revenge. But can you, Maria,   205
feel thus for others and be unkind to me alone? Is hope to
be denied the tenderest passion?

MARIA

Why will you distress me by renewing the subject?

JOSEPH

Ah, Maria, you would not treat me thus and oppose your
guardian Sir Peter's will, but that I see that profligate Charles   210
is still a favoured rival.

MARIA

Ungenerously urged! But whatever my sentiments are of
that unfortunate young man, be assured I shall not feel more
bound to give him up because his distresses have lost him
the regard even of a brother.   215

JOSEPH

Nay, but Maria, do not leave me with a frown. By all that's
honest I swear— (*Kneels*)

Enter LADY TEAZLE

(*Aside*) Gad's life, here's Lady Teazle. (*Aloud*) You must not
—no, you shall not—for though I have the greatest regard
for Lady Teazle—   220

MARIA

Lady Teazle!

JOSEPH

Yet were Sir Peter to suspect—

201 *intemperance*. So *Buckinghamshire, Crewe B, Georgetown, Banbury,
Spunge, Fawcett; Tickell* and *Murray* revert to *Lord Chamberlain's*
clearly erroneous 'interference'.

202 *ungovernable*. So all MSS; *Murray* has 'uncontrollable'—perhaps
from a late 'Dublin' edition (*1780* reads *ungovernable*).

203-5 *Undoubtedly . . . revenge*. So *Lord Chamberlain, Tickell, Murray;*
all other MSS om. A reader is no doubt grateful to be spared
Joseph's sentiment, but an actor might turn this example of his two
voices—both false but both plausible—to a virtuoso comic performance.

LADY TEAZLE *comes forward*

LADY TEAZLE

What is this, pray? (*Aside*) Does he take her for me?—
(*Aloud*) Child, you are wanted in the next room. *Exit* MARIA
What is all this, pray?   225

JOSEPH

Oh, the most unlucky circumstance in nature. Maria has
somehow suspected the tender concern I have for your happiness and threatened to acquaint Sir Peter with her suspicions,
and I was just endeavouring to reason with her when you
came in.   230

LADY TEAZLE

Indeed! But you seemed to adopt a very tender mode of
reasoning. Do you usually argue on your knees?

JOSEPH

Oh, she's a child and I thought a little bombast—but, Lady
Teazle, when are you to give me your judgment on my
library, as you promised?   235

LADY TEAZLE

No, no; I begin to think it would be imprudent, and you
know I admit you as a lover no farther than fashion sanctions.

JOSEPH

True—a mere Platonic *cicisbeo*—what every London wife
is entitled to.   240

LADY TEAZLE

Certainly one must not be out of the fashion. However, I

222 s.d. LADY TEAZLE *comes forward*. *Holl* again specifies 'through the
door in the scene'. Maria, Lady Teazle, and Joseph all have their
exits marked 'M.D.' (Middle Door?) in *Fawcett* and *Holl*. *Banbury*
has 'Exit back', *Fawcett* has 'Exit M.[iddle] D.(oor]'.

234-5 *judgment on my library*. Although no agreement is reached here,
Lady Teazle was actually to visit the new library that very evening
(in IV. iii).

237 *fashion sanctions*. A clear improvement in *Tickell* and *Murray* on
earlier texts' 'fashion requires'.

239 *a mere Platonic cicisbeo*. A cicisbeo is the recognized gallant of a
married woman, the *cavalier serviente*. Earliest instance *OED* Lady
Mary Wortley Montagu 1718. Frances Sheridan (mother of R.B.S.)
has a clever passage on the cicisbeo's privileges in the then unpub-
lished *A Journey to Bath* (cit. *Price*, p. 384).
London wife. Here *Georgetown* and *Fawcett* revert to the pre-
performance reading. The other later texts omit *London*—which,
however, is essential to the distinction between the *mores* of wives
from 'country' and in 'fashion'.

have so much of my country prejudices left that, though Sir
Peter's ill humour may vex me ever so, it shall never provoke
me to—

JOSEPH

The only revenge in your power. Well, I applaud your   245
moderation.

LADY TEAZLE

Go! You are an insinuating wretch! But we shall be missed.
Let us join the company.

JOSEPH

But we had best not return together.

LADY TEAZLE

Well, don't stay, for Maria shan't come to hear any more of   250
your reasoning, I promise you.   *Exit [back wing left]*

JOSEPH

A curious dilemma my politics have run me into! I wanted
at first only to ingratiate myself with Lady Teazle that she
might not be my enemy with Maria; and I have, I don't
know how, become her serious lover. Sincerely I begin to   255
wish I had never made such a point of gaining so very good
a character, for it has led me into so many cursed rogueries
that I doubt I shall be exposed at last.

                                    Exit [middle wing left]

Act II, Scene iii

SIR PETER TEAZLE's [*house*]

Enter SIR OLIVER SURFACE *and* ROWLEY [*right door*]

SIR OLIVER

Ha, ha, ha! So my old friend is married, hey? A young wife
out of the country. Ha, ha, ha! That he should have stood
bluff to old bachelor so long and sink into a husband at last.

242 *country prejudices.* The shift towards romanticism in Sheridan
differentiates his attitude to the country from that of the Restoration. Wycherley's *Country Wife* and Vanbrugh's Hoyden (in *The
Relapse*) were more 'natural', i.e., explicitly immoral, than their
London counterparts.
s.d. II. iii. Scene described in *Fawcett* as 'Antique Chamber' . . . 2nd
groove, with a table and two chairs.
2–3 *stood . . . bachelor.* Stood foursquare to his status as an old bachelor.
    3 *old bachelor.* Congreve's first play was *The Old Bachelor.* Sheridan
had revived it with minor expurgations at Drury Lane the preceding

ROWLEY

But you must not rally him on the subject, Sir Oliver. 'Tis a
tender point, I assure you, though he has been married only   5
seven months.

SIR OLIVER

Then he has been just half a year on the stool of repentance!
Poor Peter! But you say he has entirely given up Charles—
never sees him, hey?

ROWLEY

His prejudice against him is astonishing, and I am sure   10
greatly increased by a jealousy of him with Lady Teazle,
which he has been industriously led into by a scandalous
society in the neighbourhood, who have contributed not a
little to Charles's ill name; whereas the truth is, I believe, if
the lady is partial to either of them, his brother is the   15
favourite.

SIR OLIVER

Aye, I know there are a set of malicious, prating, prudent
gossips, both male and female, who murder characters to kill
time, and will rob a young fellow of his good name before
he has years to know the value of it. But I am not to be   20
prejudiced against my nephew by such, I promise you. No,
no, if Charles has done nothing false or mean, I shall com-
pound for his extravagance.

ROWLEY

Then, my life on't, you will reclaim him. Ah, sir, it gives me
new life to find that *your* heart is not turned against him,   25
and that the son of my good old master has one friend
however left.

SIR OLIVER

What, shall I forget, Master Rowley, when I was at his years
myself? Egad, my brother and I were neither of us very
prudent youths—and yet, I believe, you have not seen many   30
better men than your old master was.

ROWLEY

Sir, 'tis this reflection gives me assurance that Charles may
yet be a credit to his family. But here comes Sir Peter.

---

autumn. Congreve's Heartwell is described as 'surly' and has other
affinities to Sir Peter; he narrowly escapes marriage.
6 *seven months.* The contradiction with the *six months* of I. ii, 2 seems
merely careless.

SIR OLIVER

Egad, so he does! Mercy on me, he's greatly altered, and
seems to have a settled married look. One may read husband   35
in his face at this distance!

Enter SIR PETER TEAZLE [*right*]

SIR PETER

Hah! Sir Oliver—my old friend. Welcome to England a
thousand times!

SIR OLIVER

Thank you—thank you, Sir Peter! And i'faith I am as glad
to find you well, believe me.   40

SIR PETER

Oh! 'tis a long time since we met—fifteen years, I doubt,
Sir Oliver, and many a cross accident in the time.

SIR OLIVER

Aye, I have had my share. But what—I find you are married,
hey? Well, well, it can't be helped, and so I wish you joy
with all my heart.   45

SIR PETER

Thank you, thank you, Sir Oliver. Yes, I have entered into
the happy state. But we'll not talk of that now.

SIR OLIVER

True, true, Sir Peter. Old friends should not begin on griev-
ances at first meeting. No, no, no.

ROWLEY (*To* SIR OLIVER)

Take care, pray, sir.   50

SIR OLIVER

Well—so one of my nephews is a wild rogue, hey?

SIR PETER

Wild! Ah, my old friend, I grieve for your disappointment
there; he's a lost young man, indeed. However, his brother
will make you amends; Joseph is, indeed, what a youth
should be. Everybody in the world speaks well of him.   55

---

36 *at this distance.* An extreme example of the Restoration convention
   that permitted a character to be visible from the stage before his
   actual entry on to it.
41 *fifteen years.* So *Tickell, Murray* as in I. ii. 68; *Georgetown* and
   earlier texts have 'sixteen' in both passages. The changes are discussed in note to I. ii, 68.

SIR OLIVER

I am sorry to hear it; he has too good a character to be an
honest fellow. Everybody speaks well of him! Pshaw! Then
he has bowed as low to knaves and fools as to the honest
dignity of genius and virtue.

SIR PETER

What, Sir Oliver, do you blame him for not making enemies?   60

SIR OLIVER

Yes, if he has merit enough to deserve them.

SIR PETER

Well, well—you'll be convinced when you know him. 'Tis
edification to hear him converse; he professes the noblest
sentiments.

SIR OLIVER

Oh, plague of his sentiments! If he salutes me with a scrap   65
of morality in his mouth, I shall be sick directly. But, however, don't mistake me, Sir Peter; I don't mean to defend
Charles's errors. But before I form my judgment of either of
them, I intend to make a trial of their hearts; and my friend
Rowley and I have planned something for the purpose.   70

ROWLEY

And Sir Peter shall own for once he has been mistaken.

SIR PETER

Oh, my life on Joseph's honour!

SIR OLIVER

Well, come, give us a bottle of good wine, and we'll drink the
lads' health, and tell you our scheme.

SIR PETER

Allons, then!   75

SIR OLIVER

And don't, Sir Peter, be so severe against your old friend's
son. Odds my life! I am not sorry that he has run out of the
course a little. For my part I hate to see prudence clinging
to the green suckers of youth; 'tis like ivy round a sapling
and spoils the growth of the tree.   *Exeunt [right]*   80

Act III, Scene i

SIR PETER TEAZLE's *house. Scene continues*

Enter [right] SIR PETER TEAZLE, SIR OLIVER SURFACE, *and* ROWLEY
[Manservant in attendance]

SIR PETER

Well then, we will see this fellow first and have our wine
afterwards. But how is this, Master Rowley? I don't see the
jet of your scheme.

ROWLEY

Why, sir, this Mr Stanley who I was speaking of is nearly
related to them by their mother. He was once a merchant   5
in Dublin but has been ruined by a series of undeserved
misfortunes. He has applied by letter since his confinement
to both Mr Surface and Charles. From the former he has
received nothing but evasive promises of future service, while
Charles has done all that his extravagance has left him power   10
to do; and he is at this time endeavouring to raise a sum of
money, part of which, in the midst of his own distresses, I
know he intends for the service of poor Stanley.

SIR OLIVER

Ah, he is my brother's son.

SIR PETER

Well, but how is Sir Oliver personally to—   15

ROWLEY

Why, sir, I will inform Charles and his brother that Stanley
has obtained permission to apply personally to his friends;

---

s.d. III. i. The order of entry through right proscenium door (in *Fawcett*)
is Sir Oliver, Sir Peter, Rowley. Other texts have Sir Peter leading, no
doubt to emphasize that the scene is *chez lui*. The one major structural
change in the play from *Frampton Court* is the removal of Snake's
cross-examination and confession from this scene to V. iii.

3 *jet*. Point, gist (of which *jet* is a by-form).

7 *since his confinement*. Om. *Tickell* and *Murray*, perhaps because of
Sheridan's own personal experience of the indignities of a spunging-
house. He had himself 'applied by letter' to friends for help (*Letters*,
III *passim*), and no doubt obtained occasional 'permission to apply
in person' (below, l. 17). Earlier texts' greater explicitness reflects
freedom from arrest accorded to Members of Parliament. Imprison-
ment for debt was not abolished in England until the Debtors' Act
(1869).

and, as they have neither of them ever seen him, let Sir
Oliver assume his character and he will have a fair opportunity of judging at least of the benevolence of their   20
dispositions. And believe me, sir, you will find in the younger
brother one who, in the midst of folly and dissipation, has
still, as our immortal bard expresses it,

      a tear for pity and a hand ⎫
    Open as day for melting charity. ⎬   25

SIR PETER

Pshaw! What signifies his having an open hand, or purse
either, when he has nothing left to give? Well, well, make the
trial if you please. But where is the fellow whom you brought
for Sir Oliver to examine relative to Charles's affairs?

ROWLEY

Below, waiting his commands, and no one can give him   30
better intelligence. This, Sir Oliver, is a friendly Jew, who to
do him justice has done everything in his power to bring
your nephew to a proper sense of his extravagance.

SIR PETER

Pray, let us have him in.

ROWLEY (*Apart to* SERVANT)

Desire Mr Moses to walk upstairs.   35

SIR PETER

But, pray, why should you suppose he will speak the truth?

ROWLEY

Oh, I have convinced him that he has no chance of recover-
ing certain sums advanced to Charles but through the bounty
of Sir Oliver, who he knows has arrived, so that you may
depend on his fidelity to his own interest. I have also another   40
evidence in my power, one Snake, whom I have detected in

24–5 *a tear . . . charity.* 2 *Henry IV,* IV. iv, 31–2. So most texts, some
    inserting 'the' before *day.* Misquoted in *Tickell, Murray* as 'A heart
    to pity and a hand open as day for melting charity'—no doubt one
    derived by Thomas Wilkie from a peculiarly corrupt 'Dublin' text
    (not *1780*).
36 *But, pray, why.* So *Lord Chamberlain, 1778, Buckinghamshire,
    Crewe B, Banbury, Spunge, Tickell, Murray;* 'but why' *Georgetown*
    ('pray' is heavily blotted out, presumably by Sheridan, to avoid
    repetition of 'pray' in l. 34). Sir Peter's irritated courtesy requires
    such drastic repetition.
40 *his own interest.* So *Lord Chamberlain, Buckinghamshire, Crewe B,
    Banbury, Spunge, Fawcett, Tickell;* 'his own interests' *Murray;* 'his
    interest' *Georgetown* ('own' heavily blotted out by Sheridan).

a matter little short of forgery and shall speedily produce to
remove some of your prejudices.

SIR PETER

I have heard too much on that subject.

ROWLEY

Here comes the honest Israelite.   45

Enter MOSES [*right*]

This is Sir Oliver.

SIR OLIVER

Sir, I understand you have lately had great dealings with my
nephew Charles.

MOSES

Yes, Sir Oliver, I have done all I could for him; but he was
ruined before he came to me for assistance.   50

42–3 *shall . . . prejudices.* So *Tickell, Murray;* 'shall shortly produce to
    remove some of your prejudices, Sir Peter, in relation to Charles
    and Lady Teazle' *Lord Chamberlain, 1778, Georgetown, Banbury,
    Fawcett.* Alleged Charles/Lady Teazle affair, though mentioned and
    denied by Rowley in II. iii, 10ff., is more effectively reserved for the
    conclusion of this scene. To Sir Oliver it was Charles's extravagance
    and reckless generosity that was the immediate problem. The
    Tickell/Murray reading is decidedly less clumsy than that of the
    earlier texts, if less explicit.

45 *the honest Israelite.* The introduction of Moses led to the Licenser
    holding up his approval of the play's performance. The affair is dis-
    cussed in great detail in *Price*, pp. 300ff. It can be summarized
    briefly here. The City Chamberlain—one Benjamin Hopkins, sus-
    pected of usurious loans to minors—was campaigning for re-election.
    On hearing of Sheridan's Moses, he believed that this was part of
    the opposition's tactics to smear him. There was also a real Moses—
    a certain Jacob Nathan Moses—who had lent £2,000 to Willoughby
    Lacy, who was then one of the part-owners of Drury Lane Theatre,
    and he too feared that he might be caricatured by Sheridan. Under
    the circumstances the Licenser's refusal is comprehensible. But, as it
    happened, Sheridan was entirely innocent. Moses's part had been
    introduced into the play many months before these complications
    arose, and his part is in fact politically and racially inoffensive. As
    the Licenser only received the MS on 7 May, and the play was due
    to have its first night on 8 May, Sheridan had to act promptly. He
    therefore went above the Licenser's head to Lord Hertford, who was
    the Chamberlain and as such the Licenser's employer, and was able
    to satisfy him that the play could be acted without any public or
    private damage.
        And so the licence was obtained without any alteration being
    required. Many years later Sheridan was able to introduce the episode
    into one of his speeches in the House of Commons, which is to be
    found in his collected *Speeches* (IV (1816), 188).

SIR OLIVER

That was unlucky truly, for you have had no opportunity of
showing your talents.

MOSES

None at all. I hadn't the pleasure of knowing his distresses
till he was some thousands worse than nothing.

SIR OLIVER

Unfortunate, indeed! But I suppose you have done all in   55
your power for him, honest Moses?

MOSES

Yes, he knows that. This very evening I was to have brought
him a gentleman from the City, who does not know him and
will, I believe, advance him some money.

SIR PETER

What—one Charles has never had money from before?   60

MOSES

Yes. Mr Premium of Crutched Friars, formerly a broker.

SIR PETER

Egad, Sir Oliver, a thought strikes me. Charles, you say, does
not know Mr Premium?

MOSES

Not at all.

SIR PETER

Now then, Sir Oliver, you may have a better opportunity of   65
satisfying yourself than by an old romancing tale of a poor
relation. Go with my friend Moses and represent Mr
Premium, and then, I'll answer for it, you'll see your nephew
in all his glory.

SIR OLIVER

Egad, I like this idea better than the other, and I may visit   70
Joseph afterwards as old Stanley.

SIR PETER

True. So you may.

ROWLEY

Well, this is taking Charles rather at a disadvantage, to be

61 *Crutched Friars.* A small street off Aldgate in the heart of the City.
A friary had once occupied it (built 1298)—appropriately for
Premium who was a Christian if a broker.
a broker. Stockbroker, moneylender.
66 *romancing.* Fantastic, incredible (like a medieval romance); *romantic*
in the neo-classic sense, as still used by Dr Johnson (who had proposed Sheridan for 'The Club' only in April 1777), meant 'improbable,
false'.

sure. However, Moses, you understand Sir Peter and will be
faithful?   75

MOSES

You may depend upon me. This is near the time I was to
have gone.

SIR OLIVER

I'll accompany you as soon as you please, Moses. But hold,
I have forgot one thing. How the plague shall I be able to
pass for a Jew?   80

MOSES

There's no need. The principal is Christian.

SIR OLIVER

Is he? I'm sorry to hear it. But then again, a'n't I rather too
smartly dressed to look like a money-lender?

SIR PETER

Not at all; 'twould not be out of character, if you went in
your own carriage. Would it, Moses?   85

MOSES

Not in the least.

SIR OLIVER

Well, but how must I talk? There's certainly some cant of
usury and mode of treating that I ought to know.

SIR PETER

Oh, there's not much to learn. The great point, as I take it,
is to be exorbitant enough in your demands—hey, Moses?   90

MOSES

Yes, that's a very great point.

SIR OLIVER

I'll answer for't I'll not be wanting in that. I'll ask him eight
or ten per cent on the loan—at least.

MOSES

If you ask him no more than that, you'll be discovered
immediately.   95

SIR OLIVER

Hey, what the plague! How much then?

MOSES

That depends upon the circumstances. If he appears not very
anxious for the supply, you should require only forty or

---

87 *cant.* Professional lingo.
88 *treating.* 'Treatment' rather than 'hospitality'.

fifty per cent. But if you find him in great distress and want
the moneys very bad, you must ask double.   100
SIR PETER
A good honest trade you're learning, Sir Oliver.
SIR OLIVER
Truly, I think so—and not unprofitable.
MOSES
Then, you know, you haven't the moneys yourself, but are
forced to borrow them for him of an old friend.
SIR OLIVER
Oh, I borrow it of a friend, do I?   105
MOSES
Yes, and your friend is an unconscionable dog; but you can't
help it.
SIR OLIVER
My friend is an unconscionable dog, is he?
MOSES
Yes, and he himself has not the moneys by him, but is forced
to sell stock at a great loss.   110
SIR OLIVER
He is forced to sell stock at a great loss, is he? Well, that's
very kind of him.
SIR PETER
I'faith, Sir Oliver—Mr Premium, I mean—you'll soon be
master of the trade. But, Moses, wouldn't you have him run
out a little against the Annuity Bill? That would be in   115
character I should think.
MOSES
Very much.
ROWLEY
And lament that a young man now must be at years of
discretion before he is suffered to ruin himself?
MOSES
Aye, great pity!   120

---

100 *moneys.* Baddeley, the original Moses, allowed himself a more
grotesque Jewish accent than Sheridan's text permits (see above,
p. xxvi). But there are hints of foreign idiom, that differentiate
Moses's speech from that of the other characters.
115 *the Annuity Bill*, which protected minors from annual payments of
more than 10 shillings per £100 to the moneylenders, had been
passed by the House of Commons in April 1777, but did not become
an Act (below, l. 121) until 12 May.
120 *great pity.* Moses's broken English again.

SIR PETER

And abuse the public for allowing merit to an Act whose
only object is to snatch misfortune and imprudence from the
rapacious relief of usury—and give the minor a chance of
inheriting his estate without being undone by coming into
possession.   125

SIR OLIVER

So—so. Moses shall give me further instructions as we go
together.

SIR PETER

You will not have much time, for your nephew lives hard by.

SIR OLIVER

Oh, never fear: my tutor appears so able, that though
Charles lived in the next street, it must be my own fault if I   130
am not a complete rogue before I turn the corner.

Exeunt SIR OLIVER SURFACE *and* MOSES [*left*]

SIR PETER

So now I think Sir Oliver will be convinced. You are partial,
Rowley, and would have prepared Charles for the other plot.

ROWLEY

No, upon my word, Sir Peter.

SIR PETER

Well, go bring me this Snake, and I'll hear what he has to   135
say presently. I see Maria and want to speak with her.

Exit ROWLEY [*right*]

I should be glad to be convinced my suspicions of Lady
Teazle and Charles were unjust. I have never yet opened my
mind on this subject to my friend Joseph. I am determined I
will do it; he will give me his opinion sincerely.   140

Enter MARIA [*left*]

So, child, has Mr Surface returned with you?

MARIA

No, sir. He was engaged.

SIR PETER

Well, Maria, do you not reflect the more you converse with
that amiable young man what return his partiality for you
deserves?   145

MARIA

Indeed, Sir Peter, your frequent importunity on this subject

136 *presently.* Immediately.

distresses me extremely. You compel me to declare that I
know no man who has ever paid me a particular attention
whom I would not prefer to Mr Surface.

SIR PETER

So—here's perverseness! No, no, Maria, 'tis Charles only   150
whom you would prefer. 'Tis evident his vices and follies
have won your heart.

MARIA

This is unkind, sir. You know I have obeyed you in neither
seeing nor corresponding with him. I have heard enough to
convince me that he is unworthy my regard. Yet I cannot   155
think it culpable, if while my understanding severely con-
demns his vices, my heart suggests some pity for his distresses.

SIR PETER

Well, well, pity him as much as you please, but give your
heart and hand to a worthier object.   160

MARIA

Never to his brother.

SIR PETER

Go, perverse and obstinate! But take care, madam; you have
never yet known what the authority of a guardian is. Don't
compel me to inform you of it.

MARIA

I can only say you shall not have just reason. 'Tis true, by 165
my father's will I am for a short period bound to regard you
as his substitute, but must cease to think you so when you
would compel me to be miserable.   *Exit* [*right*]

SIR PETER

Was ever man so crossed as I am?—everything conspiring
to fret me! I had not been involved in matrimony a fort-   170
night before her father, a hale and hearty man, died, on
purpose I believe, for the pleasure of plaguing me with the
care of his daughter. But here comes my helpmate. She
appears in great good humour. How happy I should be if I
could tease her into loving me, though but a little.   175

162 *madam.* Sir Peter addresses Maria here for the first time as if she
was grown up, while threatening her with the authority of a
guardian. She is generally spoken to as 'child'—which would suggest
she is at most sixteen. Priscilla Hopkins, who took the part, was at
least twenty, perhaps twenty-one.

Enter LADY TEAZLE

LADY TEAZLE

Lud, Sir Peter, I hope you haven't been quarrelling with
Maria? It is not using me well to be ill-humoured when I am
not by.

SIR PETER

Ah, Lady Teazle, you might have the power to make me
good-humoured at all times.   180

LADY TEAZLE

I am sure I wish I had, for I want you to be in a charming
sweet temper at this moment. Do be good-humoured now
and let me have two hundred pounds, will you?

SIR PETER

Two hundred pounds! What, a'n't I to be in a good humour
without paying for it? But speak to me thus and i'faith   185
there's nothing I could refuse you. You shall have it, but seal
me a bond for the repayment.

LADY TEAZLE

Oh, no. There—my note of hand will do as well.

SIR PETER (*Kissing her hand*)

And you shall no longer reproach me with not giving you
an independent settlement. I mean shortly to surprise you.   190
But shall we always live thus, hey?

LADY TEAZLE

If you please. I'm sure I don't care how soon we leave off
quarrelling provided you'll own you were tired first.

SIR PETER

Well, then let our future contest be who shall be most oblig-
ing.   195

LADY TEAZLE

I assure you, Sir Peter, good nature becomes you. You look
now as you did before we were married, when you used to
walk with me under the elms and tell me stories of what a
gallant you were in your youth and chuck me under the
chin, you would, and ask me if I thought I could love an old   200
fellow who would deny me nothing—didn't you?

SIR PETER

Yes, yes, and you were as kind and attentive—

189 s.d. *Kissing her hand.* Sheridan has inserted this in *Georgetown.* Most
MSS (including *Tickell*) omit the direction. *Murray*: 'offering her
hand'. The context makes it clear that the offer is accepted.

LADY TEAZLE

Aye, so I was, and would always take your part when my
acquaintance used to abuse you and turn you into ridicule.

SIR PETER

Indeed!   205

LADY TEAZLE

Aye, and when my cousin Sophy has called you a stiff,
peevish old bachelor and laughed at me for thinking of
marrying one who might be my father, I have always
defended you and said I didn't think you so ugly by any
means—and I dared say you'd make a very good sort of   210
husband.

SIR PETER

And you prophesied right. And we shall now be the happiest
couple—

LADY TEAZLE

And never differ again?

SIR PETER

No, never. Though at the same time indeed, my dear Lady   215
Teazle, you must watch your temper very narrowly, for in
all our quarrels, my dear, if you recollect, my love, you
always began first.

LADY TEAZLE

I beg your pardon, my dear Sir Peter. Indeed you always
gave the provocation.   220

SIR PETER

Now see, my angel! Take care. Contradicting isn't the way
to keep friends.

LADY TEAZLE

Then don't you begin it, my love.

SIR PETER

There, now, you—you—are going on. You don't perceive, my
life, that you are just doing the very thing which you know   225
always makes me angry.

209–10 *so ugly by any means. Fawcett* alone inserts Sir Peter's 'Thank
      you, Lady Teazle'. An actor's gag?
216 *very narrowly.* Emended in *Tickell* and *Murray* to 'very seriously'.
      The earlier MSS' reading seems marginally preferable; it is the care
      with which she is to watch her temper with which Sir Peter is con-
      cerned. Such care need not be incompatible with good humour and
      the absence of seriousness.
224 *you—you.* Sir Peter is having difficulty in not being offensive.

LADY TEAZLE

Nay, you know if you will be angry without any reason, my
dear—

SIR PETER

There now, you want to quarrel again.

LADY TEAZLE

No, I'm sure I don't; but if you will be so peevish—   230

SIR PETER

There now! Who begins first?

LADY TEAZLE

Why, you to be sure. I said nothing; but there's no bearing
your temper.

SIR PETER

No, no, madam! The fault's in your own temper.

LADY TEAZLE

Aye, you are just what my cousin Sophy said you would be.   235

SIR PETER

Your cousin Sophy is a forward impertinent gipsy.

LADY TEAZLE

You are a great bear, I'm sure, to abuse my relations.

SIR PETER

Now may all the plagues of marriage be doubled on me if
ever I try to be friends with you any more!

LADY TEAZLE

So much the better.   240

SIR PETER

No, no, madam. 'Tis evident you never cared a pin for me
and I was a madman to marry you—a pert rural coquette
that had refused half the honest squires in the neighbourhood.

LADY TEAZLE

And I am sure I was a fool to marry you—an old dangling   245

236 *gipsy*. A general term of abuse.
237 *great bear*. Gray's *mot* about *ursa major* (=Dr Johnson) suggests
that a comparison with bears was in vogue at the time. For Sheridan's instructions to Mrs Abington on how to act this sentence, see
the reminiscences of Charles Reade's mother (above, p. liii), the
daughter of John Scott, editor of *London Magazine* and friend of
Lamb and Hazlitt. The stage directions derived from prompt copies
do not confirm her account.
243 *honest squires*. So *Tickell, Murray; Georgetown* om. 'honest'. Sir
Peter's adjective is not to be taken at face value. In his present mood
all squires were honest.
245 *dangling*. Hovering follower of women.

bachelor, who was single at fifty only because he never
could meet with anyone who would have him.

SIR PETER

Aye, aye, madam; but you were pleased enough to listen to
me. You never had such an offer before.

LADY TEAZLE

No? Didn't I refuse Sir Tivy Terrier, who everybody said   250
would have been a better match, for his estate is just as good
as yours and he has broke his neck since we have married?

SIR PETER

I have done with you, madam! You are an unfeeling, ungrateful—But there's an end of everything. I believe you
capable of everything that is bad. Yes, madam, I now believe   255
the reports relative to you and Charles, madam. Yes, madam,
you and Charles are, not without grounds—

LADY TEAZLE

Take care, Sir Peter! You had better not insinuate any such
thing. I'll not be suspected without cause, I promise you.

SIR PETER

Very well, madam, very well! A separate maintenance as   260
soon as you please. Yes, madam, or a divorce! I'll make an
example of myself for the benefit of all old bachelors. Let
us separate, madam.

LADY TEAZLE

Agreed, agreed! And now, my dear Sir Peter, we are of a
mind once more, we may be the happiest couple and never   265
differ again, you know. Ha, ha, ha! Well, you are going to
be in a passion, I see, and I shall only interrupt you; so
bye, bye!   *Exit [right]*

SIR PETER

Plagues and tortures! Can't I make her angry either? Oh, I
am the miserablest fellow! But I'll not bear her presuming   270
to keep her temper. No. She may break my heart, but she
shan't keep her temper.   *Exit [left]*

---

250 *Sir Tivy.* Abbreviation of *tantivy* (at full gallop).
270 *miserablest.* Sir Peter had already used the unusual superlative to
describe himself ('the miserablest dog', I. ii, 3): the reading 'most
miserable' is confined to *Murray* and seems to have been Thomas
Wilkie's emendation.
272 s.d. *Exit [left].* In *Banbury* Sir Peter also goes out right—perhaps to
prevent any confusion with the entries in III. ii.

Act III, Scene ii

CHARLES SURFACE's *house*

Enter TRIP, MOSES, *and* SIR OLIVER SURFACE [*left*]

TRIP

Here, Master Moses! If you'll stay a moment, I'll try
whether— What's the gentleman's name?

SIR OLIVER (*Aside* [*to* MOSES])

Mr Moses, what is my name?

MOSES

Mr Premium.

TRIP

Premium. Very well.   *Exit, taking snuff* [*right*]   5

SIR OLIVER

To judge by the servants one wouldn't believe the master was
ruined. But what—sure, this was my brother's house?

MOSES

Yes, sir; Mr Charles bought it of Mr Joseph, with the furni-
ture, pictures, etc., just as the old gentleman left it. Sir Peter
thought it a great piece of extravagance in him.   10

SIR OLIVER

In my mind the other's economy in selling it to him was
more reprehensible by half.

Enter TRIP [*right*]

TRIP

My master says you must wait, gentlemen; he has company
and can't speak with you yet.

SIR OLIVER

If he knew who it was wanted to see him, perhaps he   15
wouldn't have sent such a message.

TRIP

Yes, yes, sir; he knows *you* are here. I didn't forget little
Premium. No, no, no.

s.d. III. ii. Scenery described in prompt copies (*1778, Fawcett* as 'Drop
    Chamber')—Garrick's innovation at Drury Lane for short interiors
    (superseding the flat with wallpaper in second groove).

SIR OLIVER

Very well. And I pray, sir, what may be *your* name?

TRIP

Trip, sir. My name is Trip, at your service.   20

SIR OLIVER

Well, then, Mr Trip, you have a pleasant sort of place here,
I guess?

TRIP

Why, yes. Here are three or four of us pass our time agree-
ably enough, but then our wages are sometimes a little in
arrear—and not very great either. But fifty pounds a year,   25
and find our own bags and bouquets.

SIR OLIVER

Bags and bouquets! Halters and bastinadoes!

TRIP

But *à propos*, Moses, have you been able to get me that
little bill discounted?

SIR OLIVER (*Aside*)

Wants to raise money—mercy on me! Has his distresses   30
too, I warrant, like a lord—and affects creditors and duns.

MOSES

'Twas not to be done, indeed, Mr Trip.   *Gives the note*

TRIP

Good lack, you surprise me! My friend Brush has endorsed
it, and I thought when he put his name at the back of a bill
'twas as good as cash.   35

MOSES

No, 'twouldn't do.

TRIP

A small sum—but twenty pounds. Hark'ee, Moses, do you
think you couldn't get it me by way of annuity?

---

26 *bags and bouquets.* Footmen retained the large bag-wig fashionable
   in France ('bouquet'), with the bag of ornamented silk behind in
   which it terminated, long after their masters had discarded theirs.
29 *bill discounted.* Promissory note with commission deducted when
   cashed.
30 *raise money . . . distresses too. Tickell, Murray* alone insert *too* after
   distresses (where it is logically necessary).
35 *good as cash.* So all earlier texts; *Tickell, Murray*'s 'same as cash' is
   an unnecessary enfeeblement.

SIR OLIVER (*Aside*)

An annuity! Ha, ha! A footman raise money by way of
annuity! Well done, luxury, egad!   40

MOSES

Well, but you must insure your place.

TRIP

Oh, with all my heart! I'll insure my place, and my life too,
if you please.

SIR OLIVER (*Aside*)

It's more than I would your neck.

MOSES

But is there nothing you could deposit?   45

TRIP

Why, nothing capital of my master's wardrobe has dropped
lately; but I could give you a mortgage on some of his winter
clothes, with equity of redemption before November. Or you
shall have the reversion of the French velvet, or a post-obit
on the blue and silver. These, I should think, Moses, with a   50
few pair of point ruffles, as a collateral security—hey, my
little fellow?

MOSES

Well, well.   *Bell rings*

TRIP

Egad, I heard the bell. I believe, gentlemen, I can now
introduce you. Don't forget the annuity, little Moses! This   55
way, gentlemen. Insure my place, you know.

SIR OLIVER (*Aside*)

If the man be a shadow of the master, this is the temple of
dissipation indeed.   *Exeunt [right]*

---

40 *luxury, egad. Lord Chamberlain* and *1778* retain from *Frampton
Court*:

> MOSES
> Who would you get to join with you?
> TRIP
> You know my Lord Applicit? You have seen him, however?
> MOSES
> Yes.
> TRIP
> Very well. You must have observed what an appearance he
> makes. Nobody dresses better; nobody throws off faster. Very
> well—his own gentleman will stand my security.

The School for Scandal had been generally criticized for being too
long (above, p. xxxv); this was a passage nobody would miss. The

Act III, Scene iii

CHARLES SURFACE, CARELÉSS, *etc., at a table with wine, etc.*

CHARLES

'Fore Heaven, 'tis true—there's the great degeneracy of the
age! Many of our acquaintance have taste, spirit, and
politeness; but plague on't they won't *drink*.

CARELESS

It is so, indeed, Charles. They give in to all the substantial
luxuries of the table, and abstain from nothing but wine   5
and wit.

'cit' in Applicit suggests a City merchant who had recently been
ennobled. A vague allusion may even have been intended to Sir
Hugh Smithson, of a family of London bankers, who had in 1766
been created duke of Northumberland.

44–5 *your neck . . . But is there nothing. Lord Chamberlain, Buckinghamshire, Georgetown* insert:

TRIP

But then, Moses, it must be done before this d——d register
takes place—one wouldn't like to have one's name made public,
you know.

MOSES

No, certainly.

This is om. in *Crewe B, Banbury, Fawcett, Tickell, Murray*—no
doubt because the comment was no longer topical. The 1777
Annuity Act required the registering of all life annuities.

46–51 *capital . . . mortgage . . . equity of redemption . . . reversion . . .
post-obit . . . collateral security.* A parody of the legal jargon used
by money-lenders. A post-obit is 'a bond given by a borrower,
securing to the lender a sum of money to be paid on the death of
a specified person from whom the borrower has expectations' (*OED*).
Trip's currency is his master's clothes, which 'die' when discarded
by Charles.

56 *Insure my place, you know. Crewe B* has 'I ensure'; *Murray*'s variation is 'I'll insure' (from *1780*, or a reprint?)

s.d. III, iii. The prompt copies have 'Antique Hall Table, Wine Glasses
and Chairs' *1778*, which has also 'a Small Throne'—not really
required until IV. i. *Fawcett* omits 'throne', but adds 'Table covered
with green cloth, two decanters of Wine, plenty of glasses U.E.L.
[=upper end left?], two chairs L[eft] H[and]. Charles, Careless and
4 Gents disc[over]d at a table drinking'. *Holl* adds the interesting
detail 'Folding Doors, 3d. G[roo]v[e]. The two chairs are to be
"ready for Oliver and Moses" '.

The earlier part of the scene derives from Suckling's *The Goblins*

CHARLES

Oh, certainly society suffers by it intolerably. For now, instead of the social spirit of raillery that used to mantle over a glass of bright burgundy, their conversation is become just like the Spa-water they drink, which has all the pertness   10 and flatulence of champagne, without its spirit or flavour.

1ST GENTLEMAN

But what are they to do who love play better than wine?

CARELESS

True. There's Harry diets himself for gaming, and is now under a hazard regimen.

CHARLES

Then he'll have the worst of it. What! You wouldn't train   15 a horse for the course by keeping him from corn. For my part, egad, I am now never so successful as when I am a little merry. Let me throw on a bottle of champagne, and I never lose—at least I never feel my losses, which is exactly the same thing.   20

2ND GENTLEMAN

Aye, that I believe.

CHARLES

And then what man can pretend to be a believer in love, who is an abjurer of wine? 'Tis the test by which the lover knows his own heart. Fill a dozen bumpers to a dozen beauties, and she that floats atop is the maid that has   25 bewitched you.

CARELESS

Now then, Charles, be honest and give us your real favourite.

(1638). Sheridan can be presumed to have acquired a copy of Thomas Davies's ed. of Suckling's *Works* (2 vols., 1770). For the influence of *The Goblins* on his early *A Drama of Devils*, see *Price*, pp. 804–5. The 'Song' ('Here's to the maiden of bashful fifteen') echoes a song in *The Goblins* (II, 313, in Davies's ed.), which begins 'A health to the nut-brown lass; / With the hazel eyes; let it pass. / She that has good eyes / Has good thighs / Let it pass . . . let it pass'.

There are more short cuts in this scene from the version originally performed than in any other. In general they have been skilfully made and can be safely attributed to Sheridan. As was usual at the time the play, in addition to its own prologue and epilogue, was always followed by a farce, and there was much criticism of the play's excessive length. See, for contemporary complaints, *Price*, pp. 313, 316, 322.

CHARLES

Why, I have withheld her only in compassion to you. If I
toast her, you must give a round of her peers, which is
impossible—on earth.   30

CARELESS

Oh, then we'll find some canonized vestals or heathen god-
desses that will do, I warrant.

CHARLES

Here then, bumpers, you rogues! Bumpers! Maria! Maria!

SIR TOBY

Maria who?

CHARLES

Oh, damn the surname! 'Tis too formal to be registered in   35
love's calendar. But now, Sir Toby, beware! We must have
beauty superlative.

CARELESS

Nay, never study, Sir Toby. We'll stand to the toast though
your mistress should want an eye, and you know you have
a song will excuse you.   40

SIR TOBY

Egad, so I have, and I'll give him the song instead of the
lady.   *Sings*

SONG

Here's to the maiden of bashful fifteen;
Here's to the widow of fifty;

35 *damn the surname*. Maria is without a surname throughout the play
—as the women who are married or widowed are without Christian
names. The convention had been inherited from Restoration comedy.
43 SONG. At first assigned to Careless (in *Frampton Court* and *Lord
Chamberlain*), then to Sir Harry, perhaps the Harry of l. 13) above,
in *1778* to 'III Gent.', then to Sir Toby in *Georgetown*, which also
provides Sir Toby with the surname Bumper (though this may be
a nickname, invented on the spot by Charles, as it follows his insistence on 'bumpers' being drunk to Maria). The character is not
specified in any list of *dramatis personae* before *Murray*—which was
sub-edited by Thomas Wilkie and may be his doing—where it
appears as Sir Harry Bumper. Although most texts prefer Sir Harry
—except *Georgetown* (and *1799*)—Sir Toby Bumper is too good to
lose, as Sheridan would surely have agreed.

　　Rae's edition of *Frampton Court* has '*Exeunt* Sir Harry Bumper
and Gentlemen' at l. 107, but this is not in the MS.

　　This 'favourite song' was appended—with Thomas Linley's setting
'by permission of the Author'—to Linley's music for *The Camp* (for
which Sheridan had provided the words) in 1778. The order of
stanzas 2 and 3 differs in the various texts, that of *Georgetown*,
Tickell, and *Murray* being followed here.

Here's to the flaunting, extravagant queen,   45
And here's to the housewife that's thrifty.

CHORUS   Let the toast pass,
                    Drink to the lass,
I'll warrant she'll prove an excuse for the glass!

Here's to the charmer whose dimples we prize;   50
Now to the maid who has none, sir!
Here's to the girl with a pair of blue eyes,
And here's to the nymph with but *one*, sir!

CHORUS   Let the toast pass, etc.

Here's to the maid with a bosom of snow!   55
Now to her that's brown as a berry!
Here's to the wife with a face full of woe,
And now to the girl that is merry!

CHORUS   Let the toast pass, etc.

For let 'em be clumsy, or let 'em be slim,   60
Young or ancient, I care not a feather:
So fill a pint bumper quite up to the brim,
And let us e'en toast them together!

CHORUS   Let the toast pass, etc.

Enter TRIP [*right*] *and whispers* CHARLES SURFACE

CHARLES
Gentlemen, you must excuse me a little. Careless, take the   65
chair, will you?
CARELESS
Nay, prithee, Charles, what now? This is one of your peer-
less beauties, I suppose, has dropped in by chance?
CHARLES
No, faith! To tell you the truth, 'tis a Jew and a broker, who
are come by appointment.   70
CARELESS
Oh, damn it, let's have the Jew in.

---

58 *to the girl that is merry*. So *Tickell, Murray*; earlier texts have the
    more artificial 'for the damsel that's merry'.
69 *broker*. *Frampton Court* reading had first been 'usurer', which
    Sheridan deletes there and substitutes this more general and less
    offensive term.

1ST GENTLEMAN

Aye, and the broker too, by all means.

2ND GENTLEMAN

Yes, yes, the Jew and the broker!

CHARLES

Egad, with all my heart! Trip, bid the gentlemen walk in.

Exit TRIP

Though there's one of them a stranger, I can tell you.   75

CARELESS

Charles, let us give them some generous burgundy and
perhaps they'll grow conscientious.

CHARLES

Oh, hang 'em, no! Wine does but draw forth a man's
natural qualities, and to make them drink would only be to
whet their knavery.   80

Enter TRIP, SIR OLIVER, *and* MOSES

CHARLES

So, honest Moses! Walk in, pray, Mr Premium. That's the
gentleman's name, isn't it, Moses?

MOSES

Yes, sir.

CHARLES

Set chairs, Trip. Sit down, Mr Premium. Glasses, Trip. Sit
down, Moses. Come, Mr Premium, I'll give you a sentiment: 85
here's *Success to usury!* Moses, fill the gentleman a bumper.

MOSES

Success to usury!   *Drinks*

CARELESS

Right, Moses! Usury is prudence and industry, and deserves
to succeed.

SIR OLIVER

Then here's—*all the success it deserves!*   *Drinks*   90

---

85 *a sentiment.* Joseph has the monopoly of 'sentiments' elsewhere. The
   passage ('Set chairs . . . bumper') is in *Frampton Court* and may
   well antedate this crucial change in Joseph's moral posturings.
90 *success it deserves.* Post-performance texts cut the following exchange, presumably as irrelevant, though excusable as an attempt
   by Charles as host to gloss over Sir Oliver's indiscretion:

   CHARLES
       Mr. Premium, you and I are but strangers yet, but I hope we
   shall be better acquainted by and by.

CARELESS

No, no, that won't do. Mr Premium, you have demurred at
the toast and must drink it in a pint bumper.

1ST GENTLEMAN

A pint bumper at least.

MOSES

Oh, pray, sir, consider. Mr Premium's a gentleman.

CARELESS

And therefore loves good wine.   95

2ND GENTLEMAN

Give Moses a quart glass. This is mutiny and a high contempt for the chair.

CARELESS

Here, now for't. I'll see justice done to the last drop of my
bottle.

SIR OLIVER

Nay, pray, gentlemen. I did not expect this usage.   100

CHARLES

No, hang it, you shan't. Mr Premium's a stranger.

SIR OLIVER (*Aside*)

Odd! I wish I was well out of their company.

CARELESS

Plague on 'em, then! If they don't drink, we'll not sit down
with 'em. Come, Harry, the dice are in the next room.
Charles, you'll join us when you have finished your business   105
with these gentlemen?

CHARLES

I will! I will!   *Exeunt* [CHARLES'*s friends right*]
Careless!

SIR OLIVER

Yes, sir, I hope we shall—(*Aside*) more intimate perhaps than
you'll wish.

The dramatic irony, if scarcely subtle, was worth saving.

At this point there is a gap in *Frampton Court* to the end of the
scene. It is clear, however, from the dialogue with which IV. ii opens
that the missing pages must have had the auction of family portraits
as in *Lord Chamberlain* ('But he wouldn't sell my picture', etc.). The
suggestion that the absence of the auction in the MS proves it late
is pure speculation. The III. iii fragment ends abruptly in the aside
by Sir Oliver 'more intimate perhaps than you'll wish'.

Stylistically, the scene is perhaps more consistently mature than
the rest of the play—closer to the first act of *The Critic* than to the
horseplay of *The Rivals* or *The Duenna*.

103 *don't drink. Tickell, Murray* improve on earlier texts' 'won't drink'.

CARELESS (*Returning*)

Well?

CARELESS

Perhaps I may want *you*.   110

CARELESS

Oh, you know I am always ready: word, note, or bond, 'tis
all the same to me.   *Exit [right]*

MOSES

Sir, this is Mr Premium, a gentleman of the strictest honour
and secrecy—and always performs what he undertakes. Mr
Premium, this is—   115

CHARLES

Pshaw! Have done. Sir, my friend Moses is a very honest
fellow, but a little slow at expression. He'll be an hour giving
us our titles. Mr Premium, the plain state of the matter is
this: I am an extravagant young fellow who wants to borrow
money, you I take to be a prudent old fellow, who have got   120
money to lend. I am blockhead enough to give fifty per cent
sooner than not have it, and you, I presume, are rogue
enough to take a hundred if you can get it. Now, sir, you see
we are acquainted at once and may proceed to business without further ceremony.   125

SIR OLIVER

Exceeding frank, upon my word. I see, sir, you are not a
man of many compliments.

CHARLES

Oh, no, sir. Plain dealing in business I always think best.

---

119 *wants to borrow money.* So *Murray*; all other texts (including
Tickell) *have* 'money to borrow', criticized in *Moore* as 'by no means
idiomatic' (I, 237n), but plausibly explained in *Price*, p. 5, as a misreading in early sketch 'The Teazles' (*Price*, p. 294) where 'to
borrow' has been inserted by Sheridan over 'money' without a caret
to indicate whether it is to precede or follow it. The passage is not
in *Frampton Court*; *Lord Chamberlain*'s mistake was no doubt due
to haste with which performance version of the play was put
together. The error points decisively to all later authoritative texts
(with the one exception of *Murray*) descending from that version,
however remotely. Both 'Dublin' and American piracies have the
'idiomatic' *Murray* reading; indeed *Murray* version may be filling a gap here
from *1780* or a reprint. *Price* quotes a complaint by 'Thespes' about
this uncouth phrase in *The Oracle* (17 September 1792)—which suggests that it was retained on the stage.

SIR OLIVER

Sir, I like you the better for it. However, you are mistaken
in one thing. I have no money to lend, but I believe I could   130
procure some of a friend. But then he's an unconscionable
dog, isn't he, Moses?

MOSES

But you can't help that.

SIR OLIVER

And must sell stock to accommodate you—mustn't he, Moses?

MOSES

Yes, indeed! You know I always speak the truth, and I   135
scorn to tell a lie!

CHARLES

Right. People that speak the truth generally do: but these
are trifles, Mr Premium. What! I know money isn't to be
bought without paying for't.

SIR OLIVER

Well—but what security could you give? You have no land,   140
I suppose?

CHARLES

Not a mole-hill, nor a twig, but what's in beau-pots out of
the window!

SIR OLIVER

Nor any stock, I presume?

CHARLES

Nothing but live stock—and that's only a few pointers and   145
ponies. But pray, Mr Premium, are you acquainted at all
with any of my connections?

SIR OLIVER

Why, to say truth, I am.

CHARLES

Then you must know that I have a dev'lish rich uncle in the
East Indies, Sir Oliver Surface, from whom I have the   150
greatest expectations.

SIR OLIVER

That you have a wealthy uncle I have heard, but how your
expectations will turn out is more, I believe, than you can
tell.

---

142 *twig*. In the days of wooden ships forests were a valuable possession.
   beau-pots. Ornamental flower-vases. *Tickell* has plural reading.

CHARLES

Oh, no. There can be no doubt of it. They tell me I'm a   155
prodigious favourite and that he talks of leaving me everything.

SIR OLIVER

Indeed! This is the first I've heard on't.

CHARLES

Yes, yes, 'tis just so. Moses knows 'tis true, don't you, Moses?

MOSES

Oh, yes! I'll swear to't.   160

SIR OLIVER (*Aside*)

Egad, they'll persuade me presently I'm at Bengal.

CHARLES

Now I propose, Mr Premium, if it's agreeable to you, a post-
obit on Sir Oliver's life; though at the same time the old
fellow has been so liberal to me that I give you my word I
should be very sorry to hear that anything had happened to   165
him.

SIR OLIVER

Not more. than *I* should, I assure you. But the bond you
mention happens to be just the worst security you could
offer me—for I might live to a hundred and never recover
the principal.   170

CHARLES

Oh, yes, you would. The moment Sir Oliver dies, you know,
you would come on me for the money.

SIR OLIVER

Then I believe I should be the most unwelcome dun you ever
had in your life.

CHARLES

What? I suppose you are afraid now that Sir Oliver is too   175
good a life?

SIR OLIVER

No, indeed I am not—though I have heard he is as hale and
healthy as any man of his years in Christendom.

---

155 *doubt of it.* Sheridan has added *of it* in his own hand in *Crewe B.*
Georgetown and *Murray* are both without it, but the addition is
clearly necessary, though *Lord Chamberlain, Buckinghamshire, Banbury, Tickell,* among other early texts, also lack it. Sheridan had
presumably been anxious not to overdo the *of it, on't* or *to't* in the
passage.

161 s.d. *Aside.* Entered in Sheridan's hand in both *Crewe* MSS.

CHARLES

There again you are misinformed. No, no, the climate has
hurt him considerably, poor Uncle Oliver. Yes, yes, he breaks   180
apace, I'm told—and so much altered lately that his nearest
relations don't know him.

SIR OLIVER

No? Ha, ha, ha!—so much altered lately that his nearest
relations don't know him! Ha, ha, ha! That's droll, egad.
Ha, ha, ha!   185

CHARLES

Ha, ha! You're glad to hear that, little Premium.

SIR OLIVER

No, no, I'm not.

CHARLES

Yes, yes, you are. Ha, ha, ha! You know that mends your
chance.

SIR OLIVER

But I'm told Sir Oliver is coming over. Nay, some say he is   190
actually arrived.

CHARLES

Pshaw! Sure I must know better than you whether he's come
or not. No, no, rely on't, he's at this moment at Calcutta,
isn't he, Moses?

MOSES

Oh, yes, certainly.   195

SIR OLIVER

Very true, as you say, you must know better than I, though
I have it from pretty good authority, haven't I, Moses?

MOSES

Yes, most undoubted!

SIR OLIVER

But, sir, as I understand you want a few hundreds immediately, is there nothing you could dispose of?   200

CHARLES

How do you mean?

SIR OLIVER

For instance now, I have heard that your father left behind
him a great quantity of massy old plate.

186 *little Premium.* By now even 'Master' has been dropped. Prints and
    illustrations (see above, p. xxviii) suggest that Yates, the original Sir
    Oliver, was a small man.

CHARLES

Oh, lud, that's gone long ago. Moses can tell you how better
than I can.   205

SIR OLIVER (*Aside*)

Good lack, all the family race-cups and corporation bowls!
(*Aloud*) Then it was also supposed that his library was one
of the most valuable and complete.

CHARLES

Yes, yes, so it was—vastly too much so for a private gentleman. For my part, I was always of a communicative disposi-   210
tion; so I thought it a shame to keep so much knowledge to
myself.

SIR OLIVER (*Aside*)

Mercy upon me! Learning that had run in the family like an
heirloom! [*Aloud*] Pray what are become of the books?

CHARLES

You must inquire of the auctioneer, Master Premium, for I   215
don't believe even Moses can direct you.

MOSES

I know nothing of books.

SIR OLIVER

So, so, nothing of the family property left, I suppose?

CHARLES

Not much, indeed, unless you have a mind to the family
pictures. I have got a room full of ancestors above; and if   220
you have a taste for paintings, egad, you shall have 'em a
bargain.

SIR OLIVER

Hey! And the devil! Sure, you wouldn't sell your fore-
fathers, would you?

CHARLES

Every man of them to the best bidder.   225

SIR OLIVER

What! Your great-uncles and aunts?

---

208 *valuable and complete.* So all MSS, including *Tickell*, which all spell
    compleat. Murray's 'compact' is a misreading.
217 *I know . . . books.* So *Banbury, Tickell, Murray;* 'I never meddle
    with books', *Buckinghamshire, Crewe B, Georgetown;* om. *Lord
    Chamberlain.*
219 *the family pictures.* Sir Jeremy in Sheridan's mother's *A Journey to
    Bath* can 'thank heaven the family pictures are still extant' (cit.
    Price).

CHARLES

Aye, and my great-grandfathers and grandmothers too.

SIR OLIVER (*Aside*)

Now I give him up! [*Aloud*] What the plague, have you no
bowels for your own kindred? Odd's life, do you take me
for Shylock in the play that you would raise money of me   230
on your own flesh and blood?

CHARLES

Nay, my little broker, don't be angry. What need you care
if you have your money's worth?

SIR OLIVER

Well, I'll be the purchaser. I think I can dispose of the family
canvas. (*Aside*) Oh, I'll never forgive him this—never!   235

Enter CARELESS

CARELESS

Come, Charles; what keeps you?

CHARLES

I can't come yet. I' faith, we are going to have a sale above
stairs. Here's little Premium will buy all my ancestors.

CARELESS

Oh, burn your ancestors!

CHARLES

No, he may do that afterwards if he pleases. Stay, Careless,   240
we want you. Egad, you shall be auctioneer; so come along
with us.

CARELESS

Oh, have with you, if that's the case. I can handle a hammer
as well as a dice-box.

SIR OLIVER (*Aside*)

Oh, the profligates!   245

CHARLES

Come, Moses, you shall be appraiser if we want one. Gad's
life, little Premium, you don't seem to like the business.

234–5 *family canvas.* Om *canvas Georgetown*; *Tickell* and *Murray* revert
   to less offensive reading of earlier MSS.
235 *I'll never forgive him this—never!* A second *never!* added in *1799*.
   Tickell, Murray agree with *Crewe B, Georgetown* in inserting *this*.
   But the forgiveness denied is surely general rather than merely
   pictorial.

SIR OLIVER

Oh, yes, I do, vastly. Ha, ha, ha! Yes, yes, I think it a rare
joke to sell one's family by auction. Ha, ha! (*Aside*) Oh, the
prodigal!   250

CHARLES

To be sure! When a man wants money, where the plague
should he get assistance if he can't make free with his own
relations?   *Exeunt* [*left*]

Act IV, Scene i

Picture room at CHARLES SURFACE'*s house*

Enter [*left*] CHARLES SURFACE, SIR OLIVER SURFACE, MOSES, *and*
CARELESS

CHARLES

Walk in, gentlemen, pray walk in. Here they are, the family
of the Surfaces, up to the Conquest.

SIR OLIVER

And, in my opinion, a goodly collection.

CHARLES

Aye, Aye, these are done in the true spirit of portrait painting
—no volunteer grace and expression, not like the works of   5
your modern Raphael, who gives you the strongest resemblance, yet contrives to make your own portrait independent
of you, so that you may sink the original and not hurt the
picture. No, no; the merit of these is the inveterate likeness—
all stiff and awkward as the originals, and like nothing in   10
human nature beside.

SIR OLIVER

Ah! we shall never see such figures of men again.

s.d. IV. i. One of the 'new' scenes announced in the playbills and no
    doubt supervised by de Loutherbourg himself. In addition to
    Zoffany's portrait of Baddeley (which shows Great-Aunt Deborah
    as a shepherdess) and other portraits, there are illustrations in the
    'Dublin' editions of 1785 and 1793, and a print by Bunbury (April
    1789). The *Fawcett* stage directions add a 'pocket-book' for Sir
    Oliver and Moses, with a 'settee on' (clear in the Zoffany) and 'Great
    chair ready to bring on', a 'pedigree hung up first wing' (left). *Holl*
    adds 'banknote' for Sir Oliver.
  5 *volunteer.* So Price; 'volontiere' in *Lord Chamberlain, Georgetown*
    (before correction); 'volontier' in *Murray, Cumberland;* 'voluntiere'
    Georgetown (after correction—not apparently by Sheridan, see Net-
    tleton, p. 868n), *1799, Fawcett.* See additional note on p. 144.
  6 *modern Raphael. Murray* has 'modern Raphaels',

CHARLES

I hope not. Well, you see, Master Premium, what a domestic character I am. Here I sit of an evening surrounded by my family. But come, get to your pulpit, Mr Auctioneer. Here's   15
an old gouty chair of my grandfather's will answer the purpose.

CARELESS

Aye, aye, this will do. But, Charles, I have ne'er a hammer—and what's an auctioneer without his hammer?

CHARLES

Egad, that's true. (*Reading a roll*) What parchment have we   20
here? *Richard, heir to Thomas.* Oh, our genealogy in full. Here, Careless, you shall have no common bit of mahogany —here's the family tree for you, you rogue. This shall be your hammer, and now you may knock down my ancestors with their own pedigree.   25

SIR OLIVER (*Aside*)

What an unnatural rogue—an *ex post facto* parricide!

CARELESS

Yes, yes, here's a list of your generation indeed. Faith, Charles, this is the most convenient thing you could have found for the business, for 'twill serve not only as a hammer but a catalogue into the bargain. But come, begin. A-going,   30
a-going, a-going!

CHARLES

Bravo, Careless. Well, here's my great-uncle Sir Richard Raveline, a marvellous good general in his day, I assure you. He served in all the Duke of Marlborough's wars, and got that cut over his eye at the Battle of Malplaquet. What say   35
you, Mr Premium? Look at him—there's a hero for you! Not cut out of his feathers, as your modern clipped captains are, but enveloped in wig and regimentals, as a general should be. What do you bid?

20 s.d. *Reading a roll. Crewe B* in Sheridan's hand. *Georgetown* has 'takes down a roll', also in his hand. Other MSS omit.
21 *Richard, heir to Thomas.* Om. *Tickell, Murray.*
26 *ex post facto.* Legal jargon for retrospective.
27 *list of your generation.* The 'bit' of *Tickell* and *Murray* for *list* is a copyist's error.
33 *Raveline.* Term from fortification ('an outwork of two faces which form a salient beyond the main ditch', *OED*).
35 *Malplaquet.* The bloodiest of Marlborough's battles, 11 September 1709.

MOSES

Mr Premium would have *you* speak.   40

CHARLES

Why, then, he shall have him for ten pounds, and I'm sure
that's not dear for a staff-officer.

SIR OLIVER (*Aside*)

Heaven deliver me! His famous uncle Richard for ten
pounds! [*Aloud*] Well, sir, I take him at that.

CHARLES

Careless, knock down my uncle Richard. Here now is a   45
maiden sister of his, my great-aunt Deborah, done by
Kneller, thought to be in his best manner, and a very formid-
able likeness. There she is, you see, a shepherdess feeding
her flock. You shall have her for five pounds ten—the sheep
are worth the money.   50

SIR OLIVER (*Aside*)

Ah, poor Deborah—a woman who set such value on herself!
[*Aloud*] Five pounds ten—she's mine.

CHARLES

Knock down my aunt Deborah. Here now are two that were
a sort of cousins of theirs. You see, Moses, these pictures
were done some time ago, when beaux wore wigs, and the   55
ladies their own hair.

SIR OLIVER

Yes, truly, head-dresses appear to have been a little lower in
those days.

CHARLES

Well, take that couple for the same.

MOSES

'Tis good bargain.   60

CHARLES

Careless! This now is a grandfather of my mother's, a
learned judge, well known on the western circuit. What do
you rate him at, Moses?

MOSES

Four guineas.

48–9 *shepherdess feeding her flock*. See Pope's *Moral Essay*, II, 8, and
Goldsmith's *Vicar of Wakefield* (cit. *Price*, 405). Sir Godfrey Kneller
painted many ladies in landscapes and pastoral settings, but not as
shepherdesses, as did his contemporary Sir Peter Lely.
60 *'Tis good bargain*. Moses's broken English again.

CHARLES

Four guineas! Gad's life, you don't bid me the price of his   65
wig. Mr Premium, you have more respect for the woolsack.
Do let us knock his lordship down at fifteen.

SIR OLIVER

By all means.

CARELESS

Gone.

CHARLES

And these are two brothers of his, William and Walter   70
Blunt, Esquires, both Members of Parliament and noted
speakers; and what's very extraordinary, I believe this is the
first time they were ever bought and sold.

SIR OLIVER

That is very extraordinary, indeed! I'll take them at your
own price for the honour of Parliament.   75

CARELESS

Well said, little Premium! I'll knock them down at forty.

CHARLES

Here's a jolly fellow. I don't know what relation, but he was
Mayor of Manchester. Take him at eight pounds.

SIR OLIVER

No, no; six will do for the mayor.

CHARLES

Come, make it guineas, and I'll throw you the two aldermen   80
there into the bargain.

SIR OLIVER

They're mine.

CHARLES

Careless, knock down the Lord Mayor and aldermen. But,
plague on't, we shall be all day retailing in this manner. Do
let us deal wholesale, what say you, little Premium? Give   85

66 *the woolsack.* On which the Lord Chancellor sits as a mark of respect
   to medieval England's principal export industry; also as here a judge
   summoned to attend the House of Lords.
78 *Manchester.* So *Georgetown, Tickell, Murray; Buckinghamshire,*
   Crewe B, Banbury, 1799, Fawcett, Cumberland, have 'Norwich';
   Lord Chamberlain has 'Bristol'. Touring companies may have suited
   the town to the place where they were acting. *Price* cites *Morning*
   Chronicle (19 June 1778), on 'the crowd who pressed for places at
   Manchester'.

us three hundred pounds for the rest of the family in the
lump.

CARELESS

Aye, aye, that will be the best way.

SIR OLIVER

Well, well, anything to accommodate you. They are mine.
But there is one portrait which you have always passed over.   90

CARELESS

What, that ill-looking little fellow over the settee?

SIR OLIVER

Yes, sir, I mean that, though I don't think him so ill-looking
a little fellow by any means.

CHARLES

What, that? Oh, that's my uncle Oliver. 'Twas done before
he went to India.   95

CARELESS

Your uncle Oliver! Gad, then you'll never be friends,
Charles. That now to me is as stern a looking rogue as ever
I saw—an unforgiving eye and a damned disinheriting
countenance. An inveterate knave, depend on't, don't you
think so, little Premium?   100

SIR OLIVER

Upon my soul, sir, I do not. I think it is as honest a looking
face as any in the room, dead or alive. But I suppose Uncle
Oliver goes with the rest of the lumber?

CHARLES

No, hang it! I'll not part with poor Noll. The old fellow has
been very good to me, and egad I'll keep his picture while   105
I've a room to put it in.

SIR OLIVER (*Aside*)

The rogue's my nephew after all! (*Aloud*) But, sir, I have
somehow taken a fancy to that picture.

CHARLES

I'm sorry for't, for you certainly will not have it. Oons,
haven't you got enough of them?   110

86 *for the rest of the family.* So *Lord Chamberlain, Georgetown,*
Tickell, Murray; Buckinghamshire, Crewe B, 1799, Fawcett, Cumber-
land have 'and take all that remains on each side'—no doubt in order
to preserve Sir Oliver's own portrait (in centre 'over the settee').

91 *over the settee.* Lord Chamberlain has 'over the door', a reading that
may have created problems for the original stage-manager as 'the
door' must have been one of the proscenium doors, whereas the
portrait should clearly be at the centre of the back-flat.

So vanity over
wins out morality
(family?)
honesty + morals wins?
honour

SIR OLIVER (*Aside*)

I forgive him for everything! (*Aloud*) But, sir, when I take
a whim in my head, I don't value money. I'll give you as
much for that as for all the rest.

CHARLES

Don't tease me, master broker. I tell you I'll not part with it,
and there's an end of it.   115

SIR OLIVER (*Aside*)

How like his father the dog is! (*Aloud*) Well, well, I have
done. (*Aside*) I did not perceive it before, but I think I never
saw such a striking resemblance. [*Aloud*] Here's a draft for
your sum.

CHARLES

Why, 'tis for eight hundred pounds!   120

SIR OLIVER

You will not let Sir Oliver go?

CHARLES

Zounds, no! I tell you once more.

SIR OLIVER

Then never mind the difference, we'll balance that another
time. But give me your hand on the bargain. You are an
honest fellow, Charles. I beg pardon, sir, for being so free. 125
Come, Moses.

CHARLES (*Aside*)

Egad, this is a whimsical old fellow! (*Aloud*) But hark'ee,
Premium, you'll prepare lodgings for these gentlemen.

SIR OLIVER

Yes, yes, I'll send for them in a day or two.

CHARLES

But hold! Do, now, send a genteel conveyance for them, for,   130
I assure you, they were most of them used to ride in their
own carriages.

SIR OLIVER

I will, I will—for all but Oliver.

CHARLES

Aye, all but the little nabob.

SIR OLIVER

You're fixed on that?   135

---

134 *the little nabob*. 'One who has returned from India with a large
    fortune acquired there' (*OED*). Samuel Foote's farce *The Nabob*
    (Haymarket Theatre, June 1772) has popularized the word. The
    implication of ill-gotten gains developed later in the century.

CHARLES

Peremptorily.

SIR OLIVER (*Aside*)

A dear extravagant rogue! [*Aloud*] Good day! Come, Moses.
(*Aside*) Let me hear now who calls him profligate!

Exeunt SIR OLIVER *and* MOSES [*left*]

CARELESS

Why, this is the oddest genius of the sort I ever saw.

CHARLES

Egad, he's the prince of brokers, I think. I wonder how the   140
devil Moses got acquainted with so honest a fellow. Ha!
here's Rowley. Do, Careless, say I'll join the company in a
few moments.

CARELESS

I will; but don't let that old blockhead persuade you to
squander any of that money on old musty debts, or any such   145
nonsense; for tradesmen, Charles, are the most exorbitant
fellows!

CHARLES

Very true, and paying them is only encouraging them.

CARELESS

Nothing else.

CHARLES

Aye, aye, never fear.   *Exit* CARELESS   150
So this was an odd old fellow, indeed! Let me see, two-thirds
of this is mine by right—five hundred and thirty odd pounds.
'Fore Heaven! I find one's ancestors are more valuable
relations than I took 'em for! Ladies and gentlemen, your
most obedient and very grateful humble servant.   155

Enter ROWLEY

Ha, old Rowley! Egad, you are just come in time to take
leave of your old acquaintance.

141-2 *how the devil.* So *Crewe, Tickell*; the diabolic omission in *1799*
    and *Murray* was a concession to Puritan objections, but Sir Peter is
    allowed it later, though not Charles.
152 *five hundred and thirty odd pounds.* This presumably represents what
    was left of the £800, i.e., a third has gone to Moses as his commis-
    sion. The *Lord Chamberlain* reading 'five hundred and sixty pounds'
    assumes a mere 30 per cent commission.

ROWLEY

Yes, I heard they were a-going. But I wonder you can have
such spirits under so many distresses.

CHARLES

Why, there's the point—my distresses are so many, that I   160
can't afford to part with my spirits. But I shall be rich and
splenetic all in good time. However, I suppose you are surprised that I am not more sorrowful at parting with so
many near relations. To be sure, 'tis very affecting; but, rot
'em, you see they never move a muscle, so why should I?   165

ROWLEY

There's no making you serious a moment.

CHARLES

Yes, faith, I am so now. Hence, my honest Rowley. Here, get
me this changed, and take a hundred pounds of it immediately to old Stanley.

ROWLEY

A hundred pounds! Consider only—   170

CHARLES

Gad's life, don't talk about it! Poor Stanley's wants are
pressing, and if you don't make haste, we shall have someone
call that has a better right to the money.

ROWLEY

Ah, there's the point! I never will cease dunning you with
the old proverb—   175

CHARLES

'Be just before you're generous', hey? Why, so I would if I
could; but Justice is an old lame hobbling beldame, and I
can't get her to keep pace with Generosity for the soul of me.

ROWLEY

Yet, Charles, believe me, one hour's reflection—

CHARLES

Aye, aye, it's all very true, but, hark'ee, Rowley, while I have,   180
by Heaven I'll give. So damn your economy, and now for
hazard.   *Exeunt [left]*

---

181 *economy. Fawcett, Cumberland* add 'and away to old Stanley with
    the money'. Reading is confirmed by the 'Dublin' and American
    piracies, but om. in presentation copies, *Tickell*, and *Murray*.
182 *hazard.* Game of chance played with dice; in French hazard the players
    staked against the bank, in English (or chicken) hazard, they played
    against each other.

Act IV, Scene ii

The Parlour at CHARLES SURFACE'*s house*

Enter [left] SIR OLIVER SURFACE *and* MOSES

MOSES

Well, sir, I think, as Sir Peter said, you have seen Mr Charles
in high glory; 'tis great pity he's so extravagant.

SIR OLIVER

True, but he wouldn't sell my picture.

MOSES

And loves wine and women so much.

SIR OLIVER

But he wouldn't sell my picture.   5

MOSES

And games so deep.

SIR OLIVER

But he wouldn't sell my picture. Oh, here's Rowley.

Enter ROWLEY *[left]*

ROWLEY

So, Sir Oliver, I find you have made a purchase.

SIR OLIVER

Yes, yes, our young rake has parted with his ancestors like
old tapestry.   10

ROWLEY

And here has he commissioned me to re-deliver you part of
the purchase-money—I mean, though, in your necessitous
character of old Stanley.

MOSES

Ah, there is the pity of all. He is so damned charitable.

ROWLEY

And I left a hosier and two tailors in the hall, who, I'm sure,   15
won't be paid, and this hundred would satisfy them.

s.d. IV. ii. *The Parlour.* So most texts; *Fawcett* has 'saloon'. Original
   scenery no doubt the same backdrop as in III. ii.
10 *old tapestry. Lord Chamberlai*n adds 'sold judges and generals by
   the foot and maiden aunts as cheap as broken china'. A vivid phrase
   retained from *Frampton Court* and repeated in *Spunge,* but deleted
   there; Sheridan uses it in V. iii, 137–8.

SIR OLIVER

Well, well, I'll pay his debts—and his benevolence too. But
now I am no more a broker and you shall introduce me to
the elder brother as old Stanley.

ROWLEY

Not yet awhile. Sir Peter I know means to call there about   20
this time.

Enter TRIP [*left*]

TRIP

Oh, gentlemen, I beg pardon for not showing you out; this
way. Moses, a word.   *Exeunt* TRIP *and* MOSES [*right*]

SIR OLIVER

There's a fellow for you! Would you believe it, that puppy
intercepted the Jew on our coming and wanted to raise   25
money before he got to his master?

ROWLEY

Indeed.

SIR OLIVER

Yes, they are now planning an annuity business. Ah, Master
Rowley, in my days servants were content with the follies of
their masters, when they were worn a little threadbare; but   30
now they have their vices, like their Birthday clothes, with
the gloss on.   *Exeunt* [*right*]

Act IV, Scene iii

JOSEPH SURFACE *and* SERVANT [*in the*] *library in* JOSEPH's *house*

JOSEPH

No letter from Lady Teazle?

SERVANT

No, sir.

---

31 *Birthday clothes.* The king's official birthday, then in January, marked
    the height of the social season.
s.d. IV. iii. The scenery was 'new'; screen 'off 2nd wing', 3 chairs, a
    table, and books completed the original properties (*1778*). *Fawcett*
    adds: a 'discovery' scene, screen on left, 'upper wing', 'Pembroke
    table' with a book on it, 'two chairs before the screen and one chair
    behind it'. *Holl* adds a 'window'. This appears as a large tall French

JOSEPH (*Aside*)

I am surprised she has not sent, if she is prevented from
coming. Sir Peter certainly does not suspect me. Yet, I wish
I may not lose the heiress, through the scrape I have drawn   5
myself in with the wife; however, Charles's imprudence and
bad character are great points in my favour.

Knocking heard without [right]

SERVANT

Sir, I believe that must be Lady Teazle.

JOSEPH

Hold! See whether it is or not before you go to the door; I
have a particular message for you, if it should be my   10
brother.

SERVANT

'Tis her ladyship, sir; she always leaves her chair at the
milliner's in the next street.

JOSEPH

Stay, stay. Draw that screen before the window—that will
do. My opposite neighbour is a maiden lady of so anxious   15
a temper.   SERVANT *draws the screen, and exit [right]*
I have a difficult hand to play in this affair. Lady Teazle
has lately suspected my views on Maria, but she must by no
means be let into that secret—at least, not till I have her
more in my power.   20

Enter LADY TEAZLE *[left]*

---

window in the 1778 print in a back-flat (on actor's right) with the
rest occupied by 5 shelves packed tight with books from floor to
ceiling; window and spines of 'books' clearly painted on canvas flat.
A feature for which de Loutherbourg, Drury Lane's inventive
scene-painter-in-chief, was clearly responsible is that the wings appear
as two painted pillars on each side of the stage instead of the usual
wall-papered imitation walls. See also above, p. xxx.

12 *chair.* Sedan or Bath chair.
13 *milliner.* 'Person (usually a woman) who makes up articles of female
apparel, esp. bonnets and other headgear' (*OED*).
15 *anxious.* So *Tickell* and *Murray* alone. All earlier texts have 'curious';
but the neighbour is not only inquisitive—she fears the worst! See
above, p. xlv, for fuller discussion. If not too dark by l. 111, when
Lady Teazle hides behind the screen, what was visible through the
French window would not have allayed the neighbour's anxiety.
19 *not till l.* The *not* is inserted in Sheridan's hand in *Georgetown*; all
other texts omit, but the extra emphasis it gives is certainly an
improvement.

LADY TEAZLE

What! Sentiment in soliloquy now? Have you been very
impatient? O lud, don't pretend to look grave. I vow I
couldn't come before.

JOSEPH

Oh, madam, punctuality is a species of constancy, a very
unfashionable quality in a lady.   25

LADY TEAZLE

Upon my word, you ought to pity me. Do you know Sir
Peter is grown so ill-tempered to me of late—and so jealous
of Charles too! That's the best of the story, isn't it?

JOSEPH (*Aside*)

I am glad my scandalous friends keep that up.

LADY TEAZLE

I am sure I wish he would let Maria marry him and then   30
perhaps he would be convinced; don't you, Mr Surface?

JOSEPH (*Aside*)

Indeed I do not. [*Aloud*] Oh, certainly I do. For then my
dear Lady Teazle would also be convinced how wrong her
suspicions were of my having any design on the silly girl.
                                                          [*They*] *sit*

LADY TEAZLE

Well, well, I'm inclined to believe you. But isn't it provoking   35
to have the most ill-natured things said to one? And there's
my friend Lady Sneerwell has circulated I don't know how

---

21 *in soliloquy now.* So *Tickell, Murray* (earlier MSS have *now* after
    impatient). The convention that a soliloquy could be overheard,
    unlike the aside, is common in Restoration comedy, but with the
    increasing realism initiated in the 18th century by sentimental comedy
    critics began to condemn the practice. The half-way stage, as here,
    was to hear a character thinking aloud without understanding what
    is being said.
34 s.d. [*They*] *sit*. The direction is entered in Sheridan's hand in *George-
    town*; though plausible, it is not found in the prompt-copies.
35 *to believe you. Spunge* inserts at this point from *Frampton Court*
    some two pages of dialogue (deleted here in Sheridan's hand) which
    are not found in any other MS, and interrupt the natural transition
    to Joseph's casuistical logic, but they are of considerable psycho-
    logical interest. What is of special interest in the fragment is Lady
    Teazle's vulgar jealousy of Maria and an unexpected chivalry in
    Joseph as he comes to Maria's defence. Price has printed the pass-
    age in *Theatre Notebook* XXIX (1975), 52–3.
36 *the most ill-natured things.* Malicious gossip as distinguished from
    Sir Peter's explosions of bad temper.

·many scandalous tales of me, and all without any foundation too. That's what vexes me.

JOSEPH

Aye, madam, to be sure, that's the provoking circumstance—   40
without foundation. Yes, yes, there's the mortification, indeed; for, when a scandalous story is believed against one,
there certainly is no comfort like the consciousness of having
deserved it.

LADY TEAZLE

No, to be sure, then I'd forgive their malice. But to attack   45
me, who am really so innocent and who never say an ill-
natured thing of anybody—that is, of any friend; and then
Sir Peter, too, to have him so peevish and so suspicious,
when I know the integrity of my own heart—indeed, 'tis
monstrous!   50

JOSEPH

But, my dear Lady Teazle, 'tis your own fault if you suffer
it. When a husband entertains a groundless suspicion of his
wife and withdraws his confidence from her, the original
compact is broken; and she owes it to the honour of her sex
to outwit him.   55

LADY TEAZLE

Indeed! So that, if he suspects me without cause, it follows
that the best way of curing his jealousy is to give him reason
for it?

JOSEPH

Undoubtedly—for your husband should never be deceived
in you; and in that case it becomes you to be frail in com-   60
pliment to his discernment.

LADY TEAZLE

To be sure, what you say is very reasonable, and when the
consciousness of my own innocence—

JOSEPH

Ah, my dear madam, there is the great mistake! 'Tis this
very conscious innocence that is of the greatest prejudice to   65
you. What is it makes you negligent of forms, and careless
of the world's opinion? Why, the consciousness of your own

38 *scandalous. Frampton Court* reading 'slanderous' is preferred in
Price, perhaps because *scandalous* has been used twice already in
this passage; but latter is the reading of all later texts and is preferable to more general 'slanderous' because the play is concerned primarily with sexual tittle-tattle alone.

innocence. What makes you thoughtless in your conduct, and apt to run into a thousand little imprudences? Why, the consciousness of your own innocence. What makes you   70 impatient of Sir Peter's temper, and outrageous at his suspicions? Why, the consciousness of your innocence.

LADY TEAZLE

'Tis very true.

JOSEPH

Now, my dear Lady Teazle, if you would but once make a trifling *faux pas*, you can't conceive how cautious you would   75 grow, and how ready to humour and agree with your husband.

LADY TEAZLE

Do you think so?

JOSEPH

Oh, I am sure on't; and then you would find all scandal would cease at once, for, in short, your character at present   80 is like a person in a plethora, absolutely dying from too much health.

LADY TEAZLE

So, so; then I perceive your prescription is that I must sin in my own defence, and part with my virtue to secure my reputation?   85

JOSEPH

Exactly so, upon my credit, ma'am.

LADY TEAZLE

Well, certainly this is the oddest doctrine, and the newest receipt for avoiding calumny.

JOSEPH

An infallible one, believe me. Prudence, like experience, must be paid for.   90

LADY TEAZLE

Why, if my understanding were once convinced—

JOSEPH

Oh, certainly, madam, your understanding should be convinced. Yes, yes—Heaven forbid I should persuade you to

---

81 *plethora.* Over-abundance (esp. medically of blood).
84–5 *secure my reputation.* So *Crewe B, Tickell, Murray;* the alternative 'preserve' (*Lord Chamberlain, Buckinghamshire, Georgetown, Banbury, Fawcett,* from *Frampton Court*) suggests that the reputation is already under attack.

do anything you *thought* wrong. No, no, I have too much
honour to desire it.   95

LADY TEAZLE

Don't you think we may as well leave *honour* out of the
argument?

JOSEPH

Ah, the ill effects of your country education, I see, still
remain with you.

LADY TEAZLE

I doubt they do indeed; and I will fairly own to you that if   100
I could be persuaded to do wrong, it would be by Sir Peter's
ill usage sooner than your *honourable logic* after all.

JOSEPH

Then, by this hand, which he is unworthy of—

Taking her hand

Enter SERVANT [*left*]

'Sdeath, you blockhead—what do you want?

SERVANT

I beg your pardon, sir, but I thought you wouldn't choose   105
Sir Peter to come up without announcing him.

JOSEPH

Sir Peter! Oons—the devil!   *Both rise*

LADY TEAZLE

Sir Peter! O lud, I'm ruined! I'm ruined!

SERVANT

Sir, 'twasn't I let him in.

LADY TEAZLE

Oh, I'm undone! What will become of me now, Mr Logic?   110
Oh, mercy, he's on the stairs. I'll get behind here—and if
ever I'm so imprudent again—   [*Hides behind screen*]

JOSEPH

Give me that book.

Sits down. Servant pretends to adjust his hair

Enter SIR PETER TEAZLE [*left*]

96–7 *honour out of the argument.* The change to 'out of the question'
   is only in *Murray* and ignores the logic of Joseph's proposition.
98 *country education.* The supposed pastoral innocence of life in the
   country was a specifically pre-Romantic illusion. Lady Teazle's
   'country prejudices' were an obstacle to Joseph's designs in II. ii.
103 s.d. *Taking her hand.* So only *Georgetown* and *Murray; Price* omits.

SIR PETER

Aye, ever improving himself! Mr Surface, Mr Surface—

JOSEPH

Oh, my dear Sir Peter, I beg your pardon. (*Gaping, and*   115
throws away the book) I have been dozing over a stupid
book. Well, I am much obliged to you for this call. You
haven't been here, I believe, since I fitted up this room.
Books, you know, are the only things I am a coxcomb in.

SIR PETER

'Tis very neat indeed. Well, well, that's proper; and you   120
make even your screen a source of knowledge—hung, I
perceive, with maps.

JOSEPH

Oh, yes, I find great use in that screen.

SIR PETER

I dare say you must. Certainly when you want to find anything in a hurry.   125

JOSEPH (*Aside*)

Aye, or to hide anything in a hurry either.

SIR PETER

Well, I have a little private business—

JOSEPH (*To* SERVANT)

You needn't stay.

SERVANT

No, sir.   *Exit [right]*

114 *Mr Surface, Mr Surface. Fawcett* inserts the direction 'Taps Joseph
on the shoulder'.
115 s.d. *Gaping.* Yawning.
116 s.d. *throws away the book.* Mary Linley (mother of Elizabeth Ann
Tickell), describing the Bath performance to her sister (Sheridan's wife)
in a letter of 14 November 1777 tells her, 'I particularly observed that
instead of throwing the Book to the other end of the Room as Palmer
does he [Dimond, the Bath Joseph] very carefully pulled down the Page
he was reading and gave it to his Servant w[hi]ch is certainly more
consistent with his Character' (cit. *Price*, p. 413). The *Fawcett* reading
'Gaping and giving away the book' suggests that Drury Lane made
this change after Palmer's death in 1798.
121–2 *hung . . . with maps.* Roberts's painting of the climax of the scene,
now owned by the Garrick Club, shows the back of the screen
ornamented—not exactly hung—with maps of the world by con-
tinents. No doubt the principal countries of Europe were on the
front. (The screen is on the floor.) Roberts's painting, recently
cleaned, is reproduced in *Theatre Notebook*, VI (October–December
1951).
123 *in that screen. Holl* adds the direction 'takes Sir Peter by the left
arm and turns him round to right hand'.

JOSEPH

Here's a chair, Sir Peter. I beg—   130

SIR PETER

Well, now we are alone, there is a subject, my dear friend,
on which I wish to unburden my mind to you—a point of
the greatest moment to my peace; in short, my dear friend,
Lady Teazle's conduct of late has made me extremely unhappy.   135

JOSEPH

Indeed! I am very sorry to hear it.

SIR PETER

Aye, 'tis too plain she has not the least regard for me; but,
what's worse, I have pretty good authority to suppose she
must have formed an attachment to another.

JOSEPH

Indeed! You astonish me!   140

SIR PETER

Yes; and, between ourselves, I think I've discovered the
person.

JOSEPH

How! You alarm me exceedingly.

SIR PETER

Aye, my dear friend, I knew you would sympathize with me.

JOSEPH

Yes—believe me, Sir Peter, such a discovery would hurt me ⌉ 145
just as much as it would you. ⌋

SIR PETER

I am convinced of it. Ah, it is a happiness to have a friend

---

133 *in short, my dear friend.* So *Tickell, Murray*; earlier texts, 'good
friend' (to avoid repetition of *dear friend* earlier in sentence; but Sir
Peter is nothing if not repetitive).

138 *authority to suppose.* So *Buckinghamshire, Fawcett, Tickell, Murray*;
'suspect' in *Frampton Court, Lord Chamberlain,* both *Crewe* MSS,
Banbury. A 'pretty good authority' justifies a supposition rather than
a mere suspicion.

140 *Indeed! You astonish me.* The word *Indeed* had preceded *You* in the
earlier texts and is retained, perhaps by oversight, in *Fawcett,
Tickell,* and *Murray.* It prevents *astonish* getting the emphasis that
is needed here, and Sheridan deletes it here in own hand in *Georgetown.*

144 *Aye, my dear friend.* So *Tickell, Murray.* Earlier texts read 'Ah' for
Aye. Possibly a better reading: Sir Peter is asking for sympathy
rather than agreement.

whom one can trust even with one's family secrets. But have
you no guess who I mean?

SIR PETER

JOSEPH

I haven't the most distant idea. It can't be Sir Benjamin   150
Backbite?

SIR PETER

Oh, no! What say you to Charles?

JOSEPH

My brother! Impossible!

SIR PETER

Ah, my dear friend, the goodness of your own heart mis-
leads you. You judge of others by yourself.   155

JOSEPH

Certainly, Sir Peter, the heart that is conscious of its own
integrity is ever slow to credit another's treachery.

SIR PETER

True, but your brother has no sentiment. You never hear
him talk so.

JOSEPH

Yet I can't but think Lady Teazle herself has too much   160
principle.

SIR PETER

Aye, but what is principle against the flattery of a handsome,
lively young fellow?

JOSEPH

That's very true.

SIR PETER

And then, you know, the difference of our ages makes it very   165
improbable that she should have any very great affection for
me; and, if she were to be frail, and I were to make it public,
why, the town would only laugh at me—the foolish old
bachelor who had married a girl.

JOSEPH

That's true, to be sure. They *would* laugh.   170

SIR PETER

Laugh—aye, and make ballads and paragraphs and the devil
knows what of me.

JOSEPH

No, you must never make it public.

SIR PETER

But then, again, that the nephew of my old friend, Sir
Oliver, should be the person to attempt such a wrong, hurts   175
me more nearly.

JOSEPH

Aye, there's the point. When ingratitude barbs the dart of injury, the wound has double danger in it.

SIR PETER

Aye. I that was, in a manner, left his guardian, in whose house he had been so often entertained—who never in my   180
life denied him my advice!

JOSEPH

Oh, 'tis not to be credited! There may be a man capable of such baseness, to be sure; but, for my part, till you can give me positive proofs, I cannot but doubt it. However, if it should be proved on him, he is no longer a brother of mine;   185
I disclaim kindred with him; for the man who can break the laws of hospitality and attempt the wife of his friend,   _haha_
deserves to be branded as the pest of society.

SIR PETER

What a difference there is between you. What noble sentiments!   190

JOSEPH

Yet I cannot suspect Lady Teazle's honour.

SIR PETER

I am sure I wish to think well of her and to remove all ground of quarrel between us. She has lately reproached me more than once with having made no settlement on her, and in our last quarrel she almost hinted that she should not   195
break her heart if I was dead. Now, as we seem to differ in our ideas of expense, I have resolved she shall have her own way and be her own mistress in that respect for the future; and, if I were to die, she will find that I have not been in-
attentive to her interest while living. Here, my friend, are   200
the drafts of two deeds, which I wish to have your opinion on. By one she will enjoy eight hundred a year independent

186–7 *break the laws.* So *Tickell, Murray*; their reading is perhaps prefer-
    able to other texts' 'break through the laws' as it suggests a *success-*
    ful breach of the social code.
    attempt the wife. So all MSS, but *Murray* has *tempt.*
197–8 *have her own way and.* A judicious addition in *Tickell* and
    Murray not found in earlier text. Sir Peter's surrender is not
    impressively generous. Mrs Abington, who took the part, was paid
    'five hundred a-year for Her wardrobe [in 1781]; she received,
    besides, eighteen guineas a-week as an actress, together with a bene-
    fit' (*A Picture of England*, from the German of Wide Archenholtz
    (1797), p. 110).

while I live; and, by the other, the bulk of my fortune at my death.

JOSEPH

This conduct, Sir Peter, is indeed truly generous. (*Aside*) I   205
wish it may not corrupt my pupil.

SIR PETER

Yes, I am determined she shall have no cause to complain, though I would not have her acquainted with the latter instance of my affection yet awhile.

JOSEPH (*Aside*)

Nor I, if I could help it.   210

SIR PETER

And now, my dear friend, if you please, we will talk over the situation of your affairs with Maria.

JOSEPH (*Softly*)

Oh, no, Sir Peter! Another time, if you please.

SIR PETER

I am sensibly chagrined at the little progress you seem to make in her affection.   215

JOSEPH (*Softly*)

I beg you will not mention it. What are my disappointments when your happiness is in debate! (*Aside*) 'Sdeath, I shall be ruined every way.

SIR PETER

And though you are so averse to my acquainting Lady Teazle with your passion for Maria, I'm sure she's not your   220
enemy in the affair.

JOSEPH

Pray, Sir Peter, now, oblige me. I am really too much affected by the subject we have been speaking of, to bestow a thought on my own concerns. The man who is entrusted with his friend's distresses can never—   225

Enter SERVANT [*left*]

Well, sir?

SERVANT

Your brother, sir, is speaking to a gentleman in the street, and says he knows you are within.

203–4 *at my death.* A small improvement by *Tickell* and *Murray*; 'after my death' in earlier texts.
212 *affairs with Maria. Tickell* and *Murray* improve on earlier 'hopes'.
217–18 *shall be ruined.* So *Buckinghamshire, Crewe B, Tickell, Murray*; preferable to *Georgetown*'s 'should be ruined'.

JOSEPH

'Sdeath, blockhead—I'm not within. I'm out for the day.

SIR PETER

Stay. Hold. A thought has struck me. You *shall* be at home.   230

JOSEPH

Well, well, let him up.   *Exit* SERVANT

(*Aside*) He'll interrupt Sir Peter, however.

SIR PETER

Now, my good friend, oblige me, I entreat you. Before
Charles comes, let me conceal myself somewhere; then do
you tax him on the point we have been talking on, and his   235
answers may satisfy me at once.

JOSEPH

Oh, fie, Sir Peter! Would you have me join in so mean a
trick—to trepan my brother too?

SIR PETER

Nay, you tell me you are *sure* he is innocent; if so, you do
him the greatest service by giving him an opportunity to   240
clear himself, and you will set my heart at rest. Come, you
shall not refuse me. Here, behind this screen will be— (*Goes
to the screen*). Hey! What the devil! There seems to be *one*
listener there already. I'll swear I saw a petticoat.

JOSEPH

Ha, ha, ha! Well, this is ridiculous enough. I'll tell you, Sir   245
Peter, though I hold a man of intrigue to be a most despicable character, yet you know it doesn't follow that one is
to be an absolute Joseph either. Hark'ee, 'tis a little French
milliner, a silly rogue that plagues me—and having some
character, on your coming, sir, she ran behind the screen.   250

238 *trepan.* Trap.
247 *that one is.* So *Tickell*; 'for a man's' *Spunge,* reverting to *Frampton
Court.*
248 *an absolute Joseph.* As the Joseph of *Genesis* 39: 7–12 had rejected
the advances of Potiphar's wife. In all but Puritan families the name
was more a recollection of Our Lady's husband.
248-9 *a little French milliner.* Joseph (or Sheridan) remembers the milliner in the next street with whom, according to his Servant (IV, iii,
12–13), Lady Teazle used to leave her chair when visiting him. Since
a sedan or Bath chair required two men to carry the poles, they
must have been entertained by the milliner while Lady Teazle was
with Joseph—which at least hints that her virtue was easy. That she
was French, a fact not hitherto disclosed, would carry the same
implication.
250 *character.* Respectable reputation.

SIR PETER

Ah, you rogue! But, egad, she has overheard all I have been saying of my wife.

JOSEPH

Oh, 'twill never go any farther, you may depend upon't.

SIR PETER

No? Then i'faith let her hear it out. Here's a closet will do as well.   255

JOSEPH

Well, go in then.

SIR PETER

Sly rogue! sly rogue!   *Goes [right] into the closet*

JOSEPH

A narrow escape, indeed, and a curious situation I'm in to part man and wife in this manner.

LADY TEAZLE (*Peeping from the screen*)

Couldn't I steal off?   260

JOSEPH

Keep close, my angel.

SIR PETER (*Peeping [right]*)

Joseph, tax him home.

JOSEPH

Back, my dear friend.

LADY TEAZLE (*Peeping*)

Couldn't you lock Sir Peter in?

JOSEPH

Be still, my life.   265

SIR PETER (*Peeping*)

You're sure the little milliner won't blab?

257 s.d. *into the closet.* The prompter's notes in *Banbury* and *Fawcett* make it clear that the right-hand proscenium door was supposed at this point to provide an entrance into the 'closet'. (All entries and exits on the scene are through the left-hand proscenium door.) At l. 262 Sir Peter is 'Peeping out O.P.' [=opposite Prompter]. Lady Teazle must therefore do her 'Peeping out' from the right-hand side of the stage where the screen would make her unseen by him. The screen must be presumed to have been on the curtain-line. The *Holl* prompter has Sir Peter 'Run up to the screen, start and turn down Right—and, Lady Teazle dashing back'. *A Trip to Scarborough* (Sheridan's adaptation of Vanbrugh) has no less than three separate 'closet' scenes. Many occur in such comic dramatists as Cibber and Mrs Centlivre.

JOSEPH

In, in, my good Sir Peter. 'Fore Gad, I wish I had a key to
the door.

Enter CHARLES SURFACE [*left*]

CHARLES

Hullo, brother, what has been the matter? Your fellow
would not let me up at first. What, have you had a Jew or   270
a wench with you?

JOSEPH

Neither, brother, I assure you.

CHARLES

But what has made Sir Peter steal off? I thought he had been
with you.

JOSEPH

He *was* brother, but hearing *you* were coming he did not   275
choose to stay.

CHARLES

What! Was the old gentleman afraid I wanted to borrow
money of him?

JOSEPH

No, sir. But I am sorry to find, Charles, you have lately
given that worthy man grounds for great uneasiness.   280

CHARLES

Yes, they tell me I do that to a great many worthy men. But
how so, pray?

JOSEPH

To be plain with you, brother, he thinks you are endeavouring to gain Lady Teazle's affections from him.

CHARLES

Who, I? O lud, not I, upon my word. Ha, ha, ha! So the   285

---

268 s.d. *Enter* CHARLES. Dublin ed. of 1793—which, though in general
   derived from the unauthorized eds. headed textually by *1780*, has
   several readings from the authentic text—has here the direction
   'singing'.

269-70 *Your fellow would not let me up.* Joseph's man was fully aware
   of his master's affair with Lady Teazle, and Joseph had intended
   him to have 'a particular message' if Charles should call (see IV. iii,
   10), but she had found her own way into the library before the
   servant could be told what the message was. He must have realized
   that a visit from Charles would not be exactly welcome that afternoon.

old fellow has found out that he has got a young wife, has
he? Or, what is worse, her ladyship has found out she has
an old husband?

JOSEPH

This is no subject to jest on, brother. He who can laugh—

CHARLES

True, true, as you were going to say. Then, seriously, I   290
never had the least idea of what you charge me with, upon
my honour.

JOSEPH (*Aloud*)

Well, it will give Sir Peter great satisfaction to hear this.

CHARLES

To be sure, I once thought the lady seemed to have taken a
fancy to me; but, upon my soul, I never gave her the least   295
encouragement. Besides, you know my attachment to Maria.

JOSEPH

But sure, brother, even if Lady Teazle had betrayed the
fondest partiality for you—

CHARLES

Why, look'ee, Joseph, I hope I shall never deliberately do a
dishonourable action; but if a pretty woman was purposely   300
to throw herself in my way—and that pretty woman married
to a man old enough to be her father—

JOSEPH

Well?

CHARLES

Why, I believe I should be obliged to borrow a little of your
morality. That's all. But brother, do you know now that   305
you surprise me exceedingly by naming *me* with Lady
Teazle; for, faith, I always understood *you* were her favourite.

JOSEPH

Oh, for shame, Charles! This retort is foolish.

CHARLES

Nay, I swear I have seen you exchange such significant   310
glances—

JOSEPH

Nay, nay, sir, this is no jest—

CHARLES

Egad, I'm serious. Don't you remember, one day, when I
called here—

JOSEPH

Nay, prithee, Charles—   315

CHARLES
And found you together—
JOSEPH
Zounds, sir, I insist—
CHARLES
And another time, when your servant—
JOSEPH
Brother, brother, a word with you. (*Aside*) Gad, I must stop
him.   320
CHARLES
Informed me, I say, that—
JOSEPH
Hush! I beg your pardon, but Sir Peter has overheard all
we have been saying. I knew you would clear yourself, or I
should not have consented.
CHARLES
How, Sir Peter! Where is he?   325
JOSEPH
Softly. There!   *Points to the closet*
CHARLES
Oh, 'fore Heaven, I'll have him out. Sir Peter, come forth!
JOSEPH
No, no—
CHARLES
I say, Sir Peter, come into court. (*Pulls in* SIR PETER) What!
My old guardian! What, turn inquisitor and take evidence   330
incog.?
SIR PETER
Give me your hand, Charles. I believe I have suspected you
wrongfully; but you mustn't be angry with Joseph. 'Twas
my plan.
CHARLES
Indeed!   335
SIR PETER
But I acquit you. I promise you I don't think near so ill of
you as I did. What I have heard has given me great satis-
faction.
CHARLES
Egad, then, 'twas lucky you didn't hear any more. (*Apart to*
JOSEPH) Wasn't it Joseph?   340

331 *incog.*, i.e. *incognito* = whilst concealed.

SIR PETER
  Ah, you would have retorted on him.
CHARLES
  Aye, aye, that was a joke.
SIR PETER
  Yes, yes, I know his honour too well.
CHARLES
  But you might as well have suspected him as me in this
  matter for all that. (*Apart to* JOSEPH) Mightn't he, Joseph?   345
SIR PETER
  Well, well, I believe you.
JOSEPH (*Aside*)
  Would they were both out of the room!

  Enter SERVANT [*left*] *and whispers* JOSEPH

SIR PETER
  And in future, perhaps, we may not be such strangers.
                                          Exit SERVANT [*left*]
JOSEPH
  Gentlemen, I beg your pardon. I must wait on you down-
  stairs. Here is a person come on particular business.   350

---

350 *a person come on particular business.* In *Frampton Court* and *Lord
    Chamberlain* the 'person' is anonymous, but in a loose sheet in
    Frampton Court—presumed in *Price* to be a last-minute change in
    text of first performance (but would even Sheridan have had the
    impudence to vary the licensed text?)—'person' becomes in an
    insertion in Sheridan's hand 'Lady Sneerwell'. The necessary changes
    affect the whole passage and are repeated with minor variants in
    the *Crewe* group of MSS (superimposed in Sheridan's hand in
    Georgetown as well as the *Frampton Court* loose sheet) and repeated
    in *1799, Spunge, Fawcett, Cumberland*, the 'Dublin' and American
    piracies. *Tickell* and *Murray*, however, revert to the anonymous
    visitor and a text close to that of *Lord Chamberlain*. Sheridan's
    reasons for inserting and then discarding Lady Sneerwell here are
    not clear. The audience has not seen Lady Sneerwell since II. ii
    and, though there is a reference to 'my friend Lady Sneerwell' by
    Lady Teazle at IV. iii, 37, it is not developed. As Lady Sneerwell is
    to intervene melodramatically in the play's last scene, Sheridan may
    have thought it desirable to remind us of her sinister possibilities.
    On reflection, however, he must have realized that she is an irrel-
    evance in the screen episode—indeed, a potential distraction. Granted
    the intimacy with Joseph established in I. i, Joseph should have been
    able to refuse her or fob her off, if difficult to satisfy face to face
    in the two or three minutes between l. 350 and l. 385, on a matter
    of 'particular business'. And what can such a matter have been?
    Sheridan's plot demanded Joseph's brief absence from the stage. It

CHARLES

Well, you can see him in another room. Sir Peter and I have not met a long time, and I have something to say to him.

JOSEPH (*Aside*)

They must not be left together. [*Aloud*] I'll send this man away and return directly. (*Apart to* SIR PETER *and goes out* [*left*]) Sir Peter, not a word of the French milliner.   355

SIR PETER (*Apart to* JOSEPH)

I? Not for the world. [*Aloud*] Ah, Charles, if you associated more with your brother, one might indeed hope for your reformation. He is a Man of Sentiment. Well, there is nothing in the world so noble as a Man of Sentiment.

CHARLES

Pshaw, he is too moral by half—and so apprehensive of his   360
good name, as he calls it, that I suppose he would as soon let a priest into his house as a girl.

SIR PETER

No, no! Come, come! You wrong him. No, no, Joseph is no rake, but he is no saint either in that respect. (*Aside*) I have a great mind to tell him. We should have such a laugh.   365

CHARLES

Oh, hang him, he's a very anchorite, a young hermit.

SIR PETER

Hark'ee, you must not abuse him. He may chance to hear of it again, I promise you.

CHARLES

Why, you won't tell him?

SIR PETER

No. But this way. (*Aside*) Egad, I'll tell him. [*Aloud*]   370
Hark'ee, have you a mind to have a good laugh at Joseph?

CHARLES

I should like it of all things.

---

was both less distracting and more plausible, since the last act had already been completed, for the absence to be due to an anonymous 'person' about whose identity a theatrical audience would ask no questions. But Sneerwell's intrusion was clearly popular with actors and audience, and Sheridan may have had some difficulty in discarding her. (She is in *Fawcett* and *Cumberland*, both copied from the Drury Lane prompt-book.) See *Price*, p. 338. A case of spectator/ reader contradiction?

352 *something to say to him.* Perhaps about the 'understanding' he and Maria have reached on his renewed expectations from Sir Oliver. Or Sheridan may have been merely fumbling for an excuse to retain Charles on stage.

SIR PETER

Then, i'faith, we will! (*Aside*) I'll be quit with him for discovering me. (*Aloud*) He had a girl with him when I called.

CHARLES

What! Joseph? You jest.   375

SIR PETER

Hush! A little French milliner. And the best of the jest is—
she's in the room now.

CHARLES

The devil she is!

SIR PETER

Hush! I tell you.   *Points* [*to the screen*]

CHARLES

Behind the screen! 'Slife, let's unveil her.   380

SIR PETER

No, no, he's coming—you shan't indeed.

CHARLES

Oh, egad, we'll have a peep at the little milliner.

SIR PETER

Not for the world! Joseph will never forgive me.

CHARLES

I'll stand by you.

SIR PETER

Odds, here he is!   385

JOSEPH *enters* [*left*] *just as* CHARLES *throws down the screen*

CHARLES

Lady Teazle—by all that's wonderful!

SIR PETER

Lady Teazle, by all that's damnable!

CHARLES

Sir Peter, this is one of the smartest French milliners I ever
saw. Egad, you seem all to have been diverting yourselves
here at hide and seek—and I don't see who is out of the   390

387 *all that's damnable!* So *Banbury, 1799, Tickell, Murray; Frampton
Court, Lord Chamberlain, Georgetown* prefer 'horrible'. The piracies,
for what their evidence is worth, are similarly divided, the Dublin
group reading 'horrible' and the Americans 'damnable'. That the
latter is more Sir Peter's idiom—cf. V. ii, 185; 'Sir Oliver, we live in
a damned wicked world'—may be thought to be confirmed by the
gag at the end of this scene found in *1799, Fawcett, Cumberland*,
and the Dublin and American piracies ('SIR PETER Oh, damn your
sentiments!').

secret. Shall I beg your ladyship to inform me? Not a word!
Brother, will you be pleased to explain this matter? What!
Is morality dumb too? Sir Peter, though I *found* you in the
dark, perhaps you are not so now? All mute. Well, though
I can make nothing of the affair, I suppose you perfectly   395
understand one another. So I'll leave you to yourselves.
(*Going*) Brother, I'm sorry to find you have given that
worthy man cause for so much uneasiness. Sir Peter, there's
nothing in the world so noble as a Man of Sentiment!

Exit CHARLES [*left*]. *They stand for some time looking at
each other*

JOSEPH

Sir Peter, notwithstanding I confess that appearances are   400
against me, if you will afford me your patience, I make no
doubt—but I shall explain everything to your satisfaction.

SIR PETER

If you please, sir.

JOSEPH

The fact is, sir, that Lady Teazle, knowing my pretensions to
your ward, Maria—I say, sir—Lady Teazle, being apprehen-   405
sive of the jealousy of your temper—and knowing my
friendship to the family—she, sir, I say—called here—in
order that—I might explain these pretensions—but on your

---

398 *so much uneasiness.* So *Georgetown, Tickell*; 'grounds for so much
uneasiness' *Buckinghamshire, Crewe B*; cause for so much uneasiness
Murray.

399 s.d. *They stand for some time looking at each other.* Garrick's letter
to Sheridan, 12 May 1777, comments: 'A gentleman who is as mad
as myself about y[e] School remark'd, that the Characters upon the
stage at y[e] falling of the screen stand too long before they speak; I
thought so too y[e] first night:—he said it was the same on y[e] 2nd,
and was remark'd by others;—tho' they should be astonished, and
a little petrify'd, yet it may be carry'd to too great a length'. (*Moore,*
I, 245). This suggests that the 'time looking at each other' originally
preceded Charles's 'Lady Teazle—by all that's wonderful'. The
applause on the first night (see above, p. xlvii) would have compelled
a pause.

In the theatre Lady Teazle's exit earns its meed of virtuous
applause. The mere reader may be permitted to wonder whether,
having pushed past the inquisitive servant (an ear at the door's key-
hole?), she ventures into the dark and walks boldly round to the
milliner's in the next street, and perhaps finds her chair and its two
bearers have vanished!

coming—being apprehensive—as I said—of your jealousy—
she withdrew—and this, you may depend on it, is the whole   410
truth of the matter.

SIR PETER

A very clear account, upon my word; and I dare swear the
lady will vouch for every article of it.

LADY TEAZLE

For not one word of it, Sir Peter.

SIR PETER

How? Don't you even think it worth while to agree in the   415
lie?

LADY TEAZLE

There is not one syllable of truth in what that gentleman has
told you.

SIR PETER

I believe you, upon my soul, ma'am.

JOSEPH (*Aside* [*to* LADY TEAZLE])

'Sdeath, madam, will you betray me?   420

LADY TEAZLE

Good Mr Hypocrite, by your leave, I'll speak for myself.

SIR PETER

Aye, let her alone, sir; you'll find she'll make out a better
story than you without prompting.

LADY TEAZLE

Hear me, Sir Peter! I came hither on no matter relating to
your ward, and even ignorant of this gentleman's pretensions   425
to her. But I came seduced by his insidious arguments, at
least to listen to his pretended passion, if not to sacrifice
your honour to his baseness.

SIR PETER

Now I believe the truth is coming indeed!

JOSEPH

The woman's mad!   430

LADY TEAZLE

No, sir, she has recovered her senses, and your own arts
have furnished her with the means. Sir Peter, I do not expect
you to credit me, but the tenderness you expressed for me,
when I am sure you could not think I was a witness to it,
has penetrated so to my heart that had I left the place   435
without the shame of this discovery, my future life should
have spoken the sincerity of my gratitude. As for that
smooth-tongued hypocrite, who would have seduced the wife
of his too credulous friend, while he affected honourable

addresses to his ward—I behold him now in a light so truly   440
despicable that I shall never again respect myself for having
listened to him.   *Exit [left]*

JOSEPH

Notwithstanding all this, Sir Peter, Heaven knows—

SIR PETER

That you are a villain! And so I leave you to your con-
science.   445

JOSEPH

You are too rash, Sir Peter; you *shall* hear me. The man who ⌉
shuts out conviction by refusing to—   ⌋
              Exeunt [left] JOSEPH SURFACE *following and speaking*

Act V, Scene i

The library in JOSEPH SURFACE'*s house*

Enter [left] JOSEPH SURFACE *and* SERVANT

JOSEPH

Mr Stanley! And why should you think I would see him?
You must know he comes to ask something.

SERVANT

Sir, I should not have let him in, but that Mr Rowley came
to the door with him.

JOSEPH

Pshaw, blockhead! To suppose that I should now be in a ⌉ 5
temper to receive visits from poor relations! Well, why don't ⌋
you show the fellow up?

---

447 *refusing to*—. After Joseph's final speech, Sheridan has entered Sir
    Peter's groan ('Oh!') in his own hand in *Georgetown*; it is not found
    in any other text except *Frampton Court*.
s.d. V. i. *Fawcett*'s prompt-note is 'Scene—A Library [continues]'. No
    properties are called for. The right proscenium door no longer leads
    into the closet of the preceding scene, but more vaguely into Joseph's
    private apartments.
  1 *And why should you think. Georgetown* seems to be alone in omit-
    ting *And*—which is necessary because Joseph has two faults to find
    with this remarkable Servant (who in this Act becomes William):
    (i) Why remind me at this painful moment of Stanley's existence at
    all? (ii) Why admit him, so that he can pester me with his financial
    needs? The emphasis on *must* (l. 16 below, indicated by italics in
    Georgetown), becomes the unidiomatic consequence. A special defect
    of this MS is to rely too much on italics. In good English emphasis
    is secured *grammatically*, not by an unnatural raising of the voice.

SERVANT

I will, sir. Why, sir, it was not my fault that Sir Peter discovered my lady—

JOSEPH

Go, fool!   *Exit* SERVANT [*left*]   10
Sure, Fortune never played a man of my policy such a trick
before. My character with Sir Peter, my hopes with Maria,
destroyed in a moment! I'm in a rare humour to listen to
other people's distresses. I shan't be able to bestow even a
benevolent sentiment on Stanley.—So here he comes and   15
Rowley with him. I must try to recover myself and put a
little charity into my face, however.   *Exit* [*right*]

Enter SIR OLIVER SURFACE *and* ROWLEY [*left*]

SIR OLIVER

What, does he avoid us? That was he, was it not?

ROWLEY

It was, sir. But I doubt you are come a little too abruptly.
His nerves are so weak that the sight of a poor relation   20
may be too much for him. I should have gone first to break
you to him.

SIR OLIVER

Oh, plague of his nerves! Yet this is he whom Sir Peter
extols as a man of the most benevolent way of thinking.

ROWLEY

As to his way of thinking, I cannot pretend to decide; for,   25
to do him justice, he appears to have as much speculative
benevolence as any private gentleman in the kingdom, though
he is seldom so sensual as to indulge himself in the exercise
of it,

SIR OLIVER

Yet he has a string of charitable sentiments, I suppose, at   30
his fingers' ends.

ROWLEY

Or, rather, at his tongue's end, Sir Oliver, for I believe there

---

17 *my face, however.* The use of 'however' at the end of a sentence,
   though obsolete now, remained common in the late 18th and early
   19th centuries.
30 *I suppose.* Om. unnecessarily *Spunge, Tickell,* and *Murray*—perhaps
   because *I presume* is to follow almost immediately (l. 35). Since
   Joseph and Sir Oliver have not yet met, the latter cannot be too
   dogmatic. All other texts have the phrase, including *Frampton Court*
   and both the Dublin and American piracies.

is no sentiment he has such faith in as that 'Charity begins at home'.

SIR OLIVER

And his, I presume, is of that domestic sort which never   35
stirs abroad at all.

ROWLEY

I doubt you'll find it so. But he's coming. I mustn't seem to
interrupt you; and you know immediately as you leave him,
I come in to announce your arrival in your real character.

SIR OLIVER

True, and afterwards you'll meet me at Sir Peter's.   40

ROWLEY

Without losing a moment.   *Exit [left]*

SIR OLIVER

I don't like the complaisance of his features.

Enter JOSEPH SURFACE [*right*]

JOSEPH

Sir, I beg you ten thousand pardons for keeping you a
moment waiting. Mr Stanley, I presume.

SIR OLIVER

At your service.   45

JOSEPH

Sir, I beg you will do me the honour to sit down.—I entreat
you, sir.

SIR OLIVER

Dear sir, there's no occasion. (*Aside*) Too civil by half.

JOSEPH

I have not the pleasure of knowing you, Mr Stanley, but I
am extremely happy to see you look so well. You were   50
nearly related to my mother, I think, Mr Stanley?

SIR OLIVER

I was, sir; so nearly that my present poverty, I fear, may do
discredit to her wealthy children; else I should not have presumed to trouble you.

JOSEPH

Dear sir, there needs no apology. He that is in distress,   55
though a stranger, has a right to claim kindred with the
wealthy. I am sure I wish I was of that class and had it in
my power to offer you even a small relief.

SIR OLIVER

If your uncle, Sir Oliver, were here, I should have a friend.

JOSEPH

I wish he was, sir, with all my heart. You should not want   60
an advocate with him, believe me, sir.

SIR OLIVER

I should not need one—my distresses would recommend me.
But I imagined his bounty had enabled you to become the
agent of his charity.

JOSEPH

My dear sir, you were strangely misinformed. Sir Oliver is   65
a worthy man, a very worthy man; but avarice, Mr Stanley,
is the vice of age. I will tell you, my good sir, in confidence,
what he has done for me has been a mere nothing; though
people, I know, have thought otherwise, and for my part I
never chose to contradict the report.   70

SIR OLIVER

What! Has he never transmitted you bullion—rupees,
pagodas?

JOSEPH

Oh, dear sir, nothing of the kind! No, no. A few presents
now and then—china, shawls, congou tea, avadavats, and
India crackers. Little more, believe me.   75

SIR OLIVER (*Aside*)

Here's gratitude for twelve thousand pounds! Avadavats and
India crackers!

JOSEPH

Then, my dear sir, you have heard, I doubt not, of the extravagance of my brother. There are very few would credit
what I have done for that unfortunate young man.   80

SIR OLIVER (*Aside*)

Not I, for one!

JOSEPH

The sums I have lent him! Indeed I have been exceedingly
to blame. It was an amiable weakness; however, I don't pre-

---

63 *had enabled you.* So all texts except *Murray* ('would enable you').
Sir Oliver, knowing the facts, is able to use a form that still retained
a positive sense as well as the modern one of mere probability.

72 *pagodas.* Gold coin formerly current in South India.

74 *congou tea.* Black China tea.
avadavats. Indian song-bird, brown with white spots (usually spelled
amadavats).

75 *India crackers.* Fireworks (squibs) imported from India. Joseph's
ingenuity as a liar compels a delighted respect by this spontaneous
array of plausible detail. Sir Oliver can only compete by a final
excess of polite humility.

tend to defend it. And now I feel it doubly culpable, since it
has deprived me of the pleasure of serving you, Mr Stanley,   85
as my heart dictates.

SIR OLIVER (*Aside*)

Dissembler! (*Aloud*) Then, sir, you can't assist me?

JOSEPH

At present, it grieves me to say, I cannot; but, whenever I
have the ability, you may depend upon hearing from me.

SIR OLIVER

I am extremely sorry—   90

JOSEPH

Not more than I, believe me. To pity without the power to
relieve is still more painful than to ask and be denied.

SIR OLIVER

Kind sir, your most obedient humble servant.

JOSEPH

You leave me deeply affected, Mr Stanley. William, be ready
to open the door.   95

SIR OLIVER

Oh, dear sir, no ceremony.

JOSEPH

Your very obedient—

SIR OLIVER

Sir, your most obsequious—

JOSEPH

You may depend upon hearing from me, whenever I can be
of service.   100

SIR OLIVER

Sweet sir, you are too good!

JOSEPH

In the meantime I wish you health and spirits.

SIR OLIVER

Your ever grateful and perpetual humble servant.

JOSEPH

Sir, yours as sincerely.

SIR OLIVER (*Aside*)

Charles, you are my heir!   *Exit [left]*   105

JOSEPH (*Alone*)

This is one bad effect of a good character; it invites application from the unfortunate, and there needs no small degree
of address to gain the reputation of benevolence without

94 *William.* The first time Joseph's manservant is addressed by name.

incurring the expense. The silver ore of pure charity is an
expensive article in the catalogue of a man's good qualities;   110
whereas the sentimental French plate I use instead of it
makes just as good a show and pays no tax.

Enter ROWLEY *[left]*

ROWLEY

Mr Surface, your servant. I was apprehensive of interrupt-
ing you, though my business demands immediate attention—
as this note will inform you.   115

JOSEPH

Always happy to see Mr Rowley. (*Aside*) A rascal. (*Reads*)
How? '*Oliver Surface*'!—my uncle arrived?

ROWLEY

He is, indeed. We have just parted. Quite well after a speedy
voyage, and impatient to embrace his worthy nephew.

JOSEPH

I am astonished. William, stop Mr Stanley, if he's not gone.   120

ROWLEY

Oh, he's out of reach, I believe.

JOSEPH

Why didn't you let me know this when you came in together?

ROWLEY

I thought you had particular business. But I must be gone
to inform your brother and appoint him here to meet his
uncle. He will be with you in a quarter of an hour.   125

JOSEPH

So he says. Well, I am strangely overjoyed at his coming.
(*Aside*) Never to be sure was anything so damned unlucky!

ROWLEY

You will be delighted to see how well he looks.

JOSEPH

Oh, I'm rejoiced to hear it. (*Aside*) Just at this time!

ROWLEY

I'll tell him how impatiently you expect him.   130

JOSEPH

Do, do. Pray give my best duty and affection. Indeed, I

116 (*Aside*) *A rascal!* So *1799, Fawcett,* and *Cumberland.* This may have
originated in an actor's gag, but if so, its long theatrical history
(*1799* is textually close to *Lord Chamberlain*) presupposes Sheridan's
tolerance of it there. Not in the presentation MSS, *Tickell,* or *Murray*
—or even *Frampton Court* or the piracies.

cannot express the sensation I feel at the thought of seeing
him!   *Exit* ROWLEY [*left*]
JOSEPH [*Alone*]
Certainly his coming just at this time is the cruellest piece
of ill fortune.   *Exit* [*right*]   135

Act V, Scene ii

SIR PETER TEAZLE'S

Enter MRS CANDOUR *and* MAID [*left*]

MAID
Indeed, ma'am, my lady will see nobody at present.
MRS CANDOUR
Did you tell her it was her friend Mrs Candour?
MAID
Yes, ma'am; but she begs you will excuse her.
MRS CANDOUR
Do go again. I shall be glad to see her if it be only for a
moment, for I am sure she must be in great distress.   5
                                            Exit MAID [*right*]
Dear heart, how provoking! I'm not mistress of half the ⌐
circumstances. We shall have the whole affair in the news- ⎬
papers with the names of the parties at length before I have ⎬
dropped the story at a dozen houses.   ⌐

Enter SIR BENJAMIN BACKBITE [*left*]

Oh, Sir Benjamin, you have heard, I suppose—   10
SIR BENJAMIN
Of Lady Teazle and Mr Surface—
MRS CANDOUR
And Sir Peter's discovery—
SIR BENJAMIN
Oh, the strangest piece of business, to be sure!

---

s.d. V. ii. *Holl* calls for the same 'Antique Chamber' (2nd groove back-
flat) as in I. ii, II. i, III. i; no properties are specified or presumably
necessary.
   9 s.d. *Enter* SIR BENJAMIN. From this point, as play's action quickens
towards a climax, the elaborate ceremony of a maid—or later manservant—introducing each guest is dropped.

MRS CANDOUR

Well, I never was so surprised in my life. I am so sorry for
all parties, indeed I am,   15

SIR BENJAMIN

Now, I don't pity Sir Peter at all; he was so extravagantly
partial to Mr Surface.

MRS CANDOUR

Mr Surface! Why, 'twas with Charles Lady Teazle was
detected.

SIR BENJAMIN

No, no, I tell you; Mr Surface is the gallant.   20

MRS CANDOUR

No such thing! Charles is the man. 'Twas Mr Surface
brought Sir Peter on purpose to discover them.

SIR BENJAMIN

I tell you I had it from one—

MRS CANDOUR

And I have it from one—

SIR BENJAMIN

Who had it from one, who had it—   25

MRS CANDOUR

From one immediately. But here comes Lady Sneerwell;
perhaps she knows the whole affair.

Enter LADY SNEERWELL *[left]*

LADY SNEERWELL

So, my dear Mrs Candour, here's a sad affair of our friend
Lady Teazle.

MRS CANDOUR

Aye, my dear friend, who would have thought—   30

LADY SNEERWELL

Well, there is no trusting appearances, though indeed she
was always too lively for me.

28–9 *our friend Lady Teazle.* Sheridan has inserted 'Lady' before Teazle
in *Georgetown* in his own hand. The more realistic 'our friend
Teazle' (*Frampton Court, Lord Chamberlain, Buckinghamshire,
Crewe B, Banbury, 1799, Fawcett, Tickell, Cumberland*), though
attractive, would have broken the surface of continuous formal
politeness with deep underlying malice that Sheridan must have intended. *Murray* and *Georgetown* are here in agreement.

30 *Aye, my dear friend.* Mrs Candour's repeated 'Aye' in this scene
suggests that she is older than the other scandalmongers (except
Crabtree). See note to I. i, 273.

MRS CANDOUR
   To be sure, her manners were a little too free; but then she ⌉
   was so young!
LADY SNEERWELL
   And had, indeed, some good qualities.   35
MRS CANDOUR
   So she had, indeed. But have you heard the particulars?
LADY SNEERWELL
   No; but everybody says that Mr Surface—
SIR BENJAMIN
   Aye, there I told you Mr Surface was the man.
MRS CANDOUR
   No, no; indeed, the assignation was with Charles.
LADY SNEERWELL
   With Charles? You alarm me, Mrs Candour!   40
MRS CANDOUR
   Yes, yes; he was the lover. Mr Surface, do him justice, was
   only the informer.
SIR BENJAMIN
   Well, I'll not dispute with you, Mrs Candour; but, be it
   which it may, I hope that Sir Peter's wound will not—
MRS CANDOUR
   Sir Peter's wound! Oh, mercy! I didn't hear a word of their   45
   fighting.
LADY SNEERWELL
   Nor I, not a syllable.
SIR BENJAMIN
   No? What, no mention of the duel?
MRS CANDOUR
   Not a word.
SIR BENJAMIN
   Oh, Lord, yes. They fought before they left the room.   50
LADY SNEERWELL
   Pray let us hear.

34 *so young.* So *Tickell, Murray* and the early texts; *Georgetown* and
   Banbury have 'very young'. No doubt part of the joke was that Mrs
   Abington, who was the first Lady Teazle, was in fact forty in 1777.
50 *Oh, Lord, yes.* The early MSS (except *Lord Chamberlain*) add a
   second 'yes'; om. *Tickell, Murray* (which also om. 'Lord'). A compromise seems preferable. Sir Benjamin's account has to be emphatic,
   but a second *yes* delays the narrative speed. Benjamin has not completed his account of what occurred.

MRS CANDOUR

Aye, do oblige us with the duel.

SIR BENJAMIN

'Sir', says Sir Peter, immediately after the discovery, 'you are a most ungrateful fellow'.

MRS CANDOUR

Aye, to Charles—   55

SIR BENJAMIN

No, no, to Mr Surface. 'A most ungrateful fellow; and old as I am, sir', says he, 'I insist on immediate satisfaction'.

MRS CANDOUR

Aye, that must have been to Charles; for 'tis very unlikely Mr Surface should go to fight in his own house.

SIR BENJAMIN

Gad's life, ma'am, not at all—'Giving me immediate satis-   60
faction'. On this, ma'am, Lady Teazle, seeing Sir Peter in such danger, ran out of the room in strong hysterics, and Charles after her, calling out for hartshorn and water. Then, madam, they began to fight with swords—

Enter CRABTREE [*left*]

CRABTREE

With pistols, nephew—pistols. I have it from undoubted   65
authority.

MRS CANDOUR

Oh, Mr Crabtree, then it is all true?

CRABTREE

Too true, indeed, madam, and Sir Peter is dangerously wounded—

SIR BENJAMIN

By a thrust in segoon quite through his left side—   70

CRABTREE

By a bullet lodged in the thorax.

MRS CANDOUR

Mercy on me! Poor Sir Peter!

CRABTREE

Yes, madam; though Charles would have avoided the matter, if he could.

---

65 *pistols, nephew—pistols.* So *Tickell* and *Murray* only. Other texts 'pistols, nephew'. The duplication communicates Crabtree's self-important excitement.

70 *segoon.* Anglicized Fr. *séconde,* the second of the eight parries recognized in sword-play.

MRS CANDOUR

I knew Charles was the person.   75

SIR BENJAMIN

My uncle, I see, knows nothing of the matter.

CRABTREE

But Sir Peter taxed him with the basest ingratitude.

SIR BENJAMIN

That I told you, you know—

CRABTREE

Do, nephew, let me speak—and insisted on immediate—

SIR BENJAMIN

Just as I said—   80

CRABTREE

Odds life, nephew, allow others to know something too. A
pair of pistols lay on the bureau (for Mr Surface, it seems,
had come home the night before late from Salthill, where he
had been to see the Montem with a friend, who has a son at
Eton). So, unluckily, the pistols were left charged.   85

SIR BENJAMIN

I heard nothing of this.

CRABTREE

Sir Peter forced Charles to take one, and they fired, it
seems, pretty nearly together. Charles's shot took effect, as I
told you, and Sir Peter's missed; but, what is very extraordinary, the ball struck against a little bronze Pliny that   90
stood over the fireplace, grazed out of the window at a right
angle, and wounded the postman, who was just coming to
the door with a double letter from Northamptonshire.

SIR BENJAMIN

My uncle's account is more circumstantial, I confess; but I
believe mine is the true one, for all that.   95

---

84 *the Montem.* The triennial Whit Tuesday procession (till 1847) by
Eton boys *ad montem*, i.e. to Salthill (now part of Slough) to collect
money for the senior scholar from the school at King's College,
Cambridge.

90 *bronze Pliny.* So most of the texts except *Tickell, Murray,* and the
'Dublin' piracies, which read 'bronze Shakespeare'. After Garrick's
Stratford Jubilee (1769) miniature busts of Shakespeare may have
been available, but the improbability of a Surface Pliny consorts
better with Crabtree's other absurdities. J. R. Moore's preference for
'younger Pliny' because he wrote letters (*MLN,* 59 (1944), 164–5)
misses the necessity of a *reductio ad absurdum.*

93 *double letter.* A letter written on two sheets and charged double
postage.

LADY SNEERWELL (*Aside*)

I am more interested in this affair than they imagine and must have better information.   *Exit* LADY SNEERWELL [*left*]

SIR BENJAMIN (*After a pause looking at each other*)

Ah, Lady Sneerwell's alarm is very easily accounted for.

CRABTREE

Yes, yes, they certainly *do* say—but that's neither here nor there.   100

MRS CANDOUR

But, pray, where is Sir Peter at present?

CRABTREE

Oh, they brought him home, and he is now in the house, though the servants are ordered to deny it.

MRS CANDOUR

I believe so, and Lady Teazle, I suppose, attending him.

CRABTREE

Yes, yes. I saw one of the faculty enter just before me.   105

SIR BENJAMIN

Hey! Who comes here?

CRABTREE

Oh, this is he—the physician, depend on't.

MRS CANDOUR

Oh, certainly. It must be the physician; and now we shall know.

Enter SIR OLIVER SURFACE [*left*]

CRABTREE

Well, doctor, what hopes?   110

MRS CANDOUR

Aye, doctor, how's your patient?

SIR BENJAMIN

Now, doctor, isn't it a wound with a small sword?

CRABTREE

A bullet lodged in the thorax, for a hundred!

SIR OLIVER

Doctor! A wound with a small sword! And a bullet in the thorax? Oons! Are you mad, good people?   115

SIR BENJAMIN

Perhaps, sir, you are not a doctor?

98 s.d. *After a pause....* Inserted in Sheidan's hand in *Georgetown*. Other texts omit (inc. *Tickell* and *Murray*).
105 *the faculty.* The medical profession.

SIR OLIVER

Truly, I am to thank you for my degree, if I am.   *making everything up—assumptions.*

CRABTREE

Only a friend of Sir Peter's, then, I presume. But, sir, you must have heard of his accident?

SIR OLIVER

Not a word!   120

CRABTREE

Not of his being dangerously wounded?

SIR OLIVER

The devil he is!

SIR BENJAMIN

Run through the body—

CRABTREE

Shot in the breast—

SIR BENJAMIN

By one Mr Surface—   125

CRABTREE

Aye, the younger.

SIR OLIVER

Hey! What the plague! You seem to differ strangely in your accounts. However you agree that Sir Peter is dangerously wounded.

SIR BENJAMIN

Oh, yes, we agree there.   130

CRABTREE

Yes, yes, I believe there can be no doubt of that.

SIR OLIVER

Then, upon my word, for a person in that situation he is the most imprudent man alive; for here he comes, walking as if nothing at all was the matter.

Enter SIR PETER TEAZLE *[left]*

Odds heart, Sir Peter, you are come in good time, I promise   135
you; for we had just given you over.

SIR BENJAMIN

Egad, uncle, this is the most sudden recovery!

SIR OLIVER

Why, man, what do you out of bed with a small sword through your body, and a bullet lodged in your thorax?

SIR PETER

A small sword, and a bullet!   140

SIR OLIVER

Aye, these gentlemen would have killed you without law or physic, and wanted to dub me a doctor to make me an accomplice.

SIR PETER

Why, what is all this?

SIR BENJAMIN

We rejoice, Sir Peter, that the story of the duel is not true 145 and are sincerely sorry for your other misfortune.

SIR PETER (*Aside*)

So, so. All over the town already.

CRABTREE

Though, Sir Peter, you were certainly vastly to blame to marry at all at your years.

SIR PETER

Sir, what business is that of yours? 150

MRS CANDOUR

Though, indeed, as Sir Peter made so good a husband, he's very much to be pitied.

SIR PETER

Plague on your pity, ma'am! I desire none of it.

SIR BENJAMIN

However, Sir Peter, you must not mind the laughing and jests you will meet on this occasion. 155

SIR PETER

Sir, I desire to be master in my own house.

CRABTREE

'Tis no uncommon case; that's one comfort.

SIR PETER

I insist on being left to myself. Without ceremony I insist on your leaving my house directly!

MRS CANDOUR

Well, well, we are going—and depend on't, we'll make the 160 best report of you we can.

SIR PETER

Leave my house!

CRABTREE

And tell how hardly you have been treated.

SIR PETER

Leave my house!

SIR BENJAMIN

And how patiently you bear it. 165

SIR PETER
Fiends! Vipers! Furies! Oh, that their own venom would choke them!

Exeunt MRS CANDOUR, SIR BENJAMIN BACKBITE, CRABTREE [*left*]

SIR OLIVER
They are very provoking indeed, Sir Peter.

Enter ROWLEY [*left*]

ROWLEY
I heard high words—what has ruffled you, Sir Peter?

SIR PETER
Pshaw! What signifies asking? Do I ever pass a day without   170
my vexations?

ROWLEY
Well, I'm not inquisitive.

SIR OLIVER
Well, Sir Peter, I have seen both my nephews in the manner
we proposed.

SIR PETER
A precious couple they are!   175

ROWLEY
Yes, and Sir Oliver is convinced that your judgment was
right, Sir Peter.

SIR OLIVER
Yes, I find Joseph is indeed the man, after all.

ROWLEY
Aye, as Sir Peter says, he is a Man of Sentiment.

SIR OLIVER
And acts up to the sentiments he professes.   180

ROWLEY
It certainly is edification to hear him talk.

SIR OLIVER
Oh, he's a model for the young men of the age! But how's

---

172 *Well, I'm not inquisitive*, Tickell and *Murray* correctly assign the
sentence. As Rowley had been off stage during the previous episode,
he could not be expected to have heard what had *ruffled* Sir Peter,
whereas Sir Oliver, to whom the earlier texts assign the words, had
been present from V. ii, 109.

this, Sir Peter, you don't join us in your friend Joseph's
praise, as I expected.

SIR PETER

Sir Oliver, we live in a damned wicked world, and the fewer   185
we praise the better.

ROWLEY

What? Do you say so, Sir Peter, who were never mistaken
in your life?

SIR PETER

Pshaw! Plague on you both! I see by your sneering you
have heard the whole affair. I shall go mad among you.   190

ROWLEY

Then, to fret you no longer, Sir Peter, we are indeed
acquainted with it all. I met Lady Teazle coming from Mr
Surface's so humbled that she deigned to request *me* to be
her advocate with you.

SIR PETER

And does Sir Oliver know all this?   195

SIR OLIVER

Every circumstance.

SIR PETER

What? Of the closet and the screen, hey?

SIR OLIVER

Yes, yes, and the little French milliner. Oh, I have been
vastly diverted with the story! Ha, ha, ha!

SIR PETER

'Twas very pleasant   200

SIR OLIVER

I never laughed more in my life, I assure you. Ha, ha, ha!

SIR PETER

Oh, vastly diverting. Ha, ha, ha!

ROWLEY

To be sure, Joseph with his sentiments! Ha, ha, ha!

SIR PETER

Yes, yes, his sentiments! Ha, ha, ha! Hypocritical villain.

SIR OLIVER

Aye, and that rogue Charles to pull Sir Peter out of the   205
closet! Ha, ha, ha!

SIR PETER

Ha, ha! 'Twas devilish entertaining, to be sure.

SIR OLIVER

Ha, ha, ha! Egad, Sir Peter, I should like to have seen your
face when the screen was thrown down. Ha, ha!

SIR PETER

Yes, yes, my face when the screen was thrown down. Ha, ha,   210
ha! Oh, I must never show my head again.

SIR OLIVER

But, come, come, it isn't fair to laugh at you neither, my old
friend, though, upon my soul, I can't help it.

SIR PETER

Oh, pray don't restrain your mirth on my account. It does
not hurt me at all. I laugh at the whole affair myself. Yes,   215
yes, I think being a standing jest for all one's acquaintance
a very happy situation. Oh, yes, and then of a morning to
read the paragraphs about Mr S——, Lady T——, and Sir P——
will be so entertaining.

ROWLEY

Without affectation, Sir Peter, you may despise the ridicule   220
of fools. But I see Lady Teazle going towards the next room.
I am sure you must desire a reconciliation as earnestly as
she does.

SIR OLIVER

Perhaps my being here prevents her coming to you. Well, I'll
leave honest Rowley to mediate between you; but he must   225
bring you all presently to Mr Surface's, where I am now
returning, if not to reclaim a libertine, at least to expose
hypocrisy.

SIR PETER

Ah, I'll be present at your discovering yourself there with
all my heart, though 'tis a vile unlucky place for discoveries.   230

ROWLEY

We'll follow.   *Exit* SIR OLIVER [*left*]

215–19 *Oh, yes, and then of a morning . . . and Sir P—— will be so
entertaining.* So *Lord Chamberlain, 1799, Tickell, Murray, Cumberland.* All texts except *Buckinghamshire, Georgetown, Banbury,
Spunge, Fawcett, Tickell,* and *Murray* add 'I shall certainly leave
town tomorrow and never look mankind in the face again'. Sheridan
was anxious after the humiliation of Sir Peter's almost-cuckoldry to
restore him to the audience's sympathy. His comic overstatements
had therefore to be restrained.

226 *Mr Surface's.* Sir Oliver may be excused this oddly formal locution
—after using the first name for Joseph a minute earlier—in order to
lend dignity to the approaching finale. Sheridan's realism was uncer-
tain and intermittent. The reference in the text (ll. 233–4 below) to
Lady Teazle's brief apparition 'in tears' and leaving 'the door of
that room open'—and looking 'this way' (l. 244)—is not confirmed
as visible to the audience in any of the prompt-books.

SIR PETER

She is not coming here, you see, Rowley.

ROWLEY

No, but she has left the door of that room open, you perceive. See, she is in tears.

SIR PETER

Certainly a little mortification appears very becoming in a ·235
wife. Don't you think it will do her good to let her pine a
little?

ROWLEY

Oh this is ungenerous in you.

SIR PETER

Well, I know not what to think. You remember, Rowley,
the letter I found of hers evidently intended for Charles? 240

ROWLEY

A mere forgery, Sir Peter, laid in your way on purpose. This
is one of the points which I intend Snake shall give you
conviction on.

SIR PETER

I wish I were once satisfied of that. She looks this way.
What a remarkably elegant turn of the head she has! 245
Rowley, I'll go to her.

ROWLEY

Certainly.

SIR PETER

Though, when it is known that we are reconciled, people will
laugh at me ten times more.

ROWLEY

Let them laugh and retort their malice only by showing them 250
you are happy in spite of it.

SIR PETER

I'faith, so I will! And, if I'm not mistaken, we may yet be
the happiest couple in the country.

ROWLEY

Nay, Sir Peter, he who once lays aside suspicion—

SIR PETER.

Hold, Master Rowley! If you have any regard for me, never 255
let me hear you utter anything like a sentiment. I have had
enough of them to serve me the rest of my life.

Exeunt [*right*]

Act V, Scene the last

The library in JOSEPH SURFACE'*s house*

Enter JOSEPH SURFACE *and* LADY SNEERWELL [*left*]

LADY SNEERWELL

Impossible! Will not Sir Peter immediately be reconciled to
Charles and, of course, no longer oppose his union with
Maria? The thought is distraction to me.

JOSEPH

Can passion furnish a remedy?

LADY SNEERWELL

No, nor cunning neither. Oh, I was a fool, an idiot, to   5
league with such a blunderer!

JOSEPH

Sure, Lady Sneerwell, I am the greatest sufferer; yet you see
I bear the accident with calmness.

LADY SNEERWELL

Because the disappointment doesn't reach your heart; your
interest only attached you to Maria. Had you felt for her   10
what I have for that ungrateful libertine, neither your temper
nor hypocrisy could prevent your showing the sharpness of
your vexation.

JOSEPH

But why should your reproaches fall on me for this disappointment?   15

LADY SNEERWELL

Are you not the cause of it? What had you to do to bate in
your pursuit of Maria to pervert Lady Teazle by the way?
Had you not a sufficient field for your roguery in imposing
upon Sir Peter, and supplanting your brother but you must
endeavour to seduce his wife? I hate such an avarice of   20
crimes; 'tis an unfair monopoly, and never prospers.

JOSEPH

Well, I admit I have been to blame. I confess I deviated

---

s.d. V. Scene the last. *The library* as in V. i.
  2 *of course no longer.* So *Tickell* and *Murray*: earlier texts have the
    pretentious 'of consequence', an idiom of melodrama rather than
    polite conversation.
  16–17 *What had you . . . by the way?* So all texts exc. *Murray.*
  16 *bate.* Slacken.

from the direct road of wrong, but I don't think we're so
totally defeated neither.

LADY SNEERWELL

No!   25

JOSEPH

You tell me you have made a trial of Snake since we met,
and that you still believe him faithful to us?

LADY SNEERWELL

I do believe so.

JOSEPH

And that he has undertaken, should it be necessary, to swear
and prove that Charles is at this time contracted by vows   30
and honour to your ladyship—which some of his former
letters to you will serve to support.

LADY SNEERWELL

This, indeed, might have assisted.

JOSEPH

Come, come; it is not too late yet. (*Knocking at the door
[left]*) But hark! This is probably my uncle, Sir Oliver: 35
retire to that room; we'll consult farther when he's gone.

LADY SNEERWELL

Well, but if he should find you out too?

JOSEPH

Oh, I have no fear of that. Sir Peter will hold his tongue
for his own credit's sake—and you may depend on't I shall
soon discover Sir Oliver's weak side!   40

LADY SNEERWELL

I have no diffidence of your abilities. Only be constant to
one roguery at a time.   *Exit [right]*

JOSEPH

I will, I will! So! 'tis confounded hard, after such bad fortune, to be baited by one's confederate in evil. Well, at all
events my character is so much better than Charles's that I   45
certainly—hey! What? This is not Sir Oliver but old Stanley
again. Plague on't that he should return to tease me just
now. We shall have Sir Oliver come and find him here and—

Enter SIR OLIVER SURFACE *[left]*

Gad's life, Mr Stanley, why have you come back to plague
me just at this time? You must not stay now, upon my word.   50

SIR OLIVER

Sir, I hear your uncle Oliver is expected here, and though
he has been so penurious to you I'll try what he'll do for me.

JOSEPH

Sir, 'tis impossible for you to stay now, so I must beg—come
any other time, and I promise you, you shall be assisted.

SIR OLIVER

No. Sir Oliver and I must be acquainted.   55

JOSEPH

Zounds, sir! Then I insist on your quitting the room directly.

SIR OLIVER

Nay, sir—

JOSEPH

Sir, I insist on't. Here, William! Show this gentleman out.
Since you compel me, sir, not one moment. This is such
insolence.   *Going to push him out*   60

Enter CHARLES SURFACE *[left]*

CHARLES

Hey day! what's the matter now? What the devil have you
got hold of my little broker here? Zounds, brother, don't
hurt little Premium. What's the matter, my little fellow?

JOSEPH

So! he has been with you too, has he?

CHARLES

To be sure he has. Why, he's as honest a little—but sure,   65
Joseph, you have not been borrowing money too, have you?

JOSEPH

Borrowing? No. But, brother, you know we expect Sir Oliver
here every—

CHARLES

O Gad, that's true! Noll mustn't find the little broker here,
to be sure.   70

JOSEPH

Yet, Mr Stanley insists—

CHARLES

Stanley! Why his name is Premium.

JOSEPH

No, no, Stanley.

CHARLES

No, no, Premium.

JOSEPH

Well, no matter which. But—   75

CHARLES

Aye, aye, Stanley or Premium, 'tis the same thing, as you
say; for I suppose he goes by half a hundred names, besides
A.B. at the coffee-houses.

JOSEPH

Death! here's Sir Oliver at the door. *Knocking again* [*left*]
Now I beg, Mr Stanley—   80

CHARLES

Aye, aye, and I beg, Mr Premium—

SIR OLIVER

Gentlemen—

JOSEPH

Sir, by Heaven you shall go.

CHARLES

Aye, out with him, certainly.

SIR OLIVER

This violence—   85

JOSEPH

Sir, 'tis your own fault.

CHARLES

Out with him, to be sure.   *Both forcing* SIR OLIVER *out*

Enter SIR PETER *and* LADY TEAZLE, MARIA, *and* ROWLEY [*left*]

SIR PETER

My old friend, Sir Oliver—hey! What in the name of
wonder? Here are dutiful nephews—assault their uncle at a
first visit.   90

LADY TEAZLE

Indeed, Sir Oliver, 'twas well we came in to rescue you.

ROWLEY

Truly it was; for I perceive, Sir Oliver, the character of old
Stanley was no protection to you.

SIR OLIVER

Nor of Premium either. The necessities of the *former* could
not extort a shilling from *that* benevolent gentleman: and   95
now, egad, I stood a chance of faring worse than my ancestors and being knocked down without being bid for.

After a pause, JOSEPH *and* CHARLES *turning to each other*

JOSEPH

Charles!

78 *A.B ... houses.* Perhaps initials (not standing for a real name) acting
as a 'box number' at coffee-houses.

CHARLES
Joseph!
JOSEPH
'Tis now complete.   100
CHARLES
Very!
SIR OLIVER
Sir Peter, my friend, and Rowley, too, look on that elder
nephew of mine. You know what he has already received
from my bounty; and you know also how gladly I would
have regarded half my fortune as held in trust for him.   105
Judge then my disappointment in discovering him to be des-
titute of truth, charity, and gratitude.
SIR PETER
Sir Oliver, I should be more surprised at this declaration if I
had not myself found him to be mean, treacherous, and
hypocritical.   110
LADY TEAZLE
And if the gentleman pleads not guilty to these, pray let him
call *me* to his character.
SIR PETER
Then, I believe, we need add no more. If he knows himself,
he will consider it as the most perfect punishment that he is
known to the world.   115
CHARLES (*Aside*)
If they talk this way to Honesty, what will they say to *me*
by and by?
SIR OLIVER
As for that prodigal, his brother there—
CHARLES (*Aside*)
Aye, now comes my turn. The damned family pictures will
ruin me.   120
JOSEPH
Sir Oliver, Uncle, will you honour me with a hearing?
CHARLES (*Aside*)
Now, if Joseph makes one of his long speeches, and I might
recollect myself a little.
SIR OLIVER (*To* JOSEPH)
I suppose you would undertake to justify yourself entirely?

---

107 *truth, charity, and gratitude.* So the MSS to *Fawcett. Tickell* and
Murray's 'faith' seems an unnecessary alteration, with the objection
to it of suggesting too closely St Paul's three virtues.

JOSEPH

I trust I could.   125

SIR OLIVER

Pshaw! (*To* CHARLES) Well, sir, and you could justify yourself too, I suppose?

CHARLES

Not that I know of, Sir Oliver.

SIR OLIVER

What? Little Premium has been let too much into the secret,
I suppose?   130

CHARLES

True, sir; but they were *family secrets* and should not be
mentioned again, you know.

ROWLEY

Come, Sir Oliver, I know you cannot speak of Charles's
follies with anger.

SIR OLIVER

Odd's heart, no more I can—nor with gravity either. Sir   135
Peter, do you know the rogue bargained with me for all his
ancestors, sold me judges and generals by the foot and
maiden aunts as cheap as broken china?

CHARLES

To be sure, Sir Oliver, I did make a little free with the
family canvas, that's the truth on't. My ancestors may cer- 140
tainly rise in judgment against me, there's no denying it. But
believe me sincere when I tell you, and upon my soul I would
not say it if I was not, that if I do not appear mortified at

126 *Pshaw!*. The earlier texts (up to *Georgetown*) read 'Nay, if you
desert your roguery in its distress and try to be justified, you have
even less principle than I thought you had', a forced witticism retained in *Banbury, 1799, Fawcett,* and *Cumberland* (which suggests
Sheridan allowed it on the stage). In omitting it *Georgetown, Tickell,*
and *Murray* are once again in agreement—though *Tickell* and
Murray om. *Pshaw! Fawcett* follows it with the direction 'Turns
from him with contempt'.

137–8 *sold me judges . . . broken china.* The passage had already been
used at IV. ii, where Sir Oliver is telling Rowley about the auction
just concluded of the family portraits. It there followed in *Frampton
Court* (and in *Spunge A,* being deleted in *Spunge B*), 'Our young
rake has parted with his ancestors like old tapestry'. Realizing that
the passage would be more effective in the last scene of the play,
Sheridan instructs himself here (in *Frampton Court* margin), 'N.B.
to be altered in the 4th Act'. As might be expected, the alteration
was not made until much later. *Lord Chamberlain,* the text profess-
ing to be that of the opening performance, has the judges, generals,
and maiden aunts both in IV. ii and in V. iii.

the exposure of my follies, it is because I feel at this moment
the warmest satisfaction in seeing you, my liberal benefactor.   145

SIR OLIVER

Charles, I believe you. Give me your hand again. The ill-
looking little fellow over the settee has made your peace.

CHARLES

Then, sir, my gratitude to the original is still increased.

LADY TEAZLE

Yet I believe, Sir Oliver, here is one whom Charles is still
more anxious to be reconciled to.   150

SIR OLIVER

Oh, I have heard of his attachment there; and, with the
young lady's pardon, if I construe right that blush—

SIR PETER

Well, child, speak your sentiments!

MARIA

Sir, I have little to say, but that I shall rejoice to hear that
he is happy. For me, whatever claim I had to his affection, I   155
willingly resign to one who has a better title.

CHARLES

How, Maria!

SIR PETER

Hey day! What's the mystery now? When he appeared an
incorrigible rake, you would give your hand to no one else;
and now that he is likely to reform, I warrant you won't   160
have him.

MARIA

His own heart and Lady Sneerwell know the cause.

CHARLES

Lady Sneerwell!

JOSEPH

Brother, it is with great concern I am obliged to speak on
this point, but my regard to justice compels me, and Lady   165
Sneerwell's injuries can no longer be concealed.

Opens the door [right]

Enter LADY SNEERWELL [right]

SIR PETER

So another French milliner! Egad, he has one in every room
in the house, I suppose.

LADY SNEERWELL

Ungrateful Charles! Well may you be surprised, and feel for

the indelicate situation which your perfidy has forced me   170
into.

CHARLES

Pray, Uncle, is this another plot of yours? For, as I have
life, I don't understand it.

JOSEPH

I believe, sir, there is but the evidence of one person more
necessary to make it extremely clear.   175

SIR PETER

And that person, I imagine, is Mr Snake. Rowley, you were
perfectly right to bring him with us, and pray let him appear.

ROWLEY

Walk in, Mr Snake.

Enter SNAKE *[left]*

I thought his testimony might be wanted; however, it happens unluckily, that he comes to confront Lady Sneerwell,   180
not to support her.

LADY SNEERWELL

Villain! Treacherous to me at last! (*Aside*) Speak, fellow,
have *you* too conspired against me?

SNAKE

I beg your ladyship ten thousand pardons. You paid me
extremely liberally for the lie in question; but I unfortunately   185
have been offered double to speak the truth.

SIR PETER

Plot and counterplot, egad!

LADY SNEERWELL

The torments of shame and disappointment on you all!

LADY TEAZLE

Hold, Lady Sneerwell. Before you go, let me thank you for
the trouble you and that gentleman have taken in writing   190
letters from me to Charles, and answering them yourself.
And let me also request you to make my respects to the
scandalous college of which you are president, and inform
them, that Lady Teazle, licentiate, begs leave to return the
diploma they gave her, as she leaves off practice and kills   195
characters no longer.

187 *Plot and counterplot, egad.* So *Buckinghamshire, Crewe B, Georgetown, Banbury, Fawcett, Tickell, Murray.* But *Georgetown* adds 'I
wish your ladyship success of your negotiation', which is also found
in some 'Dublin' piracies. It comes as rather an anticlimax to the
preceding sentence.

LADY SNEERWELL

You too, madam! Provoking insolent! May your husband
live these fifty years.   *Exit [left]*

SIR PETER

Oons! what a Fury!

LADY TEAZLE

What a malicious creature it is!   200

SIR PETER

Hey! Not for her last wish?   *ehaha.*

LADY TEAZLE

Oh, no!

SIR OLIVER

Well, sir, and what have you to say now?

JOSEPH

Sir, I am so confounded to find that Lady *Sneerwell* could
be guilty of suborning Mr *Snake* in this manner, to impose   205
on us all that I know not what so say. However, lest her
revengeful spirit should prompt her to injure my brother I
had certainly better follow her directly.   *Exit [left]*

SIR PETER

Moral to the last drop!

SIR OLIVER

Aye, and marry her, Joseph, if you can. Oil and vinegar,   210
egad! You'll do very well together.

ROWLEY

I believe we have no more occasion for Mr Snake at present.

SNAKE

Before I go, I beg your pardon once for all for whatever
uneasiness I have been the humble instrument of causing to
the parties present.   215

SIR PETER

Well, well, you have made atonement by a good deed at last.

SNAKE

But I must request of the company that it shall never be
known.

SIR PETER

Hey! What the plague! Are you ashamed of having done a
right thing once in your life?   220

---

200 *What a malicious creature it is.* So *Crewe B* (Sheridan's hand),
Fawcett. This seems better than the earlier 'A malicious creature,
indeed' *(Lord Chamberlain, Buckinghamshire, Georgetown, Banbury,
Tickell, Murray)*, because of the sequel it provides to Sir Peter's
'What a Fury'.

SNAKE

Ah, sir, consider. I live by the badness of my character. I
have nothing but my infamy to depend on, and, if it were
once known that I had been betrayed into an honest action,
I should lose every friend I have in the world.

SIR OLIVER

Well, well, we'll not traduce you by saying anything in your   225
praise, never fear.   *Exit* SNAKE *[left]*

SIR PETER

There's a precious rogue! Yet that fellow is a writer and a
critic.

LADY TEAZLE

See, Sir Oliver. There needs no persuasion now to reconcile
your nephew and Maria.   CHARLES *and* MARIA *apart*   230

SIR OLIVER

Aye, aye, that's as it should be, and, egad, we'll have the
wedding tomorrow morning.

CHARLES

Thank you, dear Uncle.

SIR PETER

What, you rogue, don't you ask the girl's consent first?

CHARLES

Oh, I have done that a long time—above a minute ago—and   235
she has looked *yes*.

MARIA

For shame, Charles! I protest, Sir Peter, there has not been
a word.

SIR OLIVER

Well then, the fewer the better. May your love for each
other never know abatement!   240

SIR PETER

And may you live as happily together as Lady Teazle and I
intend to do!

CHARLES

Rowley, my old friend, I am sure you congratulate me; and
I suspect that I owe you much.

SIR OLIVER

You do, indeed, Charles.   245

227-8 *Yet that fellow . . . critic.* That this reading had originally a personal reference is probable (see above, p. 9). It seems worth retaining
in spite of its absence in *Tickell* and *Murray* as adding a pleasantly
Grub Street flavour to Snake.

ROWLEY

If my efforts to serve you had not succeeded, you would
have been in my debt for the attempt; but deserve to be
happy and you overpay me.

SIR PETER

Aye, honest Rowley always said you would reform.

CHARLES

Why, as to reforming, Sir Peter, I'll make no promises, and   250
that I take to be a proof that I intend to set about it. But
here shall be my monitor, my gentle guide. Ah, can I leave
the virtuous path those eyes illumine?

> Though thou, dear maid, shouldst waive thy beauty's
>   sway,   255
> Thou still must rule, because I will obey
> An humbled fugitive from folly view,
> No sanctuary near but love and you.
>
> *(To the audience)*
>
> *You* can, indeed, each anxious fear remove,
> For even Scandal dies, if you approve!   260

254–60 *Though thou, dear maid . . . approve.* The feeble rhymed couplets
are not found before *1778*, but as they are in *Buckinghamshire,
Crewe B, Georgetown, 1799, Tickell, Murray, Fawcett, Cumberland,*
and the Dublin and American piracies, they can therefore hardly be
omitted. In *Lord Chamberlain* the play ends pretentiously in prose:
'But here shall be my guide, my gentle pilot. Ah, can I wander with
those eyes my cynosure?' Fortunately for the modern reader there
was in *Frampton Court* (page now detached and in Library of Congress, Washington) what Moore wittily called the 'doxology'.
('Finished. Thank God! R.B.S.—Amen! W. Hopkins'). Hopkins,
whose daughter had the part of Maria, was the Drury Lane
prompter, and as such was responsible for the prompt-book, with
its notes on the scenery and properties required and the various cues
for actors' entries, etc., but also for the copying-out of the various
actors' parts. Cecil Price has a letter on the 'doxology' in *TLS*
(4 May 1962).

EPILOGUE

By MR COLMAN

Spoken by LADY TEAZLE

I, who was late so volatile and gay,
Like a trade-wind must now blow all one way,
Blend all my cares, my studies, and my vows,
To one dull rusty weathercock—my spouse!
So wills our virtuous bard—the motley Bayes   5
Of crying epilogues and laughing plays.
Old bachelors who marry smart young wives
Learn from our play to regulate your lives.
Each bring his dear to town, all faults upon her—
London will prove the very source of honour.   10
Plunged fairly in, like a cold bath it serves,
When principles relax, to brace the nerves.
Such is my case; and yet I must deplore
That the gay dream of dissipation's o'er.
And say, ye fair, was ever lively wife,   15

Epilogue. Whereas prologues were conventionally a self-contained prelude to the play they introduced, the epilogue was normally treated as expansion or postscript to a principal actor's part, being spoken as *dramatis persona* and in costume. Mrs Abington had been a favourite epiloguist of Garrick's.
By MR COLMAN. The elder George Colman (1732–94) was one of the most talented comic dramatists of the period still faithful to the Restoration mode, but with the sexual teeth drawn (*The Jealous Wife*, 1761); manager of Covent Garden Theatre, 1767–74, of Haymarket Theatre 1777–89. For his *New Brooms*, see above, p. xxi. There are some minor variant readings—perhaps by Sheridan—in the presentation MSS (*Price*, pp. 442–3).
5 *motley Bayes.* 'Bayes' was the name under which Dryden was satirized in Buckingham's burlesque *The Rehearsal* (1671). Although intended as a term of abuse, Dryden's genius turned it into a compliment—as it is used here when Mr Colman speaks of Sheridan, implying that he is the equal in comedy ('motley') of Dryden in heroic drama. The name derives from the wreath of bay laurel leaves given to a classical poet of distinction (poet laureate).
6 *crying epilogues.* A reference to Sheridan's sentimental epilogue to George Ayscough's *Semiramis* (Drury Lane, 12 December 1776); epilogue is in *Rhodes*, III, 271–2.

Born with a genius for the highest life,
Like me untimely blasted in her bloom,
Like me condemned to such a dismal doom?
Save money, when I just knew how to waste it!
Leave London, just as I began to taste it!   20
Must I then watch the early-crowing cock,
The melancholy ticking of a clock
In a lone rustic hall forever pounded,
With dogs, cats, rats, and squalling brats surrounded?
With humble curate can I now retire   25
(While good Sir Peter boozes with the squire)
And at backgammon mortify my soul,
That pants for loo or flutters at a vole?
'Seven's the main!'—dear sound that must expire,
Lost at hot cockles round a Christmas fire.   30
The transient hour of fashion too soon spent,
Farewell the tranquil mind, farewell content!
Farewell the plumèd head, the cushioned *tête*,
That takes the cushion from its proper seat!
That spirit-stirring drum! (card drums, I mean—   35
Spadille, odd trick, pam, basto, king and queen!)
And you, ye knockers that with brazen throat
The welcome visitors' approach denote.
Farewell all quality of high renown,
Pride, pomp, and circumstance of glorious town!   40
Farewell! Your revels I partake no more,
And Lady Teazle's occupation's o'er!
All this I told our bard; he smiled and said 'twas clear,
I ought to play deep tragedy next year.
Meanwhile he drew wise morals from his play   45
And in these solemn periods stalked away:
'Blessed were the fair like you, her faults who stopped,
And closed her follies when the curtain dropped—
No more in vice or error to engage
Or play the fool at large on life's great stage'.   50

28 *loo*. A fashionable game of cards.
vole. Winning all the tricks.
29 *Seven's the main*. The number called by the caster of the dice in
hazard.
32 ff. The passage parodies *Othello*, III. iii, 349.
35 *card drums*. Private card parties.
36 *Spadille*. Ace of spades in ombre.
pam. Knave of clubs in loo.
basto. Ace of clubs in quadrille and ombre.

TEXTUAL APPENDIX

I THE 'SHARGL' AND 'SPUNGE' MSS

THESE TWO MSS, both containing many corrections in Sheridan's unmistakable handwriting, were acquired by the British Library, together with the copy of an early prompt-book of the play described in a contemporary hand on the cover as *1778*, at the Clare Sheridan sale (Sotheby's, 29 November 1971). All three are of great textual interest. *Shargl* owes its grotesque title to the compiler of the sale catalogue, who misread the first (cancelled) name given to Charles's footman in the list of *dramatis personae* prefixed to the manuscript. What the copyist responsible for the manuscript wrote —it is only of Act I—was *Spangle*, but as the short account of it in *Price* (pp. 837, 850) uses the spelling *Shargl*, I have retained it. Soon after the copy was made, Sheridan gave it a thorough revision. In the *Dramatis Personae*, however, the only corrections he made were to cross out 'Spangle' and substitute 'Spunge', which is then corrected to 'Trip'. 'Tucke', a form not found in any text of the play itself, is crossed out by Sheridan who replaces it by 'Snake'; 'Miss Verjuice', whose part was to be taken over by Snake, is crossed out without any alternative name being given her. No other change was made by Sheridan in the list. Opposite the seven principal 'Men', the names of the Drury Lane actors who took the parts at the original performance are left unchanged, but the actresses' names are not given. Sheridan has not corrected 'Young Surface' to 'Joseph', though, as the part is assigned to 'Mr Palmer', the omission's only significance is that it is a left-over from the 'Young Pliant' of the early draft now known as 'The Teazles'. More immediately its source is the 'Young Surface' of *Frampton Court*, which has the same actors; there is an undeleted 'Spangle' in its *Dramatis Personae* (as well as a deleted 'Frank' from 'The Teazles').

In the *Spunge* MS, 'Young Surface' again reappears and is again uncorrected. The basic text of 'Spunge', which includes most of the play except the auction scene, appears to be in the hand of Hopkins the prompter and has most of the technical additions common in prompt-copies. These have been deleted in it—probably by Sheridan, who has also revised the text of the play in the spidery hand characteristic of his later years. *Rae* printed nine of the variants in Sheridan's hand (I, 832) and more are added in *Price* (pp. 851–2).

140

Rae was especially struck by the contrast between the dark ink Sheridan used and the faded ink of the theatrical base 'made before the comedy was first represented'. It is the latter, however, that is of greater interest.

The textual pre-history of *The School for Scandal* may well begin with the early jottings and drafts, but this is a largely speculative area. History proper is only entered with the two layers of *Frampton Court*, both in Sheridan's hand, the second layer a drastic revision and abbreviation of the first. Hitherto there has been an assumption that the gulf between this second layer and the text submitted to the Lord Chamberlain's office for a licence had been traversed in a single stupendous leap by Sheridan. *Shargl* and *Spunge* demonstrate that this is an over-simplification. *Shargl* alone consists of several layers. Its basis is a copyist's reproduction of the second layer of *Frampton Court*, much as that had been printed by Rae in *Sheridan's Plays now printed as he wrote them* (1902).

Frampton Court's first layer, or a copy of it by several lesser members or associates of the Hopkins family (possibly including William Hopkins himself), is the earliest stratum of *Shargl*. The copyist used a notebook in which the page-numbering of much larger sheets is erratically repeated. No doubt they were foolscap sheets similar to but never quite identical with those in *Frampton Court*. Sheridan's revisions ignore the page-numbers; they appear in three stages, ending in a version in black ink in which 'Snake' displaces 'Verjuice' as described above. This is a structural change of a type rare in Sheridan, though it could be compared to Snake's displacement from Act III to the end of Act V in the revised version of *Frampton Court*. *Shargl*'s changes in black ink are principally abbreviations and reduce Act I, which can be assumed to have been typical, to almost two-thirds of its earlier length. A typical example is at the beginning of the play, when Verjuice/Snake is asked by Lady Sneerwell how the scandalous gossip is prospering about Lady Brittle's affair with Captain Boastall. 'In a week', Miss Verjuice (who was then Lady Sneerwell's agent in the scandal-mongering) enthusiastically replies, 'the Men will toast her as a Demi-rep'. This passage had been carried over from *Frampton Court* into *Shargl*. For it Sheridan at first substitutes 'I shall have her toasted', then decides to restore the earlier reading with a 'stet', a favourite instruction of his, in the margin. Eventually, however, the whole sentence is deleted. Lady Sneerwell's next question undergoes a similar treatment, *Frampton Court*'s 'a certain Baronet's Lady and a certain Earl' being first deleted, with Lady Brittle's intrigue with Captain Boastall taking its place. Finally, however, this sentence

too is crossed out, as it is now superfluous. In the end the effect of
the revisions and deletions is to leave this passage as it is found in
post-performance MSS and editions. 'That's in as fine a train' now
refers back to the Brittle–Boastall scandal instead of the Baronet's
wife and the Earl. To make his intention crystal-clear Sheridan at
this point inserts a black line before and after the passage with
three even thicker vertical lines between the two horizontals.

Operations such as this are frequent in *Shargl*. A few of the
revisions are also made in red ink. (These too are certainly Sheridan's.) One or two—such as Mrs Candour's report of Maria's friend
Miss Prim (misread at first by the copyist as 'Miss Oswin') stepping
into 'the York diligence' (for the earlier 'Post Chaise')—are clearly
authentic, though not in either the copyist's or Sheridan's hand.
Perhaps 'York diligence' was picked up at a rehearsal. The manuscript has several indications that it was used as a prompt-copy, such
as the pencilled insertions 'PS' and 'OP' for an actor's entry or exit,
which are, however, in a different hand.

Several copies appear to have been made of *Shargl* as finally
revised by Sheridan, one of them being *Spunge*. This manuscript
would seem to have been found by Sheridan lying about the Drury
Lane prompter's office many years later and then used as the basis
of a total revision of the play. Its immediate interest is that it contains the later Acts or parts of them (see *Price*, p. 851). As with
Shargl, the basis of the text is *Frampton Court* as revised in that
manuscript, but it also embodies the revisions made in *Shargl* for
Act I and presumably the similar revisions in the later Acts II to V.
What those revisions were can be found in *Lord Chamberlain*, the
play as acted, which adheres closely to *Shargl*, at least in Act I. For
the first dozen pages it has all *Shargl*'s extensive deletions, an unrevised copy of the final text of *Frampton Court* having clearly
been used—no doubt to save time in preparing a copy for the
Licenser.

Spunge shares the same early mis-spelling ('Pharagraphs') as
Shargl and *Lord Chamberlain*, but it is not corrected as in them.
Before Sheridan made the late additions, however, its text was essentially that of the revised *Shargl* and *Lord Chamberlain*. An oddity
that has not been noticed is that a long deleted passage early in
IV. iii—between Lady Teazle's 'Well—well I'm inclined to believe
you' and her 'But isn't it provoking'—is not from either of these
manuscripts, but from *Frampton Court*. A leaf may have been lost
here from the manuscript *Spunge* was using and, not finding any
other copy of the beginning of the scene, the copyist (or Sheridan)
may have had to use a leaf from *Frampton Court*, which is followed

with minute accuracy here. The revisions in Sheridan's hand in *Spunge* are certainly much later than the copyist's base on which they are superimposed. A date immediately preceding the 1787–88 season has been suggested in the Introduction (above, pp. xiv, xliii). The textual evidence gives the date a certain plausibility. Of the nine variants listed by *Rae* (I, 323) and the sixty-six added in *Price* (pp. 851–2) no less than forty-one are not found elsewhere. They are not in general of much interest, and my collation has not included them all. The base manuscript seems to have been closer to the 'Lady Crewe' (*Crewe B*) MS than to any other.

II INDIFFERENT POST-PERFORMANCE READINGS

By *indifferent readings* I mean those in which no clear-cut superiority is discernible between two or more different versions of a single word or passage, all of which are unquestionably authorial. Until recently it was the habit of editors of the English classics to take it for granted that an author's last revision was invariably to be preferred to those he had made at some earlier date. The presupposition was labour-saving, but irrational. Each revision or reading, it would now be generally agreed, needs to be considered on its own merits.

But supposing the balance of preferability between two readings—both unquestionably authentic and equally plausible in their different ways—is *exactly* equal. What is the editor to do then?

A recurrent problem in *The School for Scandal* is the divergence of texts over whether or not to abbreviate the present indicative's third person singular. As early as Sneerwell's second sentence an editor must decide whether 'That's in as fine a train' (*Tickell/Murray*) is or is not preferable to *Georgetown*'s 'That is in as fine a train'. And the answer in this case and the hundreds similar to it must surely be that it doesn't really matter. But Price prints 'That is' and I print 'That's': a compromise between the two readings isn't possible on a printed page—or if possible, would be infuriating (e.g., 'That's (That is)').

Some guidance, however, is provided by considerations of statistical probability. The following table is confined to the two hitherto most generally favoured texts of *The School for Scandal*.

The immediately significant fact in these figures is the greater preferability of the *Murray* text; the *Georgetown* text is decidedly behind it in the number of preferable readings it supplies, except in Act IV where they almost equal the number in *Murray*. As IV. i was apparently the last scene to be written, this may account for

	Act I	Act II	Act III	Act IV	Act V	Totals of readings
Preferable original readings in Crewe (Georgetown) MS	13	11	11	31	19	85
Preferable original readings in Murray (1821) text	20	16	21	33	34	124
Indifferent readings in both Georgetown and Murray texts	19	16	15	6	21	77
Totals per Act	52	43	47	70	74	

the difference from the other acts, and as there are only six indifferent readings in Act IV, they do not pose any special problem. It is the 71 other indifferent readings that are the crux, on which an editor may find himself crucified.

Since the number of preferable readings is so much greater in *Murray*, there must be a marginal *a priori* probability that an editor who thinks hard enough will find a good reason for promoting some at least of the 'indifferents' into the preferable category. The figures should certainly encourage him to do so. The general rule—which is not strictly a rule at all—is merely to give the benefit of any doubt to the *Murray* reading and include it in the text, while admitting in a footnote the precariousness of the particular decision. Since the choice between two or more indifferent readings—*was*, for example, and the more old-fashioned (subjunctive) *were*, or *ha, ha,* as against *ha, ha, ha*—makes little or no difference to the meaning, the rival forms are often left to look after themselves in this edition. *De minimis non curat criticus*.[1]

[1] When making the preceding calculations I had not seen *Tickell*, but as virtually all the preferable original readings in *Tickell* derive from the same text as *Murray*, the conclusion is not affected.

Additional note to commentary on line 5, page 79; Act IV. i

This is Sheridan's tribute to Sir Joshua Reynolds, the 'modern Raphael', who attended the first night of *The School for Scandal* and who was not only a friend of Sheridan's but also of Frances Abington, who created the part of Lady Teazle. Reynolds' admiration for Raphael was well known, as was his opinion that, even in portrait painting, a minute attention to the detail of what was being painted must yield to the grandeur of the general idea which was being expressed, so that what Sheridan calls 'the inveterate likeness' should not be the painter's chief aim. Charles Surface (and Sheridan) pretend here a satiric attack on Reynolds' style of portraiture, in which the freely arising ('volunteer') grace and vigour of a noble idea moderates the attempt at exact resemblance.